Behavior Genetics Principles

Behavior Genetics Principles

Perspectives in Development, Personality, and Psychopathology

Edited by Lisabeth F. DiLalla

2000-2010
DECADE
of BEHAVIOR

American Psychological Association
Washington, DC

Published by
American Psychological Association
750 First Street, NE
Washington, DC 20002
www.apa.org

To order
APA Order Department
P.O. Box 92984
Washington, DC 20090-2984

Tel: (800) 374-2721, Direct: (202) 336-5510
Fax: (202) 336-5502, TDD/TTY: (202) 336-6123
Online: www.apa.org/books/
Email: order@apa.org

In the U.K., Europe, Africa, and the Middle East, copies may be ordered from
American Psychological Association
3 Henrietta Street
Covent Garden, London
WC2E 8LU England

Typeset in Century Schoolbook by NOVA Graphic Services, Jamison, PA

Printer: Edwards Brothers, Ann Arbor, MI
Cover Designer: Mercury Publishing Services, Rockville, MD
Project Manager: NOVA Graphic Services, Jamison, PA

The opinions and statements published are the responsibility of the authors, and such opinions and statements do not necessarily represent the policies of the American Psychological Association.

Library of Congress Cataloging-in-Publication Data
Behavior genetics principles : perspectives in development, personality, and psychopathology / edited by Lisabeth F. DiLalla.
      p. cm. — (Decade of behavior)
Proceedings of a festschrift conference held in honor of Irving I. Gottesman.
Includes bibliographical references and indexes.
  ISBN 1-59147-083-8
  1. Personality—Genetic aspects. 2. Behavior genetics. 3. Personality development. 4. Psychology, Pathological. I. DiLalla, Lisabeth F. II. Gottesman, Irving I. III. Series.

  BF698.9.B5B44 2004
  155.7—dc22
                                                            2003021356

British Library Cataloguing-in-Publication Data
A CIP record is available from the British Library.

Printed in the United States of America
First Edition

APA Science Volumes

APA Decade of Behavior Volumes

Contents

Contributors

Aksel Bertelsen, MD, Institute of Psychiatric Demography, Aarhus Psychiatric Hospital, Risskov, Denmark

Thomas J. Bouchard Jr., PhD, Department of Psychology, University of Minnesota, Minneapolis

Gregory Carey, PhD, Department of Psychology and Institute for Behavioral Genetics, University of Colorado at Boulder

David L. DiLalla, PhD, Department of Psychology, Southern Illinois University at Carbondale

Lisabeth F. DiLalla, PhD, Department of Family and Community Medicine, Southern Illinois University School of Medicine, Carbondale

L. Erlenmeyer-Kimling, PhD, Department of Medical Genetics, New York State Psychiatric Institute; Department of Psychiatry and Department of Genetics and Development, College of Physicians and Surgeons, Columbia University, New York

Marilyn J. Essex, PhD, Department of Psychiatry, University of Wisconsin, Madison

Anne Farmer, MD, FRCPsych, Institute of Psychiatry, Kings College, London

H. Hill Goldsmith, PhD, Department of Psychology, University of Wisconsin—Madison

Irving I. Gottesman, PhD, Hon. FRCPsych, Bernstein Professorship in Adult Psychiatry, Senior Fellow in Psychology, University of Minnesota, Minneapolis; Sherrell J. Aston Professor of Psychology Emeritus, University of Virginia, Charlottesville

Daniel R. Hanson, PhD, MD, Department of Psychiatry, University of Minnesota, Minneapolis

Leroy Hood, PhD, MD, The Institute for Systems Biology, Seattle, WA

William G. Iacono, PhD, Department of Psychology, University of Minnesota, Minneapolis

Margaret Keyes, PhD, Department of Psychology, University of Minnesota, Minneapolis

Robert Krueger, PhD, Department of Psychology, University of Minnesota, Minneapolis

Kathryn S. Lemery, PhD, Department of Psychology, Arizona State University, Tempe

Linheng Li, PhD, Stowers Institute for Medical Research, Kansas City, MO

Brendan A. Maher, PhD, Edward C. Henderson Professor of the Psychology of Personality, Professor Emeritus, Department of Psychology, Harvard University, Cambridge, MA

Matt McGue, PhD, Department of Psychology, University of Minnesota, Minneapolis

Peter McGuffin, MD, PhD, FRCPsych, MRC Social and Developmental Psychiatry Centre, Institute of Psychiatry, King's College, London

Hans Moises, MD, Molecular Genetics Laboratory, Department of Psychiatry, University of Kiel, Germany

Simone A. Roberts, BA, Department of Medical Genetics, New York State Psychiatric Institute, New York

Donald Rock, PhD, Educational Testing Service, Princeton, NJ

Nancy L. Segal, PhD, Department of Psychology, California State University, Fullerton

Auke Tellegen, PhD, Professor Emeritus, Department of Psychology, University of Minnesota, Minneapolis

Susan L. Trumbetta, PhD, Department of Psychology, Vassar College, Poughkeepsie, NY

Eric Turkheimer, PhD, Department of Psychology, University of Virginia, Charlottesville

Tómas Zoega, MD, Department of Psychiatry, National University of Iceland, Reykjavik

Series Foreword

In early 1988, the American Psychological Association (APA) Science Directorate began its sponsorship of what would become an exceptionally successful activity in support of psychological science—the APA Scientific Conferences program. This program has showcased some of the most important topics in psychological science and has provided a forum for collaboration among many leading figures in the field.

The program has inspired a series of books that have presented cutting-edge work in all areas of psychology. At the turn of the millennium, the series was renamed the "Decade of Behavior Series" to help advance the goals of this important initiative. The Decade of Behavior is a major interdisciplinary campaign designed to promote the contributions of the behavioral and social sciences to our most important societal challenges in the decade leading up to 2010. Although a key goal has been to inform the public about these scientific contributions, other activities have been designed to encourage and further collaboration among scientists. Hence, the series that was the "APA Science Series" has continued as the "Decade of Behavior Series." This represents one element in APA's efforts to promote the Decade of Behavior initiative as one of its endorsing organizations. For additional information about the Decade of Behavior, please visit http://www.decadeofbehavior.org.

Over the course of the past years, the Science Conference and Decade of Behavior Series has allowed psychological scientists to share and explore cutting-edge findings in psychology. The APA Science Directorate looks forward to continuing this successful program and to sponsoring other conferences and books in the years ahead. This series has been so successful that we have chosen to extend it to include books that, although they do not arise from conferences, report with the same high quality of scholarship on the latest research.

We are pleased that this important contribution to the literature was supported in part by the Decade of Behavior program. Congratulations to the editors and contributors of this volume on their sterling effort.

Kurt Salzinger, PhD
Executive Director for Science

Virginia E. Holt
Assistant Executive Director for Science

Volume Foreword

I have known Irving I. Gottesman as a friend and colleague since 1960. We both came to the Department of Social Relations at Harvard as new faculty members at that time, and we were assigned neighboring offices at the attic level in the Victorian house on Divinity Avenue that served as the Center for Research in Personality. This was the home of personality psychology and clinical psychology. Our offices at the top of the building brought with them the special features of no air-conditioning and gray metal war surplus furniture, dented in battles that had apparently involved direct assaults on the desks of the opposing sides. We had many more important things in common, but especially the commitment to psychology as an empirical, quantitative science.

This was not in keeping with the core culture of the department. Personality psychology, clinical psychology, and psychopathology at Harvard (and many other places) were dominated by reductionist theories. All behavior could be traced to one basic single causative factor. The basic factor might be the manner in which hypothetical intrapsychic conflicts of infancy had been handled in later life or it might have been the history of rewards and punishments for particular activities. Students took their identities from the great names attached to the theories that they favored; they were Eriksonians, Freudians, Skinnerians, Maslovians, and so forth. The task of the acolyte was to learn how to demonstrate the validity of the theory in every case, using methods (notably projective techniques) to illuminate the demonstration but never to challenge the fundamentals of the theory. Failure to demonstrate it was a failure on the part of the clinician, never a failure of the theory. One implicit dictum could be detected: "Circumstances do not alter cases." The enormous complexity of the biological and environmental combinations that determine individual differences in human behavior in the real world was ignored, and the differences were dismissed as irrelevant error.

I emphasize all this chiefly to portray the kind of intellectual atmosphere in which Gottesman began the outstanding career that this volume celebrates. He was swimming against the current of a stream that was flowing calmly and confidently into a historical backwater, and there were few cheering him on. He was also confronted with what he himself has termed the "despoiled history of the nature–nurture controversy." Not only had the study of genetics and behavior in the United States been largely abandoned in personality and clinical psychology, it had acquired unattractive connotations from the history of Nazi racism and the euthanasia programs of the Third Reich.

Gottesman persevered as a good scientist would, depending on empirical data to deliver the verdict. Time has delivered the data and has done so handsomely. Gottesman's lifetime contributions to psychological science are not only evidence of his talent and energy. They are a reflection of the integrity of his intellectual standards. He never compromised these standards by seeking to curry the favor of influential colleagues for career advantage or easy academic popularity. Facing the vicissitudes of a setting in which the intellectual levitations of Timothy Leary were interspersed with visits by Beat poets (complete with incense sticks), he coped by recourse to the wry humor with which he delights his friends. He was then as now a warm friend and a wonderful colleague.

The impressive list of his published contributions reflects perhaps the most significant theme that runs through of all of them: gene–environment interaction. When the American Psychological Association awarded Gottesman the Gold Medal for Distinguished Scientific Contributions, the opening sentence of the citation began, "For elucidating the genetic and environmental causes of schizophrenia and criminality . . . ." It is in developing the "and" in genetic and environmental causes and by taking seriously the combination of these two sources of influence that Gottesman has been a pioneer, moving the field forward from the simple-minded goal of ultimate reductionism to a sophisticated recognition of the complexity of the interactive influences that create real people in the real world.

My own first exposure to this was in our early collaboration as contributors to N. R. Ellis's *Handbook of Mental Deficiency*.[1] I recently reread Gottesman's chapter, "Genetic Aspects of Intelligent Behavior," and was struck by how well the subsequent 40 years have validated the ideas that he expressed in it.[2] Also striking was the development of a basic model of gene–environment interaction diagrammed to illustrate the concept of reaction range in his 1963 chapter to the later complex diagram of multiple genetic–environmental interactions as the framework within which the concept of reaction surface is placed.[3] His first principles were sound, and his later development of their central theme reflects the systematic movement of his thought from the simple to the complex that is the mark of real scientific progress.

In this connection, it is worthwhile to reflect on a common misunderstanding of the principle of parsimony. When William of Ockham proposed that it was a mistake to hypothesize invisible entities as explanations of natural phenomena, he was castigating metaphysics and not asserting that the most valid explanations are those that assume that "nature" prefers simplicity. He was urging that knowledge be derived from empirical observation, and if observation showed that a phenomenon was complicated, then the task of the scientist was to describe the complexity accurately. It is one of the less attractive legacies of Francis Galton that we have been taught by him the parsimonious principle that the mean of a distribution is the "truth" and that the variance is "error." This belief has been a source of discouragement to the painstaking identification of the components of the heterogeneity that is characteristic of so many categories of behavior. In the field of psychopathology heterogeneity is evident in many disorders, and the identification of the com-

---

[1]*Handbook of Mental Deficiency*, by N. R. Ellis, 1963, New York: McGraw-Hill.
[2]"Genetic Aspects of Intelligent Behavior," by I. I. Gottesman, in *Handbook of Mental Deficiency* (pp. 253–296), edited by N. R. Ellis, 1963, New York: McGraw-Hill.
[3]"Twins en Route to QTLs for Cognition," by I. I. Gottesman, 1997, *Science, 276*, pp. 1522–1523.

ponents of this is a central task of the psychopathologist. Gottesman has shown us how to go about it. In doing so, he has moved the field forward in ways that are evident in the contributions presented in this book.

Gottesman's work has required a true understanding of and sympathy with interdisciplinary concepts. The scope of the contributions and the disciplinary spectrum of their authors is a clear illustration of this. Medical geneticists, molecular biologists, psychologists, psychiatrists, epidemiologists, and members of many other disciplines have worked on the range of issues that Gottesman has illuminated in his work. His interests have taken him wherever some part of the solution might be found. The topics discussed in the chapters that follow indicate the spread of the influence that he has had in psychology and psychiatry. Here are some examples: the genetic implications of the multifactorial model of genetic–environmental interaction on the neurodevelopmental model of pathology in schizophrenia, the computer modeling of a simulation of environmental variables interacting with different genotypes, the role of genetic factors in the relationship between normal personality traits and psychopathology, the gene–environment interaction in depression, the identification of vulnerability to later schizophrenia, and many other areas.

When looking back at the early work of a scientist and comparing it with his or her later crowning achievements, it is tempting to make the assumption that the years between encompassed one giant stride. Archimedes with his bathtub insights gave us the romantic model of the "eureka" phenomenon, the sudden brilliant insight that produces an instant solution to an age-old problem. The decades of patience and care that go into the systematic development of the ideas and techniques that produced ultimate scientific triumphs in the real world often go unremarked. Pavlov said it well: "From the very beginning of your work, school yourself to severe gradualness in the accumulation of knowledge."[4] Gottesman has done this. He has pursued and extended his ideas over many years, and this book is a sample of the consequences. There have, however, been several landmark events that stand amid the steady accumulation of evidence over the years. One that has been often cited in this way is the now classic paper, "A Polygenic Theory of Schizophrenia."[5] As one group of contributors to this volume (Moises, Zoega, Li, & Hood, chapter 10, this volume) points out, the question of how schizophrenia was genetically transmitted had been a mystery for more than a century, but the puzzle was solved by Gottesman and Shields, and their model has become the central paradigm in modern psychiatry. This is as close to a eureka phenomenon as the behavioral sciences get.

Our knowledge of genetics has expanded enormously, and with it has come an appreciation that the link from genes to behavior is vastly more complicated than was hitherto assumed. Much of the progress in genetics research has arisen from the development of sophisticated techniques of measurement and analysis in the past two or three decades. To gather the mature fruit of

---

[4]*The Practical Cogitator* (p. 98), by C. P. Curtis and F. Greenslet, 1962, Boston: Houghton Mifflin.
[5]"A Polygenic Theory of Schizophrenia," by I. I. Gottesman and J. Shields, 1967, in *Proceedings of the National Academy of Sciences, USA, 58*, pp. 199–205.

these efforts through a comprehensive and systematic effort will require the parallel development of equally fine-grained techniques for the analysis of behavior. These techniques for the fine-grained analysis of genetic data are, unfortunately, not yet at the level that will permit us to define and measure environmental variables with an acceptable degree of precision and with methods that are not dependent on defining the quality or quantity of such variables by reference to normative behavioral reactions to them. As progress is made in this, we may come to an even clearer appreciation of the importance of Gottesman's contributions.

Gottesman's work has been recognized by many honors and awards. They were hard-earned and well deserved. Through his perceptive analysis of the multifactorial nature of the gene–environment question and his persistent energy in following the facts, Gottesman provided leadership in the process of mapping out the genetic terrain in which the fine-grained factors are to be identified and measured. The road ahead is clear, and we can be confident that systematic gradualism will carry us along it. This volume, which takes us part of the way, stands as a testimony to the work of a remarkable scientist and to the breadth of his influence on his field.

Brendan A. Maher

Preface: A Tribute to Irving I. Gottesman

Irving I. Gottesman

This book is an amalgamation of ideas, histories, theories, and predictions. Together, the chapters explore the behavior genetics literature on psychopathology, development, and personality. Irving I. Gottesman has been a leading figure in this work since his early days as a psychologist, and his many students and colleagues continue to work with him and with others to advance the field. This volume is a testament to the enormous impact of these scientists on current conceptualizations of human development and psychopathology. No longer do we concern ourselves with whether nature or nurture is responsible for behavior. We now accept that both are critical aspects of behavior and that the interesting questions concern how they work together to produce individual differences in behavior. The research of Gottesman and his colleagues has been a cornerstone for this field of inquiry.

This book represents a tribute to Irving I. Gottesman, a pioneer in the fields of psychopathology and behavior genetics. The Festschrift that preceded this volume was a celebration of Gottesman's many years of dedicated and innovative research in the fields of clinical psychology, developmental psychology, and behavior genetics. That conference and this volume together represent a compendium of work by researchers who have been mentored and influenced by Gottesman. The coverage extends to the sometimes diverse areas of developmental psychology, personality, and psychopathology, but all have in common the study of genetic influences on behavior and the ways in which the influences of genes and environment are interwoven. Gottesman's work includes groundbreaking research in all of these areas.[1] Most important, Gottesman and his students and colleagues continue to add to this body of research and to publish many of the most influential reports in these areas.

Gottesman's extensive work in psychopathology has been acknowledged and celebrated in many ways. He has been awarded many prestigious honors, including the Distinguished Scientific Contributions Award from the American Psychological Association, reflecting the committee consensus that he is "at the absolute top of the field." The list of Gottesman's awards during his academic career is impressive and reflects the high regard in which he is held by his peers. Some of the more impressive awards include the Lifetime Achievement Award from the Japanese Society for Biological Psychiatry (2000); the Lifetime Achievement Award in Psychiatric Genetics from the International Society for Psychiatric Genetics (1997), the only time a psychologist has been accorded this honor; the William James Book Award from the American Psychological Association (APA) Society for General Psychology; the Theodosius Dobzhansky Award (for lifetime contributions to behavioral genetics) from the Behavior Genetics Association; the Stanley R. Dean Research Award for Contributions to Schizophrenia Research from the American College of Psychiatrists; the Distinguished Scientist Award from the Society for a Science of Clinical Psychology (APA); the Kurt Schneider Prize from the University of Bonn (Germany); the Hofheimer Prize for Research from the American Psychiatric Association; and the Stephen V. Logan Award

---

[1]"The Efficiency of Several Combinations of Discrete and Continuous Variables for the Diagnosis of Zygosity," by I. I. Gottesman, in *Proceedings, Second International Congress of Human Genetics* (pp. 346–347), 1963, Rome, Italy: G. Mendel Institute; *Schizophrenia Genesis: The Origins of Madness*, by I. I. Gottesman, 1991, New York: W. H. Freeman; "Twins—en Route to QTLs for Cognition," by I. I. Gottesman, 1997, *Science, 276*, pp. 1522–1523; *Schizophrenia and Genetics: A Twin Study Vantage Point*, by I. I. Gottesman and J. Shields, 1972, New York: Academic Press; *Schizophrenia: The Epigenetic Puzzle*, by I. I. Gottesman and J. Shields, 1982, New York: Cambridge University Press; "Commentary—Some Conceptual Deficiencies in 'Developmental' Behavior Genetics," by E. Turkheimer, H. H. Goldsmith, and I. I. Gottesman, 1995, *Human Development, 38*, 142–153.

Speakers at the Festschrift in Minneapolis, MN, June 2001, and chapter authors of this volume. *From left:* Gregory Carey, Eric Turkheimer, David L. DiLalla, Peter McGuffin, Thomas J. Bouchard Jr., Anne Farmer, Hans Moises, Lisabeth F. DiLalla, Aksel Bertelsen, Irving I. Gottesman, H. Hill Goldsmith, Susan L. Trumbetta, William G. Iacono, L. Erlenmeyer-Kimling, and Daniel R. Hanson. (Matt McGue is absent.)

for research on schizophrenia and bipolar illnesses from the National Alliance for the Mentally Ill. He also is a fellow of the American Association for the Advancement of Science, the Academy of Clinical Psychology, the Royal College of Psychiatrists (London; honorary), and the Center for Advanced Study in the Behavioral Sciences in Stanford, California, and he was a Guggenheim Fellow at the University of Copenhagen from 1972 to 1973.

Gottesman has been actively involved in societies that form the basis for much of the research in these areas. For example, he has been a member of APA since 1958 and a fellow since 1975. He currently is the chair of the Twin Committee of the Institute of Medicine/National Academy of Sciences and is a member of the Medical Follow-Up Agency of the Institute of Medicine of the National Academy of Sciences. He was president of the Behavior Genetics Association in 1976. He served as the president of the Society for Research in Psychopathology in 1993. Gottesman also has served as an associate or consulting editor for 7 journals and has been on the editorial board of another 10.

The list of Gottesman's publications is outstanding by any criteria. He has published 185 journal articles, 19 books and monographs, 77 book chapters, and 23 book reviews. His collaborators include other eminent psychologists, including some of his own students, many of whom have gone on to amass an impressive list of publications in their own right.

These awards and accomplishments attest to the eminent and prolific career that Gottesman has had thus far, and his plans for continued research and teaching following his retirement from the University of Virginia in 2001 ensure that his productivity will continue to enlighten the field. Gottesman currently is professor emeritus at the University of Minnesota. He continues work on twin projects and psychopathology with colleagues and students from around the globe. This volume affords a reflection of his influences on the work of a number of his former students and colleagues and lights the path to future discoveries.

Acknowledgments

I gratefully acknowledge my colleagues whose collaborations created this exciting volume. Herein are stimulating discussions that began as Festschrift presentations held in Irving I. Gottesman's honor. This volume showcases the intellectual exchanges that occurred among researchers and students from all over the world. I am grateful for our collective efforts in bringing those discussions to a broad audience.

I sincerely acknowledge the cooperation and assistance of my colleagues who helped make the Festschrift an academically enlightening environment and thereby a resounding success. Additionally, I gratefully acknowledge those who provided financial support for this festschrift, including the Science Directorate of the American Psychological Association (APA), the University of Minnesota Medical School, and the Southern Illinois University School of Medicine. I also would like to recognize the wonderful APA staff who assisted with this volume, especially Kristine Enderle, Mary Lynn Skutley, and Sangeeta Panicker, as well as Robin Bonner at NOVA Graphic Services.

Finally, I would like to thank Irving I. Gottesman for . . . everything. For his sensitive and brilliant mentoring, for his contributions to science, and for sharing his ineffable wit and wisdom with his students, his colleagues, and his discipline all these years.

Part I

Introduction

1

Behavioral Genetics: Background, Current Research, and Goals for the Future

Lisabeth F. DiLalla

Behavioral genetics, the study of genetic and environmental origins of individual differences in behavior, has been an organized method of study in psychology for some time but has only been widely accepted by psychologists in the past decade or two as a means for understanding the etiology of mental illness as well as normal development. Earlier, learning theory provided the predominant explanation for behavior, with the prevailing belief being that the environment was the cause of all behaviors (e.g., Mischel, 1968). It is true that for all psychological variables studied to date, environmental influences have been found that explain a portion of the observed individual differences in the behaviors (Carey, 2003), but that does not mean that the environment is the only (or even the primary) influence on behavior. Behavioral geneticists believe that both genes and environment affect behavior, a radical view when first expressed. Since that time, this has become a leading perspective in the psychology literature, with research around the globe demonstrating the influence of both genotype (genetic makeup) and environment on various phenotypes (measurable behaviors; Carey, 2003).

A relatively few researchers were responsible for leading behavioral genetics to its current status as a scientifically accepted area of study. One of those pioneers was Dr. Irving I. Gottesman, whose investigations into the genesis of schizophrenia have resulted in the delineation of several models of the development of psychopathology that neatly account for the ways in which genes and environment interact. He incorporated concepts used in the physical sciences, such as reaction range, endophenotypes, and threshold models, and these terms have now become standard psychological nomenclature. His threshold model (Gottesman & Shields, 1967) applied polygenic/threshold models of inheritance to the field of psychopathology by positing an underlying continuum of genetic and environmental risks for psychopathology. Psychopathology becomes evident when an accumulation of sufficient risks causes an individual to cross the threshold from "normal" to "abnormal." Dr. Gottesman's reaction range, or reaction threshold, model (Gottesman & Goldsmith, 1994; Turkheimer, Goldsmith, & Gottesman, 1995) describes the importance of genetic, environmental, and developmental factors that work together, resulting in behaviors that are multiply determined but have upper and lower limits as a function of both genetic and environmental influences. His use of the term "endophenotype," meaning internal phenotypes that are intermediate between the genes and the more easily measured and observed behaviors (Gottesman & Gould, 2003), has important implications for future research. With a focus on endophenotypes, underlying genetic influences on behaviors may be discovered more easily.

The field of behavioral genetics offers an important perspective on psychological phenomena and has sometimes challenged conventional wisdom. For example, research performed on intelligence in children in the 1960s found that those who came from homes with more books also tended to excel in school, which led to the conclusion that increasing the number of books in children's homes would produce a rise in their academic achievement. Behavioral genetics has shown that this is only part of the picture. More intelligent parents provide an environment for their children that is more conducive to intellectual development (e.g., more books in the home) as well as genotypes that contribute to greater academic achievement, and they also respond to their children's own cognitive levels, with brighter children eliciting appropriate behaviors from their environment (DiLalla, 2000). These two sources, environment and genotype, together lead to the child's higher academic achievement. In fact, heritable factors have been shown to explain much more of the variance in intellectual development than does shared rearing environment and may be the most important contributors to shared IQ among family members (Rowe, 1994).

Similarly, behavioral genetic research informs the application of psychopathology research, and this is something for which Dr. Gottesman has been an active advocate. His approach to research has included a healthy mixture of science and compassion, which is especially important in a field that has been misinterpreted in the past as supporting genetic determinism. Dr. Gottesman was called to China in a recent court case involving three men interested in jobs with the Fire Services Department and the Customs and Excise Department. Their parents were schizophrenic, and therefore the government believed that these men were not qualified to work in the disciplinary forces and had denied them access to these jobs. Dr. Gottesman called this policy "totally intolerable" (Yee, 2000, p. A1), pointing out that genetic determinism does not exist and that genetic influence is only one factor in the etiology of psychopathology. He has also been an advocate for the personal liberties of individuals with psychopathology (Gottesman & Moldin, 1999) and an outspoken proponent of the view that behaviors are probabilistic rather than genetically determined (Healy, 1998). An important task of behavioral geneticists is to present their research in humane and ethical ways and to avoid deterministic interpretations.

A significant research goal involves understanding the ways in which genes and environment work together to shape behaviors. This has been the focus of Dr. Gottesman's research since he began his career, well before the general excitement for and acceptance of this form of research blossomed. Currently, there is an enormous amount of interest in this area of research, with new findings emerging from research labs around the world at a rapid rate. The differential effects of genetic and environmental influences and the ways in which these work together are still a puzzle, but one that Dr. Gottesman and the contributors to this volume are attempting to solve.

Behavioral Genetics Methodology

The field of human behavioral genetics uses several methodologies to study the origin of individual differences. The primary concern is to separate genetic from environmental influences on the behaviors under study. Of course, there is no ethical experimental way to accomplish this with humans. However, there are several "experiments of nature" that allow researchers to separate genetic and environmental influences statistically and thus to study their relative importance for behavioral outcomes.

Twin Studies

The first of these "experiments of nature" is the twin study. This is the methodology most often used by Dr. Gottesman in his research and is the basis for much of the research described in this volume. There are two types of twins: identical or monozygotic (MZ) twins, who share 100% of their genetic makeup, and fraternal or dizygotic (DZ) twins, who share on average approximately 50% of their genetic makeup. A comparison between MZ and DZ twin similarity provides an estimation of heritability. Figure 1.1 presents a path diagram that demonstrates this concept.

In the figure, A refers to additive genetic influences, C refers to common or shared environmental influences, and E refers to nonshared environmental influences. A fourth variable, D (dominant genetic influences), is sometimes included, but only three of these can be included in a twin model or else the model will not be identified. (Note that some researchers use G for genetic influence rather than A or D, e.g., chapter 6.) Thus, the ACE model (shown in Figure 1.1) is one in which A, C, and E are variables that directly influence the phenotype being studied. This is a commonly applied behavioral genetics model. If the path h, the square root of the heritability of the phenotype, is not significant, it can be dropped from the model, resulting perhaps in a CE model, one without genetic influence. Similarly, the path from C to the phenotype is c, the square root of the shared environmental influence, and the path from E to the phenotype is e, the square root of the nonshared environmental influence.

The correlation between identical twins (the degree to which they are similar to each other) is a function of their genetic makeup (they are genetically identical) and the environmental influences that they share (common environment). These are designated as h^2 and c^2, respectively. The algebraic equation for this correlation is

$$r_{MZ} = h^2 + c^2.$$

This can also be seen using Figure 1.1 and Wright's Rules (Wright, 1960) for calculating the correlation between two variables. The correlation between Twin 1 and Twin 2 can be found by tracing the paths from Twin 1 up to A (path h), across the link from the first A to the second A (1.0 for MZ twins), and down from A to Twin 2 (path h). Multiplying these paths gives us h^2. Then we add the values obtained by tracing the paths from Twin 1 through C to Twin 2, which gives us c^2. There is no link between the twins via the E variable because E represents aspects of the environment that the twins do not

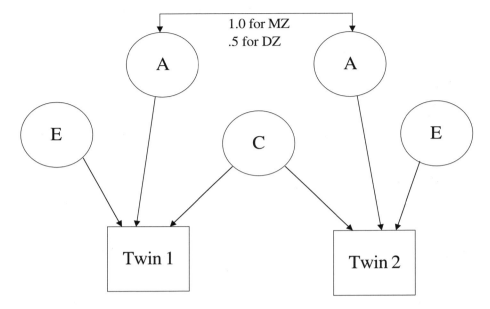

Figure 1.1. Typical ACE path diagram for twins. A = additive genetic influence, C = common (shared) environment, E = nonshared environment.

share, and therefore it does not contribute to their correlation, or what makes them similar. The correlation between fraternal twins also is a function of their genetic makeup (they share approximately 50% of their genes) and the common environmental influences that they share. Their correlation can be obtained using the tracing rules and the path diagram in Figure 1.1, or algebraically,

$$r_{DZ} = \left(\tfrac{1}{2}\right) h^2 + c^2.$$

An estimate of heritability can be achieved statistically by using structural equation modeling to estimate h in the path diagram and then squaring it or algebraically by subtracting the two equations ($r_{MZ} - r_{DZ} = [\tfrac{1}{2}]h^2$) and then doubling the difference:

$$h^2 = 2(r_{MZ} - r_{DZ}).$$

There are a few assumptions upon which twin methodologies depend. One of the most important is the "equal environments assumption." This states that identical and fraternal twins share comparable environments with respect to the characteristic of interest. That is, identical twins are not more similar on that characteristic simply as a function of being treated more similarly, except to the extent that more similar twins evoke or choose more similar environments (reflecting evocative or active gene–environment correlation), which becomes an effect of genes and not only environment. It is certainly possible that there are basic differences between the environments of identical twins and fraternal twins, but the equal environments assumption states that these differences are not relevant for the psychological traits studied. Most of the research that has explored the equal environments assumption has supported its applicability (Hettema, Neale, & Kendler, 1995; Loehlin & Nichols, 1976; Scarr & Carter-Saltzman, 1979).

A second concern for behavioral genetic studies (with twins as well as adoptees, described below) is the phenomenon of assortative mating. If parents of twins mate based in part on similarity of a certain behavior, for instance personality type, then fraternal twins will share more genes for this personality type than expected by chance, assuming that the personality type is influenced by genotype. (Identical twins, of course, still share 100% of their genetic makeup.) This would increase the similarity between fraternal twins, reducing the difference between identical and fraternal twin correlations and yielding a deflated heritability estimate.

Adoption Studies

A second behavior genetics methodology is the adoption method, which involves studying children who are adopted by nonrelatives, preferably having been placed away from their biological parents as soon after birth as possible. Because this method is not covered in the chapters in this volume, the following explanation is brief. More details can be found in texts such as Carey (2003) or Plomin, DeFries, McClearn, and McGuffin (2001). An examination of the correlation between adopted children and adoptive parents and the correlation between adopted children and biological parents yields information about the relative influences of environment and genes on the behaviors under study. The adoptive child theoretically shares genes but no environment with the biological parents and shares environment but no genetic makeup with the adoptive parents. Basically, any similarity between the adopted child and biological parents reflects the influence of genetic factors, and any similarity between the adopted child and adoptive parents reflects the influence of environmental factors on the trait being measured. This methodology is less frequently employed than the twin methodology simply because it is more difficult to obtain an adoption sample than a twin sample. Potential confounds with the adoption method include selective placement, prenatal environment from the biological mother, assortative mating, and isomorphism of the child and adult measures used in the study. For more information see Coon, Carey, and Fulker (1990), DiLalla (2002), or Fulker and DeFries (1983).

Identifying Specific Genes

Finally, a third method for exploring genetic influences on human behavior is linkage analysis, which involves locating genes on particular chromosomes that are related to certain traits. Linkage analysis examines huge family pedigrees and looks for the association between DNA marker alleles and particular disorders (Plomin et al., 2001). If a marker allele is found to co-occur with a particular disorder within members of a family, then it can be assumed that the gene responsible for that disorder is close to the marker gene on that chromo-some. This is a useful technique for traits that are caused by a single gene, but it becomes much more complicated when there are multiple genes involved in the transmission of the disorder. For these more complicated, and more typical, behaviors or traits, the affected sibling-pair linkage design is more effective (Plomin et al., 2001). In this design, siblings who share a trait or disorder are identified, and their alleles for marker genes are assessed. If the marker gene is associated with the gene(s) that influence the disorder, then the siblings will have a greater than 25% chance of sharing two alleles for the marker gene. If the marker gene is not associated with the disorder, then any two siblings have a 25% chance of sharing zero or two alleles for a given gene and a 50% chance of sharing one allele (based on Mendelian inheritance). Progress in locating genes that affect specific behaviors is slow because the effects of individual genes is small when many genes influence a given behavior or trait, but progress is evident as researchers locate genes responsible for disorders such as reading disability and dementia (Plomin & McGuffin, 2003).

Once a specific gene is located as a likely contributor to a trait, association studies can further examine this. An affected sample and a control sample can be compared on the presence of a specific allele to determine whether there is an increased prevalence of that allele in the affected group. However, one problem with this strategy is that there may be population differences in the frequency of the allele in question that may differ between the affected and control samples (Carey, 2003), thus rendering the comparison less meaning-ful. Alternatively, using a family association design circumvents that particu-lar problem (Carey, 2003). Rather than comparing an affected sample with a random control sample, comparing them with their unaffected siblings controls for potential population genetic differences. Association studies are therefore superior to linkage studies because they can pinpoint the exact gene that is associated with a disorder or trait. When the exact gene to be investi-gated is not yet known, however, linkage studies are valuable in attempting to identify a potential gene for further investigation.

We have acquired much information over the past few decades about genetic influences on various behaviors and pathologies. We are now at an exciting stage in this journey, ready to ask new, more complicated questions. Future behavioral genetic research needs to focus on identifying specific genes responsible for the traits we wish to study, as well as on exploring the intricately complex ways in which genes and environments interact to produce behaviors.

Introduction to the Present Volume

The chapters in this book are offshoots of the presentations at the Festschrift honoring Dr. Gottesman in June 2001. Twelve invited speakers addressed the primary areas covered in this volume: Developmental Behavioral Genetics, Personality and Genetics, Genetic Influences on Psychopathology, and Molec-ular Genetics and the Future of the Field. These areas recapitulate the essence of Dr. Gottesman's work in psychology and behavioral genetics. The study of behavioral genetics has been applied to normal psychological development and the study of normal personality traits and development, as covered in the first two sections of this book. It also has been highly influential in the study of psychopathology. The future of the field rests in new discoveries of molecular genetics as we explore connections between specific genes and behaviors. As Dr. Gottesman was a pioneer in the study of behavioral genetics, so too he continues his involvement in research on molecular genetics and psychology. This volume enhances our understanding of these aspects of psychology and behavioral genetics through a variety of means, some more historical and some representing explorations into new territory. The chapters vary in style and content, with some taking a broader perspective of the field and others describing specific research relating directly to the type of work that Dr. Gottesman has either conducted or influenced.

This book demonstrates how behavioral genetics as a science has augmented our understanding of many areas of psychology. The specific topics covered herein are those that Dr. Gottesman has studied throughout his career. It is noteworthy that they run the gamut from normal development and personality to psychopathology, demonstrating both the varied research in which Dr. Gottesman has been engaged and the importance of behavioral genetics for many fields of psychology. Some of the chapters provide broad overviews of specific aspects of the field, whereas others report research studies that have grown out of collaborations with Dr. Gottesman. The richness of this volume lies in the diversity of the contents of the various chapters. This has allowed the volume to cover novel approaches to the study of behavioral genetics and psychopathology, summaries of past work that represents the building blocks for future endeavors, and perspectives on the future of the field. Some of the historical sections provide a human-interest aspect to give the reader insight into the history of much research in the field. Together, these chapters represent a compendium of ideas and knowledge about behavioral genetics and development, personality, and psychopathology that summarize and extend Dr. Gottesman's influence on these fields.

This volume is divided into four broad sections: developmental behavioral genetics, personality and genetics, genetic influences on psychopathology, and the future of the field. The overarching theme is the study of genetic and environmental influences on behavior, utilizing methodologies and theories that were originated, influenced, or endorsed by Dr. Gottesman. We begin with the study of behaviors at the normal end of the spectrum in the first two sections, then move to psychopathology, and finally end with ruminations on novel approaches and forward thinking for the next wave of behavioral genetics researchers to consider.

Developmental Behavioral Genetics

The field of developmental psychology has been greatly augmented by the incorporation of behavioral genetics into its methodology. This was first popularized by Plomin, DeFries, and Loehlin (1977) and Scarr and McCartney (1983), when they described the developmental interplay between genes and environment throughout development. They defined passive gene–environment correlation as beginning in infancy, when infants receive both their genotype and their environment from their parents. Thus, genotype and environment are correlated, e.g., when a highly reactive infant inherits a "reactive" temperament from a parent with that type of personality and also is raised in a "reactive" environment by that same parent. Reactive or evocative gene–environment correlation can begin in infancy and can continue throughout life. This occurs when an individual's genetically influenced phenotype (perhaps an aggressive personality type) causes those around him or her to react to this phenotype in a particular way (perhaps responding aggressively in turn), thus causing the individual's environment to be correlated with his or her genotype. Finally, active gene–environment correlation begins after infancy and continues throughout the life span. This occurs when an individual actively chooses his or her own environment (for example, an art college) based in part on genetically influenced personal characteristics (great artistic ability). The resulting correlation between genes and environment leads to enhanced artistic ability.

A few researchers have examined stability and change of genetic influences on normal development (Wilson, 1983). Genes do not simply exist at birth and exert an unchanging influence throughout the life span. Rather, genes turn on and off through life and therefore may change in their influences on certain behaviors at different times or stages in development. The most obvious example of this is puberty, when genes for adult sexual development turn on and cause the growth of secondary sexual characteristics. Another obvious example is menopause. However, genetic influences on psychological variables appear to be more responsible for stability than for change, although these genetic influences may be amplified over time. For example, a study of adolescent twins and siblings demonstrated that genotype contributed to the stability of self-worth over a 3-year period (McGuire et al., 1999). Similarly, a study of reading performance in 7-year-old and adolescent adoptees tested in the Colorado Adoption Project (CAP) showed that genetic influences were responsible for most of the phenotypic stability across ages, with no new genetic influence appearing at the adolescent ages (Wadsworth, Corley, Hewitt, & DeFries, 2001). Continuity in intelligence also appears to be driven primarily by genetic influence (Bartels, Rietveld, Van Baal, & Boomsma, 2002).

The study of genetic influences on development can benefit from incorporation of Gottesman's theoretical work on such concepts as reaction range (Gottesman & Goldsmith, 1994) and threshold model (Gottesman & Shields, 1967). The threshold model allows consideration of development as an accumulation of genetic and environment liabilities and assets that collectively can cause a child to cross the threshold from normal behavior or personality to abnormal behaviors or disorders. Reaction range also is useful developmentally because it represents the range of possible phenotypes that an individual with a given genotype may exhibit. This awareness can provide a greater understanding of the role of the environment in influencing specific behaviors and the degree to which those behaviors can be expected to be mutable (DiLalla, 1998). Thus, although genotype may be a limiting factor in expression of a behavior, for instance intelligence, environmental influences are essential for determining exactly where within those limits the individual falls. This concept may be most useful developmentally for intervention programs that attempt to structure the environment in such a way as to change developmental outcomes such as poor school performance or behavior problems.

The chapters in this section focus on normal behaviors at different stages of the life span. H. Hill Goldsmith and colleagues (chapter 2) focus on temperament as a liability to psychopathology, not only in childhood but throughout the life span. The authors explore the possibility that temperament and childhood psychopathology share similar physiological endophenotypes, suggesting that some genetic etiology may be shared. The example of a link between ADHD and difficult temperament is proposed in the chapter. Matt McGue and William G. Iacono (chapter 3) explore substance use and abuse among adolescents in the Minnesota Twin Family Study. This chapter specifically covers findings related to the age that adolescents first tried alcohol, demonstrating that trying alcohol at an earlier age is indicative of greater problem drinking and other substance abuse longitudinally. The use of twins in this study allows an examination of whether earlier drinking is heritable and whether it appears to cause later substance abuse or whether both are caused by a common underlying factor. The authors' conclusions suggest that a disinhibitory factor accounts for both early drinking and later substance abuse, and this factor is at least partially genetically mediated. Finally, Susan Trumbetta (chapter 4) focuses specifically on health, marriage, and divorce in a middle-aged sample of twins from the National Academy of Sciences-National Research Council World War II Veteran Twin Registry. The twin sample is used to demonstrate an interaction between genes and environment, with marriage lowering the heritability estimates for exercise and increasing heritability estimates for smoking. Marriage may act as a main effect on exercise, overriding any genetic influence that may exist, but phenotypic expression of an underlying "smoking" genotype may be augmented by marriage, perhaps because of assortative mating.

Personality and Genetics

The study of underlying genetic influence on normal variation in personality is also relevant to researchers who study psychopathology because of the likelihood that some psychopathology represents the extreme end of a continuous and normal distribution of personality (Jang & Livesley, 1999; Livesley, Jang, & Vernon, 1998; Nigg & Goldsmith, 1998). Across a large number of research studies, approximately 40%–50% of the variation in most personality traits has been shown to be caused by genetic influence, with a very small amount of the variation caused by shared environment (Plomin, Happe, & Caspi, 2002). Assuming that most psychological disorders are caused in part by multiple genes (rather than by single genes), which seems to be the case, it is most likely that combinations of alleles of these genes result in different degrees to which the disorders or traits associated with them are expressed. Dr. Gottesman's threshold model (Gottesman & Shields, 1967) speaks directly to this concept. The more alleles that an individual has that lead to expression of pathology and the more the individual encounters an environment that is maladaptive, the more that individual will be accumulating genetic and environmental liabilities that can eventually cause him or her to cross the threshold from normal personality to psychopathology. Thus, the study of the genetic underpinnings of normal personality, interesting in its own right in terms of personality theory, is also relevant for the study of psychopathology.

This section of the book provides an overview of current issues in the study of personality and genetics. The first chapter provides a broad overview of the topics of statistical methods in studying personality, and the second is more specific in demonstrating genetic effects on attitudes. David DiLalla and Greg Carey (chapter 5) discuss statistical methods for studying the covariation between personality and psychopathology. They stress the importance of considering genotype as a common variable that influences both personality and psychopathology rather than assuming that personality per se leads to psychopathology. Thomas Bouchard and colleagues (chapter 6) utilize data from the Minnesota Study of Twins Reared Apart (MISTRA) to discuss the unexpected finding that genetic effects account for a large proportion of variance in attitude scores. Specifically, religiosity, authoritarianism, and conservatism appear to have heritability estimates of about 40%–50%. These two chapters compel us to reconsider traditional views of personality and to include effects of genotype in theories of personality.

Psychopathology and Genetics

Psychopathology has been a major focus for behavioral genetic research and has been the area on which most of Dr. Gottesman's work has focused. Research on twins and adoptees has made it clear that genetic influences exist for most psychopathologies that have been studied. The search for the causes of psychopathology, and schizophrenia in particular, have led Dr. Gottesman and other researchers to explore a variety of possibilities, including single-gene causes of specific pathologies, multiple-gene causes of pathology, and the interface between genes and environment (Gottesman & Shields, 1967, 1984). No environment has been found that clearly causes schizophrenia (Gottesman, 1984), further strengthening findings that genes are important, though not sufficient, contributors to the disorder.

The third section of this book serves to highlight some of the behavioral genetic research on depression and schizophrenia and to provide the reader with a sense of where this field has been and what the key questions are that remain to be addressed. Anne Farmer (chapter 7) emphasizes the importance of considering environmental influences as they interact and co-act with genes, specifically for depression. Two European samples, representing Farmer's own research on family members, are used to demonstrate a mediation by personality or cognitive style on the relation between hazardous life events and depression. Chapter 8, by Aksel Bertelsen, provides a compendium of the studies he and Dr. Gottesman have performed on Danish populations. This historical perspective represents a tribute to Dr. Gottesman and their years of working together, as well as a background for better understanding the historical means by which the invaluable data sets based on the Danish registries were obtained. The results of their twin study research on criminality, schizophrenia, bipolar disorder and other psychiatric illnesses contribute considerable insight into psychopathology and psychiatric genetics. Their novel use of disease-discordant twins has provided information about the effects of various environmental influences on these psychiatric illnesses.

L. Erlenmeyer-Kimling and colleagues (chapter 9) address the issue of longitudinal prediction of schizophrenia, a subject that has been one of Dr. Gottesman's primary areas of study over the course of his career. This chapter presents the ongoing results of a large longitudinal sample, the New York High-Risk Project, that assesses possible predictors of adult psychopathology from information gathered when participants were 7 to 12 years old. Specifically, three childhood neurobehavioral tests predict schizophrenia-related disorders but not other psychopathology. This chapter further deals with variables that may act as a buffer against these early risks. Finally, Hans Moises and colleagues (chapter 10) highlight the relations between genetic and neurodevelopmental models of the origins of schizophrenia. A series of hypotheses are put forth to explain familial incidences of schizophrenia and other mental disorders, beginning with traditional Darwinian and Mendelian explanations and culminating in state-of-the-art research using linkage association techniques. A model integrating genetic and environmental interaction is proposed to account for genetic transmission of schizophrenia.

The Future of the Field

The final section of this book is dedicated to considerations of the future of the fields of behavioral genetics and psychology. It is clear from the myriad studies conducted on genetic effects on psychopathology and normal behavior that genetic influences are significant for most behaviors, but they are not sufficient to produce the behaviors without the contribution of other, environmental factors as well (Owen, McGuffin, & Gottesman, 2002). Behavioral genetic studies have traditionally used twin or adoption designs, as described previously. As the Human Genome Project progresses and more is learned about the effects of specific genes, we will be able to better understand which genes contribute to different behaviors and possibly we will learn more about the interactive effects of genes. Linkage analysis and association studies, also described earlier, are techniques that allow current exploration of specific genes' effects on behaviors. The future of the field of behavioral genetics lies in discovering specific genes that influence behaviors as well as exploring the ways in which genes interact with genes and with the environment to affect behavior. This challenge is immense, but it is one that researchers already are beginning to conquer.

The chapters presented in this section provide groundbreaking ideas for future research and for conceptualizations of the concepts most central to this field of research. Eric Turkheimer (chapter 11) urges us to reexamine our notions of causality in terms of genetic and environmental influences on behavior. He specifically considers definitions of shared and nonshared environment. Through the use of computer simulations, he demonstrates the importance of distinguishing between systematic nonshared environmental influences and nonsystematic shared environmental influences. Peter

McGuffin (chapter 12) addresses issues involved in identifying genes that influence susceptibility to abnormal behavior and the subsequent influences such knowledge will have on the ways clinicians deal with mental illness. He presents convincing evidence for genetic influences on mental disorders, most of which will be polygenic or involve rare mutations or anomalies. This chapter concludes with a description of the positive impact of this knowledge on the psychological and psychiatric professions, suggesting that a greater understanding of the role of genes in the ontogeny of mental disorders should lead to increased acceptance of mental disorders by the public and increased ability to treat these disorders by professionals.

Daniel Hanson (chapter 13) takes a novel and speculative approach to conceptualizing the causes of schizophrenia by considering the disorder as an infectious disease. He suggests that the genetic liability toward schizophrenia may reflect genetic influence on resistence to fairly common causes of schizophrenia rather than the existence of rare genes that cause the disease. This chapter encourages us to entertain new ideas as we search for the ultimate causes of psychopathology. Finally, Dr. Gottesman (chapter 14) offers a brief summary of his thoughts about his personal scientific journey and the future research of the field. This chapter puts Gottesman's own research in perspective and utilizes current research on schizophrenia as a springboard for discussion of current behavioral genetic breakthroughs. Gottesman ends by considering the future of behavior genetic research and the importance of keeping an open, clear mind ready for the next wave of technological and theoretical advances.

These chapters integrate many of the basic issues in the behavioral genetics literature as it applies to development, personality, and psychopathology. At the heart of this volume are important questions such as how genes and environment correlate and interact and at what level of analysis we should be gearing our research questions. The intent of this book is to provide a means for extending the impact of Dr. Gottesman's contributions by allowing students and colleagues whom he has already influenced to share their knowledge and ideas with a new generation of researchers. To the extent that this volume provokes thought and excites new research ideas, it will have achieved its purpose.

References

Bartels, M., Rietveld, M. J. H., Van Baal, G. C. M., & Boomsma, D. I. (2002). Genetic and environmental influences on the development of intelligence. *Behavior Genetics, 32,* 237–249.

Carey, G. (2003). *Human genetics for the social sciences.* Thousand Oaks, CA: Sage Publications.

Coon, H., Carey, G., & Fulker, D. W. (1990). A simple method of model fitting for adoption data. *Behavior Genetics, 20,* 385–404.

DiLalla, L. F. (1998). Developmental neuropsychology: A behavioral genetic perspective. *Developmental Neuropsychology, 14,* 1–6.

DiLalla, L. F. (2000). Development of intelligence: Current research and theories. *Journal of School Psychology, 38,* 3–7.

DiLalla, L. F. (2002). Behavior genetics of aggression in children: Review and future directions. *Developmental Review, 22,* 593–622.

Fulker, D. W., & DeFries, J. C. (1983). Genetic and environmental transmission in the Colorado Adoption Project: Path analysis. *British Journal of Mathematical and Statistical Psychology, 36,* 175–188.

Gottesman, I. I., & Goldsmith, H. H. (1994). Developmental psychopathology of antisocial behavior: Inserting genes into its ontogenesis and epigenesis. In C. A. Nelson (Ed.), *Threats to optimal development: Integrating biological, psychological, and social risk factors. The Minnesota symposia on child psychology* (Vol. 27, pp. 69–104). Hillsdale, NJ: Erlbaum.

Gottesman, I. I., & Gould, T. D. (2003). The endophenotype concept in psychiatry: Etymology and strategic intentions. *American Journal of Psychiatry, 160*, 636–645.

Gottesman, I. I., & Moldin, S. (1999). *Schizophrenia and genetic risks: A guide to genetic counseling for consumers, their families, and mental health workers.* Arlington, VA: National Alliance for the Mentally Ill.

Gottesman, I. I., & Shields, J. (1967). A polygenic theory of schizophrenia. *Science, 156*, 537–538.

Gottesman, I. I., & Shields, J. (1984). *Schizophrenia: The epigenetic puzzle.* Cambridge, UK: Cambridge University Press.

Healy, D. (1998). Irving Gottesman (USA): Predisposed towards predispositions. In D. Healy (Ed.), *The psychopharmacologists II* (pp. 377–408). London: Chapman & Hall.

Hettema, J. M., Neale, M. C., & Kendler, K. S. (1995). Physical similarity and the equal-environment assumption in twin studies of psychiatric disorders. *Behavior Genetics, 25*, 327–335.

Jang, K. L., & Livesley, W. J. (1999). Why do measures of normal and disordered personality correlate? A study of genetic comorbidity. *Journal of Personality Disorders, 13*, 10–17.

Livesley, W. J., Jang, K. L., & Vernon, P. A. (1998). Phenotypic and genetic structure of traits delineating personality disorder. *Archives of General Psychiatry, 55*, 941–948.

Loehlin, J. C., & Nichols, R. C. (1976). *Heredity, environment and personality: A study of 850 sets of twins.* Austin: University of Texas Press.

McGuire, S., Manke, B., Saudino, K. J., Reiss, D., Hetherington, E. M., & Plomin, R. (1999). Perceived competence and self-worth during adolescence: A longitudinal behavioral genetic study. *Child Development, 70*, 1283–1296.

Mischel, W. (1968). *Personality and assessment.* New York: John Wiley.

Nigg, J. T., & Goldsmith, H. H. (1998). Developmental psychopathology, personality, and temperament: Reflections on recent behavioral genetics research. *Human Biology, 70*, 387–412.

Owen, M. J., McGuffin, P., & Gottesman, I. I. (2002). The future and post-genomic psychiatry. In P. McGuffin, M. J. Owen, & I. I. Gottesman (Eds.), *Psychiatric genetics and genomics* (pp. 445–460). Oxford, UK: Oxford University Press.

Plomin, R., DeFries, J. C., & Loehlin, J. C. (1977). Genotype-environment interaction and correlation in the analysis of human behavior. *Psychological Bulletin, 84*, 309–322.

Plomin, R., DeFries, J. C., McClearn, G. E., & McGuffin, P. (2001). *Behavioral genetics: A primer* (4th ed.). New York: W. H. Freeman.

Plomin, R., Happe, F., & Caspi, A. (2002). Personality and cognitive abilities. In P. McGuffin, M. J. Owen, & I. I. Gottesman (Eds.), *Psychiatric genetics and genomics* (pp. 77–112). Oxford, UK: Oxford University Press.

Plomin, R., & McGuffin, P. (2003). Psychopathology in the postgenomic era. *Annual Review of Psychology, 54*, 205–228.

Rowe, D. C. (1994). *The limits of family influence: Genes, experience, and behavior.* New York: Guilford Press.

Scarr, S., & Carter-Saltzman, L. (1979). Twin method: Defense of a critical assumption. *Behavior Genetics, 9*, 527–542.

Scarr, S., & McCartney, K. (1983). How people make their own environments. *Child Development, 54*, 424–435.

Turkheimer, E., Goldsmith, H. H., & Gottesman, I. I. (1995). Commentary—Some conceptual deficiencies in "developmental" behavior genetics. *Human Development, 38*, 142–153.

Wadsworth, S. J., Corley, R. P., Hewitt, J. K., & DeFries, J. C. (2001). Stability of genetic and environmental influences on reading performance at 7, 12, and 16 years of age in the Colorado Adoption Project. *Behavior Genetics, 31*, 353–359.

Wilson, R. S. (1983). The Louisville Twin Study: Developmental synchronies in behavior. *Child Development, 54*, 298–316.

Wright, S. (1960). Path coefficients and path regressions: Alternative or complementary concepts? *Biometrics, 16*, 189–202.

Yee, Mo Pui. (2000, April 1). Schizophrenics ban under attack. *South China Morning Post*, p. A1.

Part II

Developmental Behavior Genetics

2

Temperament as a Liability Factor for Childhood Behavioral Disorders: The Concept of Liability

H. Hill Goldsmith, Kathryn S. Lemery, and Marilyn J. Essex

One of Dr. Gottesman's signal contributions to the study of psychopathology has been to lay out a conceptual framework for relating risk factors to overt psychopathology. This contribution has taken many forms, one of which was the components of liability to schizophrenia model (Gottesman & Shields, 1972). In its ordinary language sense, liability equates to the ideas of predisposition or potential. The term also has a technical, statistical meaning that dates to D. S. Falconer's (1965, 1967) seminal explication. Falconer provided methods for estimating the inheritance of a continuous dimension of liability to complex human diseases such as diabetes from kinship and epidemiological risk data. Psychological traits or disorders are considered to be complex because they involve some combination of genetic and environmental contributors and perhaps a heterogeneous array of causal factors. Gottesman and Shields (1967; Gottesman, 1974) recognized that Falconer's work, growing out of plant and animal breeding, could help bridge the gap between concepts for studying Mendelizing traits (single-gene traits that conform to Mendel's laws of transmission) and concepts for studying continuous or quasi-continuous entities where a threshold effect could be inferred. The concept of liability has evolved over time and found service in advancing our understanding of somatic phenotypes such as coronary artery disease (Sing, Zerba, & Reilly, 1994) and psychiatric disorders (Moldin, 1994; Pogue-Geile, 1991).

The contributors to the genetic liability can be differentiated hypothetically as specific genetic liability, general genetic liability, and genetic assets. The environmental contributors can likewise be differentiated into specific environmental liability, general environmental liability, and environmental assets. Both genetic and environmental liabilities and their components can be weighted differentially as a function of empirical research. A liability approach to causal understanding does not deny nonlinear interactions and correlated causes although these factors certainly complicate the estimation of models with empirical data. The concept of a statistical "threshold" of liability that best delineates individuals with and without the disorder might, hypothetically, mark individuals with and without relevant biological markers.

As explained to this point, the contributors to liability are abstract. Still, we seek to identify specific structures, processes, and events that contribute to liability. Identification of these structures, processes, and events in terms of candidate genes is in its early stages, and some progress is also being made in identifying specific types of experience that impact the development of behavioral phenotypes. However, some structures intermediate between genes and disorders and causally related to both are useful in elucidating liability; these structures are called endophenotypes. Gottesman and Shields (1972) introduced the concept of endophenotype into behavioral science from basic genetics (John & Lewis, 1966). Among the desirable properties of a good endophenotype for genetic analysis are (a) an etiologic association with the complex behavioral phenotype, (b) presence in some unaffected relatives, and (c) being amenable to objective measurement. Endophenotypes can be biochemical, neurological, anatomical, psychophysiological, endocrine, sensorimotor, perceptual, cognitive, or affective in nature. Recently, the notion of endophenotype, or "intermediate phenotype," has gained considerable currency (e.g., Almasy & Blangero, 2001) as a concept for connecting genetics and neuroscience, and the concept has been updated (Gottesman & Gould, 2003). Pertinent to the current chapter, various domains of temperament and child psychopathology might plausibly share physiological endophenotypes.

In this chapter, we entertain the notion that temperament might be part of the liability to childhood psychopathology, although we do not view the association as simple. This chapter's focus is childhood, but we emphasize that these issues have parallels in the relation of adult personality traits to personality (Axis II) and affective disorders (Akiskal, 1998; Akiskal, Hirschfeld, & Yerevanian, 1983; Slater & Slater, 1944). Because our goal is to consider how temperament might be related to child psychopathology, we need to consider the meaning of temperament briefly.

Temperament: Definition, Genetics, Continuity, and Physiology

Defining Temperament

Temperament can be defined as individual differences in characteristic emotional reactivity, including differences in internal systems regulating that reactivity. Temperament can legitimately be defined in fewer, broader terms or more, narrower terms. In our view, a useful definition specifies five key temperamental domains, including four aspects of behavioral reactivity and one broad domain of emotional/behavioral regulation. The four aspects of reactivity are withdrawal-related negative affect (fear, sadness); approach-related negative affect (anger); approach-related positive affectivity (sometimes called "exuberance" in the temperament literature); and non-approach-related positive affect, or contentment. The positive affect domain is less well charted than other aspects of temperament. The distinction that we observe here is between high-energy exuberance and low-energy contentment. Another related distinction is between pre-goal-attainment anticipatory positive affect and post-goal-attainment pleasure (Davidson, 1994).

The regulatory domain of temperament includes the ability to inhibit behavior when requested to do so, the ability to deploy attention effectively to cope with mild stressors, and, more generally, the ability to dampen negative affect. Impulsivity is one of the major behavioral manifestations of this domain. Of course, the regulatory domain is likely to be multidimensional, but the dampening of approach and negative affect is the only aspect that has been well explored empirically. The aspects of temperament and behavioral disorders listed in Table 2.1 are meant to capture the most salient phenomena but not to be comprehensive. Of interest in this section are the domains of temperament in the left-hand column and the specific aspects of temperament in the middle column. Most of the predictions are straightforward. For instance, a tendency to react with sadness might be predictive of depression or other internalizing disorders, and early anger proneness might be predictive of conduct disorders or oppositional disorders. These aspects of temperament—particularly the reactive and regulatory aspects—might well interact in their prediction of behavioral problems. For instance, the ability to regulate negative affect, perhaps by flexibly deploying attention, might buffer the effects of some reactive temperamental characteristics that otherwise would predict disorders.

We return to the association of temperament and childhood psychopathology later in this chapter. First, we need to consider genetic influences on temperament and the continuity of temperament. Without evidence of genetic influence and continuity across time, temperament would not be very plausible as a contributor to liability for heritable disorders.

Table 2.1. Temperamental Domains and Possibly Related Childhood Behavioral Disorders

Domain	Specific constructs	Possibly related child disorders
Withdrawal-related negative affect	Fearfulness, sadness, disgust	Internalizing, anxiety, depression, OCD
Approach-related negative affect	Anger	ODD, conduct disorder
Non-approach-related positive affect	Contentment	Depression
Approach-related positive affect	Exuberance	(None)
Emotion regulation	Inhibitory control, attention allocation, control	Externalizing, ADHD, ODD, conduct disorder

Table 2.2. Mean Twin Correlations for Infant, Toddler, and Childhood
Temperament Scales

Parental report scales	MZ r	DZ r
Withdrawal-related negative affect scales		
Infant Distress to Novelty	.59	.28
Toddler Social Fearfulness	.61	.18
Childhood Fear	.77	.32
Childhood Shyness	.59	.01
Childhood Sadness	.69	.31
Emotion regulation scales		
Effortful Control at 5 years	.60	.18
Effortful Control at 7 years	.65	.26

Genetics of Temperament

Evidence for genetic variance associated with individual differences in temperament has accumulated to a convincing degree for parental report measures and to varying degrees for other types of assessment (Emde & Hewitt, 2001; Goldsmith, 1983, 1989). In Table 2.2, we present twin similarity data for two domains of temperament, withdrawal-related negative affect and emotional regulation. Depending on the age of the child, the scales employed are from the *Infant Behavior Questionnaire* (IBQ; Rothbart, 1981), the *Toddler Behavior Assessment Questionnaire* (TBAQ; Goldsmith, 1996), or the *Children's Behavior Questionnaire* (CBQ; Rothbart, Ahadi, Hershey, & Fisher, 2001). The correlations come from different studies by our research group (Goldsmith, Buss, & Lemery, 1997; Goldsmith, Lemery, Buss, & Campos, 1999; Lemery, 1999) as well as unpublished data. The correlations in Table 2.2 are means of correlations from the various samples.

As the relative size of the intraclass correlations in Table 2.2 shows, identical twin similarity coefficients for both of these domains of temperament tend to fall into the .60s; this range of values can be viewed as upper boundary estimates of broad heritability. Fraternal twin correlations are about one half the identical twins' values, or less in some cases. Thus, genetic influences are strongly implicated for variability in these dimensions. Similar but less extensive results support the existence of genetic influences on more objective measures of withdrawal-related negative affect and emotion regulation.

Continuity of Temperament

Researchers sometimes seem to define continuity as an inherent part of temperament. However, there are multiple meanings of the continuity of personality or temperament, and these have been explicated by many authors over the years (Caspi, 1998). Regardless of definition, temperamental traits in childhood are developing phenotypes. Even for behavioral inhibition, one of the classic temperamental traits, change in mean level, rank order of individuals, and even extreme group membership over periods of a few years is at least as common as strong continuity (Kagan, Snidman, & Arcus, 1998; Pfeifer, Goldsmith, Davidson, & Rickman, 2002).

As with personality self-report in adulthood, parental report of temperament tends to be stable, with correlations in the .50s to .70s, over periods of several months to a few years during middle and late childhood. We demonstrated that the statistical model that best fit such longitudinal data was often an autoregressive simplex, whereby stability is mediated through intermediate forms (Lemery, Goldsmith, Klinnert, & Mrazek, 1999). As we view the accumulated data, with good enough measures and large enough samples, significant correlational stability can be demonstrated for practically every temperamental trait after the early infancy period.

With this background on temperament in place, we now turn to its association with child psychopathology. We forego an extensive definition of child psychopathology, instead referring to the DSM-IV formulation (American Psychiatric Association, 2000). However, the DSM-IV formulation for childhood disorders needs to be open to revisions because of several factors, the most fundamental of which is the meager knowledge of these disorders that existed when the categories and their criteria were derived. DSM-IV largely lacks a developmental orientation, in the sense that it can be unclear how to evaluate a 4-year-old versus a 10-year-old for the same disorder when features of the phenotype change with maturation. Atypical symptoms and subthreshold degrees of impairment abound in the realm of childhood disorders, and the extensive degree of comorbidity suggests that the current boundaries between disorders might not be optimally drawn or that the concept of a categorical approach might need to be reconsidered.

Hypotheses Relating Temperament to Child Psychopathology

Given the complexity in both domains, it seems unlikely that a single, general principle will account for the relation between temperament and child psychopathology. There is phenotypic complexity in both domains, with hierarchical structure and overlap within the temperament domain and extensive comorbidity and spectrum manifestations within the child psychopathology domain. Of course, other investigators have addressed this question. Different but partially overlapping conceptualizations of how temperament and disorders might be related have been offered. Rothbart and Bates (1998) outline a dozen ways that the constructs might be related, both directly and indirectly, and as part of temperament × temperament or temperament × environment interactions. For instance, they noted that temperament and experience might interact in a statistical sense to influence the development of a disorder, as shown in a study in which temperamental "resistance to control" interacted with restrictive parenting to predict externalizing behavioral problems (Bates, Pettit, Dodge, & Ridge, 1998). An earlier treatment of the issue by Clark, Watson, and Mineka (1994) specified four general models for the relationship between personality and affective disorders, including vulnerability models, which are conceived very similarly to the liability models in this chapter.

Our approach draws from Dr. Irving I. Gottesman's view of liability and divides the ways that temperament and child psychopathology might be related into those in which temperament is or is not part of the liability to psychopathology. In this section, we briefly describe these hypotheses. Later in the chapter, we bring some evidence to bear on the hypotheses, but we will see, as did Clark et al. (1994), that present evidence usually does not allow us to distinguish among them.

We conceive of at least four ways that temperament could be part of the liability to a disorder. These ways are listed below, with a brief explanation of each. (In the material in this chapter, we use the term "risk factor" in its usual epidemiological sense that does not imply a causal association with a disorder.)

1. Temperamental predisposition as part of the "specific etiology" of disorder.

The idea of specific etiology implies a distinctive causal nexus of influences on the development and manifestation of a disorder. Temperament might be part of that causal nexus. Specific etiology is best discussed in conjunction with the concept of general liability.

2. Temperamental predisposition as part of the "general liability" of disorder.

The distinction between specific etiology (Meehl, 1972) and general liability depends on causal processes of other disorders. Specific etiology refers to the pathophysiology of a disorder, including any genes that increase the risk for the disorder uniquely. Specific etiology is much easier to understand for single-gene disorders such as Rett syndrome (Amir et al., 1999; Milunsky et al., 2001) than for complex multifactorial disorders, such as idiopathic autism, ADHD, anxiety disorder, and depression. Operationally, when studying a putative heritable liability factor (such as temperament) and the polygenic disorder that it is associated with, researchers can fit bivariate biometric models. A series of these models could pair each putative liability factor with each disorder. A liability factor that contributes genetic variance to only one disorder is a good candidate for the specific etiology of the disorder. On the other hand, a liability factor that contributes genetic variance to several disorders might be part of the general genetic liability. Pursuing this line of reasoning, a putative liability factor that is genetically associated with an endophenotype that is unique for the disorder is also a candidate for the specific genetic liability. What this approach entails, then, is a series of genetically informative studies relating a risk factor to a series of disorders at the behavioral level and at endophenotypic levels.

3. Extreme temperament as constituting the actual disorder.

In an editorial accompanying a report on personality disorders, T. A. Widiger (1998) wrote that "personality disorders are not qualitatively distinct from normal personality functioning, they are simply maladaptive, extreme variants of common personality traits" (p. 865). Similarly, Akiskal (1998) views the GAD (generalized anxiety disorder) as an extreme version of a normal personality type characterized by a generally anxious temperament. These are excellent examples of the third possibility of how temperament might be part of the liability to disorder. Of course, this is also the possibility that holds the most salient role for temperament. The implication is that studying normal range variation will be directly informative for understanding the etiology of the disorder. Among childhood disorders, perhaps ADHD is the most likely candidate to fit this hypothesis.

The idea of temperament as disorder implies no biological, or perhaps even clinical, reality to the *threshold* between the diagnosed cases and the continuum of functioning in the normal range. In the case of ADHD, normal range variation in impulsivity, activity level, and inattention can be viewed as extending into the problematic range. Setting the joint thresholds on these three dimensions is partly done for practical reasons, i.e., when the benefit to risk ratio of treatment versus nontreatment is favorable (Lahey et al., 1994). In this sense, the diagnostic threshold of a disorder that fits this definition of liability can change depending on the availability, safety, and efficacy of interventions, as well as the contextual demands for normative behavior.

4. Temperament related to disorder when its expression is dysregulated (i.e., when emotional expression occurs outside its typical contexts).

This hypothesis is similar to point 3, but it emphasizes the regulatory aspects of temperament and offers routes to empirical testing. One version of this notion derives from primate research on fearfulness and defensive behavior (Kalin, Larson, Shelton, & Davidson, 1998). About 5% of young rhesus monkeys displayed fearful freezing in contexts in which other monkeys tended to display threat. In this small group, out-of-context freezing had biological correlates, such as higher basal cortisol levels and greater right than left prefrontal activation in the EEG.

In human research, inadequate emotion regulation has been empirically linked to externalizing problems fairly clearly and to internalizing problems less clearly (e.g., Eisenberg et al., 2001). Well-elaborated theory has described the clinical implications of problems in emotional regulation (Cole, Michel, & O'Donnell-Teti, 1994). Nevertheless, many questions remain. For instance, does the failure to down-regulate, say, high levels of fear, in appropriate contexts have the same neural substrates as expression of fear in inappropriate contexts?

These four ways that temperament can be viewed as part of the liability to psychopathology may not be a comprehensive list, and the possibilities are certainly not mutually exclusive. There are also ways that temperament might be related to disorder, but not as a liability factor. These include the following:

5. Measurement confounding of temperament and disorder.

One of the least interesting but most vexing possibilities is that putative relations between temperament and child psychopathology are attributable to overlapping content of measures. We have recently treated this issue at length

(Lemery, Essex, & Smider, 2002). Here, we simply note that the possibility of measurement confounding, as well as other forms of artifactual association, is most plausible when a single informant is the source for both temperament and psychopathology assessment.

6. The disorder affecting the subsequent development of temperament, referred to as the "scar hypothesis" by Clark et al. (1994).

Psychotic illness clearly pervades much of personality, and it is plausible that other disorders will also affect personality, even in children. Although this topic has not been researched much, longitudinal designs with appropriate occasions of assessment can rule it out. A related issue is whether prodromal features of a disorder can affect the development of temperament. This issue might be less tractable because prodromal features are likely to be less distinct from temperament than frank symptoms of the disorder.

7. Temperament as a contributor to symptom features but not to the disorder's etiological process.

This rather subtle possibility has also been recognized by others in the realm of affective disorders (Akiskal et al., 1983). It is probably impossible to eliminate the hypothesis that temperament simply colors the expressed behavioral features of a disorder without affecting its pathogenesis unless we know something about etiology and perhaps simultaneously measure endophenotypes.

8. Temperament as a risk factor only for age of onset or course of the disorder.

This plausible hypothesis can be tested empirically by, quite obviously, incorporating measures of age of onset and course within a design that measures premorbid temperament.

9. Temperament as a risk factor for a disorder only because of its association with comorbid conditions.

As an example, anger-prone temperament is likely a risk factor for ADHD, but only because ADHD is frequently comorbid with Oppositional Defiant Disorder (ODD) and Conduct Disorder (CD), assuming that the comorbid condition is not actually an unrecognized, unitary diagnostic entity.

Hypotheses 5 through 9 seem plausible for many data sets in which we might seek to infer that temperament is a real liability factor for psychopathology. In practice, the "nonliability" explanations can be difficult to rule out.

Finally, like strong intellectual abilities, temperament can be a risk-reducing factor for psychopathology. Two broad domains of temperament are likely candidates as protective factors: emotion regulation abilities and positive affectivity. Regulatory measures are of particular importance in this domain (Zahn-Waxler, Schmitz, Fulker, Robinson, & Emde, 1996); they include approach/avoidance tendencies, the ability to focus and shift attention, and the ability to inhibit ongoing behavior. Many authors have noted that deficiencies in positive affective responding (or, the capacity to experience and express pleasure) are an important ingredient in determining vulnerability to depression (Meehl, 1975; Watson et al., 1995). By the same token, the neural substrates of high positive affect may act in part by "short-circuiting" the duration of negative affective responses (Davidson & Irwin, 1999).

Thus, the nature of the relation of temperament to childhood psychopathology can take many possible forms, and we suggest that these possibilities can usefully be divided into liability-related and non-liability-related classes. Of particular interest will be cases in which the liability is genetic. First, however, we must consider the evidence for nonartifactual associations of temperament and childhood psychopathology from studies without a genetically informative design.

Relating Temperament and Child Psychopathology at the Phenotypic Level

Most of the literature on this topic is largely uninformative concerning the nuanced ways in which temperament and psychopathology might be related. Information on links between temperament and psychopathology often involves only simple concurrent correlational approaches, using parent report of temperament and symptoms or parent report of temperament and psychiatric diagnoses. Several studies have used a longitudinal approach, which partially protects against situation-specific bias and measurement confounding. We briefly review the results from some of these longitudinal projects and then turn to results from one of our own studies. We shall see that the strongest evidence is for prediction of externalizing behavior problems by temperamental negative affect measures, largely approach-oriented, and poor emotion regulation. Outcome in the larger studies tends to be symptoms of behavioral problems rather than actual diagnoses.

The Dunedin Multidisciplinary Health and Development Study demonstrated the predictive power of early temperament for later personality, psychopathology, and interpersonal relationships. In an unselected sample of more than 800 3-year-olds, five temperament groups were identified from examiner rating scales: Undercontrolled, Inhibited, Confident, Reserved, and Well-adjusted. These examiner ratings of temperament predicted behavior problems at 13 and 15 years of age (Caspi, Henry, McGee, Moffitt, & Silva, 1995) and psychiatric diagnoses at 21 years (Caspi, Moffitt, Newman, & Silva, 1996). For instance, undercontrolled children were more likely to be diagnosed with antisocial personality disorder and inhibited children were more likely to be depressed, although effects sizes over this long time span were small. In this same sample, Jaffee et al. (2002) showed that undercontrolled temperament in males predicted juvenile-onset major depressive disorder.

In a review of the longitudinal, multicohort Pittsburgh Youth Study, Loeber et al. (2001) studied temperamental characteristics along with family process, demographic, educational, and school achievement factors in males. In the context of these other variables, a lack of guilt, hypothesized to reflect poor internal inhibition, predicted later internalizing and especially externalizing problems.

The documentation of early behavioral inhibition, reflected in rather extreme shyness, as a risk factor for later internalizing problems has now emerged from a fairly coherent literature using multiple designs (Biederman et al., 1993; Rosenbaum et al., 1993; Schwartz, Snidman, & Kagan, 1999). Some of these studies implicate genetic/familial factors in the causal nexus.

With a large community sample from the Australian Temperament Project followed from infancy to 7 years, Prior, Smart, Sanson, Pedlow, and Oberklaid (1992) showed that children with stable behavior problems had more difficult temperaments and showed more aggressive behavior from 2 to 4 years. Children with more transient behavior problems showed a lesser degree of temperamental difficulty, and children with no behavior problems had the least difficult temperament. In a smaller longitudinal study, Earls and Jung (1987) showed that age-2 maternal report of low adaptability and high intensity accounted for 30% of the variance in behavior problems 1 year later.

In the Bloomington Longitudinal Study, Bates, Bayles, Bennett, Ridge, and Brown (1991) found that difficult temperament measured in infancy and toddlerhood predicted internalizing and externalizing problems in preschool and middle childhood. In addition, unadaptability predicted internalizing problems, and resistance to control predicted externalizing problems. A follow-up at 17 years of age showed that caregivers' perceptions of toddlers as difficult and resistant to control still predicted externalizing behavioral problems.

These longitudinal projects, and others that we have not reviewed here, have demonstrated the predictive power of early temperament for later behavioral problems, with the prediction from temperament measured in infancy weaker than temperament measured at later ages. In addition, different dimensions of temperament predict different behavioral problems (Krueger, Caspi, Moffitt, Silva, & McGee, 1996) although this finding is certainly not well documented because of the widespread use of very global measures of temperament. Previously we have demonstrated the importance of considering focal aspects of temperament when identifying developmental pathways (Goldsmith et al., 1999), and more attention to focal measures of temperament is needed in studying links to psychopathology. Our concern here is only with temperament, but we emphasize that a larger body of literature, in the externalizing domain, suggests that the highest risk lies in a small percentage of boys with multiple risk factors including aggression and early hyperactivity who also experience high levels of negative parenting and family stress (Campbell, Shaw, & Gilliom, 2000).

We now turn to a more detailed description of results from our own research, with a focus on ADHD.

Prediction of ADHD Symptoms From Temperament in the Wisconsin Study of Families and Work

Sample

In an ongoing research project, we have a unique window on possible precursors of ADHD as well as other childhood behavioral disorders. As background, we briefly describe the Wisconsin Study of Families and Work. The original aim of this large-scale longitudinal study was to investigate how maternity leave, subsequent employment, and a variety of psychosocial factors (e.g., parental attitudes, personality, family characteristics, child characteristics, childcare quality) impact the physical, mental, and social health of women, children, and families. The sample includes 570 women recruited in the second trimester of pregnancy, 550 of their husbands/partners, and their infants. Participants were recruited through physicians' offices and clinics in Milwaukee (80% of sample) and Madison (20% of sample). Initial response rates were 76% for mothers (570/752); 96% of their husbands/partners also agreed to participate, resulting in an initial response rate of 73% for fathers (550/752). An important goal of the study was to recruit as great a diversity of participants as possible in regard to socio-economic status, subject to the constraint that mothers and fathers had to be living together at the time of the first interview. Other criteria for exclusion from the sample were the woman being (a) age 18 or under (teenage pregnancy, although an important problem, was not the focus of this research), (b) unemployed, (c) students, or (d) disabled (a disabled woman will have very different work and parenting experiences). At the time of pregnancy, the average age of the women was 29 years (range, 20–43); the median family income was $45,000 a year, comparable with the U.S. average for dual-earner families at the time (84% of the sample were dual-earner families, boosting family income over what might be expected in a sample that included more single-earner families); 95% of the sample were married; 39% were first-time parents. A strength of this sample for investigating issues of children's behavioral symptoms is that by recruiting families during pregnancy, the children were not preselected in any way, other than possibly via parental characteristics. At age 4.5 years, when some key assessments were conducted, the size of the remaining subject pool was 451, and this varied somewhat depending on the variables analyzed.

The children in this sample were also studied when they were in kindergarten and again in first grade. At those crucial points of transition, we assessed behavioral problems from the perspectives of parents and teachers, and when they had reached first grade, the children themselves. These problems included symptoms of inattention, hyperactivity, and impulsivity, although no formal diagnostic evaluation for ADHD was planned at this stage of this project. Nevertheless, there is considerable value in examining the predictors of ADHD symptoms in this group. To anticipate the results (described later), several associations of earlier child, parent, and family variables with kindergarten or first-grade ADHD symptoms were found. Most of these associations were modest in magnitude, as one might expect for a common, complex disorder such as ADHD. There are two virtues of examining these associations in a sample such as ours. First, very few—perhaps no—studies of ADHD have begun before the child was born. Second, because the sample was a large one, it was possible to examine a comparison group of children who exhibit the same pattern of predictors as the children eventually diagnosed with ADHD but who themselves do not develop ADHD symptoms. Differences between these two groups helped us identify protective factors.

Overview of Assessment

Assessments in this project were conducted during pregnancy and at ages 1 month, 4 months, 12 months, 2 years, 3.5 years, 4.5 years, and kindergarten age and in first grade and third grade, with fifth-grade assessments underway and others planned, depending on funding. A wide array of child, parent, and family variables were assessed, and these varied across occasions. For child variables related to temperament, emotions, and symptoms, we used multi-source data, including maternal, paternal, caregiver, teacher, and child reports, videotaped structured vignettes designed to highlight behaviors of interest, and in some cases, physiological measures. Not all sources could feasibly be tapped at each age.

The key ADHD outcome measure in the study thus far is the ADHD symptoms scale on the Health and Behavior Questionnaire (HBQ; Ablow et al., 1999; Essex et al., 2002; Luby et al., 2002). The ADHD scale comprises inattention and impulsivity subscales. The HBQ item content overlaps considerably with Achenbach and Edelbrock's (1983) well-known Child Behavior Checklist (CBCL). Both mothers and teachers completed the HBQ during spring term of both kindergarten and first grade, yielding four "outcome measures." Our preliminary findings mainly take the form of correlations between early predictors and later scores on the ADHD composite from the HBQ. The behavioral measures are drawn from the Laboratory Temperament Assessment Battery (Lab-TAB), preschool version, initially developed by Goldsmith, Reilly, Lemery, Longley, and Prescott (1993), and modified for this study by the authors.

Results

Concurrent mother and teacher ADHD scores were correlated about .45. Stability from kindergarten to first grade was .79 for mothers and .50 from the kindergarten and the first-grade teachers.

Several measures were significantly correlated with these ADHD scores. The associations held for both maternal and teacher report of ADHD symptoms. Higher ADHD scores in kindergarten were predicted by (a) lower maternal education; (b) previous hostile/aggressive behaviors, as rated by mothers (averaged over assessments at 3.5 and 4.5 years); (c) maternal report on temperament questionnaire scales tapping low inhibitory control and high anger (from the CBQ); and (d) several temperament measures derived from a home-based, videotaped observational assessment conducted at age 4.5 years. Table 2.3 displays some of the observational temperament measures, each derived from multiple situations, along with relevant, significant correlations (Ns ranging from 381 to 467) with mother and teacher report of ADHD symptoms rated a year later in kindergarten.

The observational measures in Table 2.3 also predicted maternal and teacher ADHD symptom ratings from age 4.5 to approximately age 6.5 years, during the spring semester of first grade. The prediction of ADHD symptoms from prior, objective videotaped measures of temperament is an important

Table 2.3. Longitudinal Prediction of ADHD Symptoms in Kindergarten by Behavioral Measures of Temperament

Behavioral measures of temperament	Teacher report	Maternal report
Inhibitory control	−.27	−.23
Anger[a]	.24	.14
Anticipatory behavior	.25	.10
Approach[b] (high)	.37	.19

Note. All correlations shown in the table are significant ($p < .05$, two tailed).
[a]Anger was much more predictive for boys than girls.
[b]Approach is usually hedonically positive in these measures, and it was also more predictive for boys.

Table 2.4. Concurrent Prediction of ADHD Symptoms in First Grade by Behavioral Measures of Temperament

Behavioral measures of temperament	Teacher report		Maternal report	
	Inattention	Impulsivity	Inattention	Impulsivity
Inhibitory control	−.37	−.35	−.37	−.32
Anger	.29	.30	.34	.35
On-task behavior	−.22	−.19	−.41	−.35
Anticipatory positive affect	.21	.21	.26	.35
Activity level	.20	.23	—	.27

Note. All correlations shown in the table are significant ($p < .05$, two tailed).

finding, given that much evidence in the field depends on parent, teacher, or observer reports. We sought to confirm the key findings with a concurrent videotaped measure of temperament, conducted when the children were in first grade (for a subsample of the group). In this case, we examined HBQ inattention and impulsivity subscales separately.

As Table 2.4 shows, objective, videotaped measures of temperament-related behavior in the home were related with both maternal and teacher report of ADHD. We also noted that maternal infant and toddler temperament ratings of irritability and anger (from 1 month to 3.5 years of age) were associated with later ADHD ratings, but only when the ADHD ratings were made by mothers (not when teachers made them). These infant and toddler temperament ratings were related to inhibitory control rated at age 4.5 years. Then, the age 4.5 years inhibitory control measure mediated the association of earlier irritability and anger with later ADHD symptoms.

We also screened various family stress, parenting, and mother–infant interaction measures for association with kindergarten and first grade inattention and impulsivity, rated on the HBQ by both mothers and teachers. Marital and parenting stress was rated by the mother five times between 1 month and 4.5 years of age. This stress rating was correlated with both the inattention and impulsivity subscales, rated by the mother, at both kindergarten and first grade. These correlations ranged from .18 to .37, and they increased as they became nearer in time to the ADHD measures. Most of family stress measures were not correlated with teacher report of ADHD. Parenting practices, reported on Block's Childrearing Practices Report at age 4.5

years, were also correlated very modestly with later ADHD measures, extensively for mother report and somewhat less so for teachers. The aspects of parenting practice that related to later ADHD concerned negative affect, negative control strategies, and lack of autonomy granting. It is important not to infer direction of effect from these findings.

Mother–child episodes of structured interaction were videotaped at ages 4 months, 12 months, and 4.5 years. Even the infant–mother interaction measures correlated with maternal ADHD ratings at kindergarten and first grade. A lack of positivity in the dyadic interaction was the strongest predictor, but the correlations from infancy were all below .20. Dyadic positivity at age 4.5 years was slightly more predictive of later ADHD ratings, but correlations were still under .25. Some of these correlations were also related at the same or lower levels to teacher report of ADHD.

In interpreting these findings, it is essential to remember that the prediction was for ADHD symptoms in a relatively unselected sample. From a recent three-city study that employed both the HBQ and clinical diagnoses (Luby et al., 2002), we know optimal cut-offs on the HBQ ADHD scale that likely identify clinical cases. For maternal report at kindergarten and first grade, 7% and 8%, respectively, exceeded this threshold. For teacher report at kindergarten and first grade, 5% and 9%, respectively, exceeded this threshold. Boys comprised 70% to 80% of the children above the threshold. Analyses with these putative cases have not yet been conducted, in part because we prefer to wait until structured diagnostic interviews confirm the diagnoses.

It is also critical to realize that the magnitude of prediction observed in this study makes accurate individual prediction highly problematic and inadvisable. Future work would be needed to determine whether prediction improves substantially in the clinical range at the extremes of lack of regulatory control.

Temperament and Child Psychopathology Within a Behavior-Genetic Framework

Background Literature

Despite the evidence for longitudinal prediction of psychopathology from temperament, relatively little research on this topic has employed a genetically informative design with children. One such study was a 2-year follow-up of a large sample of Norwegian twins, ages 7 to 17 years, whose parents reported first on three temperament traits and later on behavioral problems (Gjone & Stevenson, 1997). Temperamental emotionality showed a genetic link with later attentional problems and aggressive behavior. Another report is from the Colorado-based MacArthur Longitudinal Twin Study, which used assessments of temperament and behavioral problems very similar to the Norwegian study but had constant ages of assessment, including four occasions from 14 to 36 months for temperament and 4 years for behavioral problems. Schmitz, Fulker, Emde, and Zahn-Waxler (2001) found the very modest common variance among temperament and later behavioral problems was largely associated with genetic differences, with earlier emotionality (mainly negative affect) showing genetic correlations averaging about .50 with both later externalizing and internalizing. Earlier ratings of shyness and later internalizing also shared genetic variance.

Twin Study Findings on Temperamental Liability Factors for ADHD Symptoms

SAMPLE AND OVERVIEW OF ASSESSMENT. We report a set of twin data that expands this line of inquiry with different measures of temperament and behavioral problems in early to middle childhood. Our findings come from the first stage of the Wisconsin Twin Study (Van Hulle, Lemery, & Goldsmith, 2002). The sample was recruited from statewide birth records and represented a wide range of potential risk factors. For these analyses, we had 106 pairs of MZ twins and 161 DZ pairs. The initial assessment was at ages 3 to 7 years of age, and the follow-up was at 5 to 9 years. The temperament measure was a shortened version of Rothbart et al.'s (2001) Children's Behavior Questionnaire (CBQ). Here, we focus on two CBQ scales that best define the Effortful Control factor: Attentional Focusing and Inhibitory Control. The items on these scales emphasize children's reactions in specific, age-appropriate situations. The behavior problem that we consider is the ADHD scale from the HBQ (described previously in the chapter). Other results from these data, as well as the documentation of the good psychometric quality of the measures, are given by Goldsmith and Lemery (2000) and Lemery (1999). Model-fitting for the genetic analyses used the Mx program (Neale & Cardon, 1992).

RESULTS. To address the possibility of measurement confounding of temperament and related behavioral problems, we eliminated items from both the CBQ and HBQ that did not covary with the intended latent variable in a confirmatory factor analysis (for details, see Lemery et al., 2002). The analyses presented here use these "purified" scales. Both mothers and fathers provided reports, which correlated in the .50 range. The substantive results were generally the same for maternal and paternal report; here we report only the maternal data. First, we considered the phenotypic overlap of Effortful Control and ADHD. For concurrent measurement, this correlation was .58; for longitudinal prediction (Effortful Control to ADHD), the correlation was .41 across an average 2.5-year interval.

With the phenotypic correlation established, we move to genetic analyses, using the temperament data from the initial occasion and the ADHD symptom measure at the follow-up. First, we fitted univariate models for the two variables. The best-fitting model for Effortful Control was an ADE model, where A = additive genetic variance, D = dominant (nonadditive) genetic variance, and E = nonshared (unique) environmental variance. The standardized parameter estimates were as follows: A = .09, D = .48, and E = .43. For HBQ ADHD symptoms, the same model had the best fit, with parameters estimated as A = .22, D = .43, and E = .34. In model fitting with twin data, there is little leverage to apportion genetic variance between additive and nonadditive sources; thus, the exact relative size of A and D estimates cannot be taken too seriously. What we can conclude, however, is that both Effortful Control and ADHD symptoms appeared to have similar levels of genetic influence. This observation and the phenotypic correlation cited previously led us to test whether these two variables share genetic variance. If the answer is positive with these longitudinal data using unconfounded item content, then a reasonable interpretation is that the Effortful Control contributes to the genetic liability to ADHD symptoms.

We fitted a bivariate biometric model to test this possibility. The model, its fit statistics, and the parameter estimates are shown in Figure 2.1. First, we note that the overall fit of the model was quite good. None of paths shown in Figure 2.1 could be dropped without significantly worsening the fit. The first point to note in the figure is that the ADE components for Effortful Control (left side of the figure) were quite similar to those in the univariate model, as we would expect. Moreover, all three of the sources of variance in Effortful Control also accounted for variance in later ADHD symptoms; in fact, collectively they accounted for 76% of the variance (10% + 58% + 8%) in ADHD symptoms. Perhaps the most notable result was that *all* of the residual variance in ADHD symptoms was of nonshared environmental variety; that is, all of the shared variance (genetic and environmental) in ADHD could be predicted from genetic and environmental sources of variation in earlier Effortful Control.

This finding is consistent with an interpretation that extreme levels of temperamental Effortful Control carry the genetic liability to ADHD symptoms. Some limitations attach to these findings, however. First, this was not a risk sample for ADHD, and findings might change with clinical cases (which we are currently testing in a follow-up study). Second, despite our

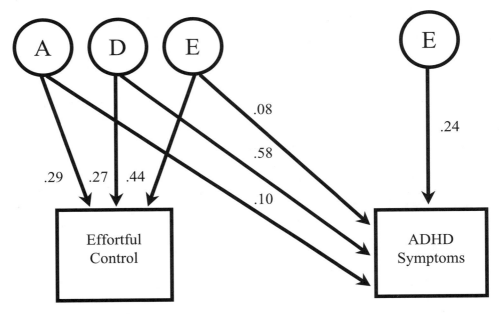

Figure 2.1. Bivariate biometric model of the prediction of ADHD symptoms from temperamental effortful control. Fit statistics: χ^2 (13) = 10.63, p = .64, AIC = −15.37.

attempt to unconfound item content and our longitudinal design, mothers were the source of information on both temperament and symptoms. We did repeat the analyses described previously with data from fathers, with very similar results. This demonstrates that the findings do generalize beyond mothers, but evaluations from others besides parents are still needed (and are being collected in a follow-up study). Finally, our analyses did not take into account conduct problems that undoubtedly accompany ADHD symptoms in some children in our sample. If Effortful Control also predicts conduct problems, then hypothesis number 2 (contribution to a more general liability) might be more likely than hypothesis number 1 (contribution to the specific etiology).

Implications

Questions easily outnumber answers in this domain. The interplay of typical developmental variation and incipient psychopathology is poorly understood. Let us close this chapter by considering a realm of child psychopathology that we have not yet treated: depression. We know that children vary considerably in the temperamental trait of positive affectivity, or positive hedonic capacity. Very low positive affect is, of course, a feature of depression, but is "very low" positive affect qualitatively, or only quantitatively, different from "moderately low" positive affect? As we have seen earlier in this chapter, the generic version of this question can be cast in genetic terms—do the same genes that influence typical variation in positive affect also influence liability to childhood depression? This question can be applied to protective as well as risk factors.

A related issue is the interface of dysphoric mood that is not very dysfunctional and diagnosed conditions such as dysthymic disorder or major depression. Is the distinction qualitative or quantitative? Does the answer to this question depend on the level of analysis (e.g., behavioral or neurophysiological) or on factors such as gender differences? Is childhood depression like ADHD, where the triad of inattention, hyperactivity, and impulsivity are generally considered to be quantitative traits that show no clear biologically specified thresholds between typical and clinical levels? Another issue about depression is that the constellation of symptoms of depression in young children (e.g., less sleep disturbance and less psychomotor retardation than in adults) needs to be better understood. Similarly, the cognitive components of adult depression (e.g., attributions of helplessness, "depressive realism") have been studied extensively, but little is known about these cognitive components prior to adolescence. It is important to fill this gap in our knowledge because known cognitive dysfunction should be a good guide for a theoretically rich cognitive neuroscience of depression, and such a neuroscience needs to have a developmental facet.

These brief comments about childhood depression indicate that the issues raised previously in the chapter on ADHD are more general to the field of developmental psychopathology. From Gottesman's work (Gottesman & Goldsmith, 1994; LaBuda, Gottesman, & Pauls, 1993), we know that the developmental facet will be enhanced by a genetic approach and the genetic implications will be richer in developmental perspective.

References

Ablow, J. C., Measelle, J. R., Kraemer, H. C., Harrington, R., Luby, J., Smider, N., et al. (1999). The MacArthur three-city outcome study: Evaluating multi-informant measures of young children's symptomatology. *Journal of the American Academy of Child and Adolescent Psychiatry, 38,* 1580–1590.

Achenbach, T. M., & Edelbrock, C. (1983). *Manual for the child behavior checklist and revised child behavior profile.* Burlington, VT: University of Vermont, Department of Psychiatry.

Akiskal, H. S. (1998). Toward a definition of generalized anxiety disorder as an anxious temperament type. *Acta Psychiatrica Scandinavica. Supplementum, 393,* 66–73.

Akiskal, H. S., Hirschfeld, R. M., & Yerevanian, B. I. (1983). The relationship of personality to affective disorders. *Archives of General Psychiatry, 40,* 801–810.

Almasy, L., & Blangero, J. (2001). Endophenotypes as quantitative risk factors for psychiatric disease: Rationale and study design. *American Journal of Medical Genetics (Neuropsychiatric Genetics), 105,* 42–44.

American Psychiatric Association (2000). *Diagnostic and statistical manual of mental disorders* (4th ed.). Washington, DC: Author.

Amir, R. E., Van den Veyver, I. B., Wan, M., Tran, C. Q., Francke, U., & Zoghbi, H. Y. (1999). Rett syndrome is caused by mutations in X-linked MECP2, encoding methyl-CpG-binding protein 2. *Nature Genetics, 23,* 185–888.

Bates, J. E., Bayles, K., Bennett, D. S., Ridge, B., & Brown, M. M. (1991). Origins of externalizing behavior problems at eight years of age. In D. J. Pepler & K. H. Rubin (Eds.), *The development and treatment of childhood aggression* (pp. 93–120). Hillsdale, NJ: Erlbaum.

Bates, J. E., Pettit, G. S., Dodge, K. A., & Ridge, B. (1998). Interaction of temperamental resistance to control and restrictive parenting in the development of externalizing behavior. *Developmental Psychology, 34,* 982–985.

Biederman, J., Rosenbaum, J. F., Bolduc-Murphy, E. A., Faraone, S. V., Chaloff, J., Hirshfeld, D. R., et al. (1993). A 3-year follow-up of children with and without behavioral inhibition. *Journal of the American Academy of Child and Adolescent Psychiatry, 32,* 814–821.

Campbell, S. B., Shaw, D. S., & Gilliom, M. (2000). Early externalizing behavior problems: Toddlers and preschoolers at risk for later maladjustment. *Developmental Psychopathology, 12,* 467–488.

Caspi, A. (1998). Personality development across the life course. In N. Eisenberg (Vol. Ed.), *Social, emotional, and personality development* (Vol. 3). In W. Damon (Ed.), *Handbook of child psychology* (5th ed., pp. 311–388). New York: Wiley.

Caspi, A., Moffitt, T., Newman, D., & Silva, P. (1998). Behavioral observations at age 3 years predict adult psychiatric disorders: Longitudinal evidence from a birth cohort. In M. E. Hertzig & E. A. Farber (Eds.), *Annual progress in child psychiatry and child development: 1997* (pp. 319–331). New York: Brunner-Routledge.

Caspi, A., Henry, B., McGee, R. O., Moffitt, T. E., & Silva, P. A. (1995). Temperamental origins of child and adolescent behavior problems: From age three to age fifteen. *Child Development, 66,* 55–68.

Clark, L. A., Watson, D., & Mineka, S. (1994). Temperament, personality, and the mood and anxiety disorders. *Journal of Abnormal Psychology, 103,* 103–116.

Cole, P. M., Michel, M. K., & O'Donnell-Teti, L. O. (1994). The development of emotion regulation and dysregulation: A clinical perspective. *Monographs of the Society for Research in Child Development, 59* (Serial No. 240), 73–100.

Davidson, R. J. (1994). Asymmetric brain function, affective style and psychopathology: The role of early experience and plasticity. *Development and Psychopathology, 6,* 741–758.

Davidson, R. J., & Irwin, W. (1999). The functional neuroanatomy of emotion and affective style. *Trends in Cognitive Science, 3,* 11–21

Earls, F., & Jung, K. G. (1987). Temperament and home environment characteristics as causal factors in the early development of childhood psychopathology. *Journal of the American Academy of Child and Adolescent Psychiatry, 26,* 491–498.

Eisenberg, N., Cumberland, A., Spinrad, T. L., Fabes, R. A., Shepard, S. A., Reiser, M., et al. (2001). The relations of regulation and emotionality to children's externalizing and internalizing problem behavior. *Child Development, 72,* 1112–1134.

Emde, R. N., & Hewitt, J. K. (Eds.) (2001). *The transition from infancy to early childhood: Genetic and environmental influences in the MacArthur Longitudinal Twin Study.* New York: Oxford University Press.

Essex, M. J., Boyce, W. T., Goldstein, L. H., Armstrong, J. M., Kraemer, H. C., Kupfer, D. J., et al. (2002). The confluence of mental, physical, social, and academic difficulties in middle childhood. II: Developing the MacArthur Health and Behavior Questionnaire. *Journal of the American Academy of Child and Adolescent Psychiatry, 41,* 588–603.

Falconer, D. S. (1965). The inheritance of liability to certain diseases, estimated from the incidence among relatives. *Annals of Human Genetics, 29,* 51–76.

Falconer, D. S. (1967). The inheritance of liability to diseases with variable age of onset with particular reference to diabetes mellitus. *Annals of Human Genetics, 31,* 1–20.

Gjone, H., & Stevenson, J. (1997). A longitudinal twin study of temperament and behavior problems: Common genetic or environmental influences? *Journal of the American Academy of Child & Adolescent Psychiatry, 36,* 1448–1456.

Goldsmith, H. H. (1983). Genetic influences on personality from infancy to adulthood. *Child Development, 54,* 331–355.

Goldsmith, H. H. (1989). Behavior-genetic approaches to temperament. In G. A. Kohnstamm, J. E. Bates, & M. K. Rothbart, (Eds.), *Temperament in childhood* (pp. 111–132). Chichester, UK: Wiley.

Goldsmith, H. H. (1996). Studying temperament via construction of the Toddler Behavior Assessment Questionnaire. *Child Development, 67,* 218–235.

Goldsmith, H. H., Buss, K. A., & Lemery, K. S. (1997). Toddler and childhood temperament: expanded content, stronger genetic evidence, new evidence for the importance of environment. *Developmental Psychology, 33,* 891–905.

Goldsmith, H. H., & Lemery, K. S. (2000). Linking temperamental fearfulness and anxiety symptoms: A behavior-genetic perspective. *Biological Psychiatry, 48,* 1199–1209.

Goldsmith, H. H., Lemery, K. S., Buss, K. A., & Campos, J. J. (1999). Genetic analyses of focal aspects of infant temperament. *Developmental Psychology, 35,* 972–985.

Goldsmith, H. H., Reilly, J., Lemery, K. S., Longley, S., & Prescott, A. (1993). *Preliminary manual for the preschool temperament assessment battery* (version 1.0; Tech. Rep.)., University of Wisconsin–Madison, Department of Psychology.

Gottesman, I. I. (1974). Developmental genetics and ontogenetic psychology: Overdue detente and propositions from a matchmaker. In A. Pick (Ed.), *Minnesota Symposium on Child Psychology.* (pp. 55–80). Minneapolis: University of Minnesota Press.

Gottesman, I. I., & Goldsmith, H. H. (1994). Developmental psychopathology of antisocial behavior: Inserting genes into its ontogenesis and epigenesis. In C. Nelson (Ed.), *Threats to optimal development: Integrating biological, social, and psychological risk factors: Vol. 27 Minnesota symposium on child development* (pp. 69–104). Hillsdale, NJ: Erlbaum.

Gottesman, I. I., & Gould, T. D. (2003). The endophenotype concept in psychiatry: Etymology and strategic intentions. *American Journal of Psychiatry, 160,* 636–645.

Gottesman, I. I., & Shields, J. (1967). A polygenic theory of schizophrenia. *Proceedings of the National Academy of Sciences, 58,* 199–205.

Gottesman, I. I., & Shields, J. (1972). *Schizophrenia and genetics: A twin study vantage point.* New York: Academic Press.

Jaffee, S. R., Moffitt, T. E., Caspi, A., Fombonne, E., Poulton, R., & Martin, J. (2002). Differences in early childhood risk factors for juvenile-onset and adult-onset depression. *Archives of General Psychiatry, 59,* 215–222.

John, B. & Lewis, K. R. (1966). Chromosome variability and geographic distribution in insects. *Science, 152,* 711–721.

Kagan, J., Snidman, N., & Arcus, D. (1998). Childhood derivatives of high and low reactivity in infancy. *Child Development, 69,* 1483–1493.

Kalin, N. H., Larson, C., Shelton, S. E., & Davidson, R. J. (1998). Asymmetric frontal brain activity, cortisol, and behavior associated with fearful temperament in rhesus monkeys. *Behavioral Neuroscience, 112,* 286–292.

Krueger, R. F., Caspi, A., Moffitt, T. E., Silva, P. A., & McGee, R. (1996). Personality traits are differentially linked to mental disorders: A multitrait–multidiagnosis study of an adolescent birth cohort. *Journal of Abnormal Psychology, 105,* 299–312.

LaBuda, M. C., Gottesman, I. I., & Pauls, D. L. (1993). Usefulness of twin studies for exploring the etiology of childhood and adolescent psychiatric disorders. *American Journal of Medical Genetics, 48,* 47–59.

Lahey, B. B., Applegate, B., McBurnett, K., Biederman, J., Greenhill, L., Hynd, G. W., et al. (1994). DSM-IV field trials for attention deficit hyperactivity disorder in children and adolescents. *American Journal of Psychiatry, 151,* 1673–1685.

Lemery, K .S. (1999). *Exploring the etiology of the relationship between temperament and behavior problems in children.* Unpublished doctoral dissertation, University of Wisconsin–Madison.

Lemery, K. S., Essex, M. J., & Smider, N. A. (2002). Revealing the relationship between temperament and behavior problem symptoms by eliminating measurement confounding: Expert ratings and factor analyses. *Child Development, 73,* 867–882.

Lemery, K. S., Goldsmith, H. H., Klinnert, M. D., & Mrazek, D. A. (1999). Developmental models of infant and childhood temperament. *Developmental Psychology, 35,* 189–204.

Loeber, R., Farrington, D. P., Stouthamer-Loeber, M., Moffitt, T. E., Caspi, A., & Lynam, D. (2001). Male mental health problems, psychopathy, and personality traits: Key findings from the first 14 years of the Pittsburgh Youth Study. *Clinical Child and Family Psychology Review, 4,* 273–297.

Luby, J. L., Heffelfinger, A., Measelle, J. R., Ablow, J. C., Essex, M. J., Dierker, L., et al. (2002). Differential performance of the MacArthur HBQ and DISC-IV in identifying DSM-IV internalizing psychopathology in young children. *Journal of the American Academy of Child and Adolescent Psychiatry, 41,* 458–466.

Meehl, P. E. (1972). Specific genetic etiology, psychodynamics, and therapeutic nihilism. *International Journal of Mental Health, 1,* 10–27.

Meehl, P. E. (1975). Hedonic capacity: Some conjectures. *Bulletin of the Menninger Clinic, 39,* 295–307.

Milunsky, J. M., Lebo, R. V., Ikuta, T., Maher, T. A., Haverty, C. E., & Milunsky, A. (2001). Mutation analysis in Rett syndrome. *Genetic Testing, 5,* 321–325.

Moldin, S. O. (1994). Indicators of liability to schizophrenia: Perspectives from genetic epidemiology. *Schizophrenia Bulletin, 20,* 169–184.

Neale, M. C., & Cardon, L. R. (1992). *Methodology for genetic studies of twins and families.* Dordrecht, The Netherlands: Kluwer.

Pfeifer, M., Goldsmith, H. H., Davidson, R. J., & Rickman, M. (2002). Continuity and change in inhibited and uninhibited children. *Child Development, 73,* 1474–1485.

Pogue-Geile, M. F. (1991). The development of liability to schizophrenia: Early and late developmental models. In E. F. Walker (Ed.), *Schizophrenia: A life-course developmental perspective* (pp. 277–298). New York: Academic Press.

Prior, M., Smart, D., Sanson, A., Pedlow, R., & Oberklaid, F. (1992). Transient versus stable behavior problems in a normal sample: Infancy to school age. *Journal of Pediatric Psychiatry, 17,* 423–443.

Rosenbaum, J. F., Biederman, J., Bolduc-Murphy, E. A., Faraone, S. V., Chaloff, J., Hirshfeld, D., et al. (1993). Behavioral inhibition in childhood: A risk factor for anxiety disorders. *Harvard Review of Psychiatry, 1,* 2–16.

Rothbart, M. K. (1981). Measurement of temperament in infancy. *Child Development, 52,* 569–578.

Rothbart, M. K., Ahadi, S. A., Hershey, K. L., & Fisher, P. (2001). Investigations of temperament at three to seven years: The Children's Behavior Questionnaire. *Child Development, 72,* 1394–1408.

Rothbart, M. K., & Bates, J. E. (1998). Temperament. In N. Eisenberg (Vol. Ed.), *Social, emotional and personality development* (Vol. 3). In W. Damon (Ed.), *Handbook of child psychology* (5th ed., pp. 105–176). New York: Wiley.

Schmitz, S., Fulker, D. W., Emde, R. N., & Zahn-Waxler, C. (2001). Early predictors of problem behavior at age four. In R. N. Emde & J. K. Hewitt (Eds.), *Infancy to childhood: Genetic and environmental influences on developmental change* (pp. 329–351). New York: Oxford University Press.

Schwartz, C. E., Snidman, N., & Kagan, J. (1999). Adolescent social anxiety as an outcome of inhibited temperament in childhood. *Journal of the American Academy of Child and Adolescent Psychiatry, 38,* 1008–1015.

Sing, C. F., Zerba, K. E., & Reilly, S. L. (1994). Traversing the biological complexity in the hierarchy between genome and CAD endpoints in the population at large. *Clinical Genetics, 46,* 6–14.

Slater, E., & Slater, P. (1944). A heuristic theory of neurosis. *Journal of Neurology and Psychiatry, 7,* 49–55.

Van Hulle, C. A., Lemery, K. S., & Goldsmith, H. H. (2002). Wisconsin Twin Panel. *Twin Research, 5,* 1–4.

Watson, D., Clark, L. A., Weber, K., Assenheimer, J. S., Strauss, M. E., & McCormick, R. A. (1995). Testing a tripartite model: II. Exploring the symptom structure of anxiety and depression in student, adult, and patient samples. *Journal of Abnormal Psychology, 104,* 15–25.

Widiger, T. A. (1998). Personality disorders. In D. F. Barone, M. Hersen, & V. B. Van Hasselt (Eds.). Advanced personality. The Plenum series in social/clinical psychology (pp. 335–352). New York: Plenum.

Zahn-Waxler, C., Schmitz, S., Fulker, D., Robinson, J., & Emde, R. (1996). Behavior problems in 5-year-old monozygotic and dizygotic twins: Genetic and environmental influences, patterns of regulation, and internalization of control. *Development and Psychopathology, 8,* 103–122.

3

The Initiation of Substance Use in Adolescence: A Behavioral Genetics Perspective

Matt McGue and William G. Iacono

Findings from family, twin, adoption, and, increasingly, molecular investigations converge on establishing the existence of substantial heritable influences on nicotine dependence (Heath & Madden, 1995; Kendler et al., 1999), alcoholism (Heath, Slutske, & Madden, 1997; Kendler, Heath, Neale, Kessler, & Eaves, 1992; McGue, 1999; Prescott, Aggen, & Kendler, 1999), and illicit substance abuse and dependence (Ball & Collier, 2002; Kendler & Prescott, 1998; Lynskey et al., 2002; McGue, Elkins, & Iacono, 2000; Tsuang et al., 1996). Findings similarly converge in unequivocally implicating the importance of environmental influences. The challenge is no longer in determining whether but rather how genetic and environmental factors contribute to risk for substance use disorders (SUDs; Rutter, Pickles, Murray, & Eaves, 2001). Meeting this challenge will require adopting a developmental perspective that recognizes the links between SUDs and the broader array of externalizing and internalizing psychopathology.

Developmental approaches emphasize the adolescent origins of (at least some forms of) SUDs, the need to investigate the progression of substance use and abuse within the broader context of adolescent and early-adult development, and the importance of both individual-level and contextual risk (Sher, Trull, Bartholow, & Vieth, 1999; Tarter & Vanyukov, 1994; Windle & Davies, 1999; Zucker, Boyd, & Howard, 1994). Normative trajectories in alcohol (Colder, Campbell, Ruel, Richardson, & Flay, 2002) and drug use (White, Pandina, & Chen, 2002) during adolescence have been carefully described. Typically, substance use begins with experimentation in middle adolescence, escalates in frequency and density through late adolescence and the early 20s, and moderates in the mid to late 20s (Bachman, Johnston, O'Malley, & Schulenberg, 1996). However, substantial individual differences about this typical course exist and can have profound long-term consequences.

Figure 3.1 illustrates a heuristic developmental model that guides our research on SUDs. The model posits the existence of both substance-specific

This research is supported in part by USPHS grants # AA00175, AA09367, and DA05147.

41

and substance-nonspecific risk factors. Substance-specific risk refers to factors that increase the likelihood of the use and abuse of a particular substance, likely reflecting differential pharmacological sensitivity, and that are hypothesized to exert a stronger influence during late-stage than early-stage transitions. Nonspecific risk refers to factors that increase the likelihood of the use and abuse of all drugs, regardless of the specific substance involved. These factors are hypothesized to be relatively more important during the early stages of substance use/abuse and would include the broad range of psychological and mental health variables that are associated with SUDs regardless of substance.

Of particular interest to our current work, as well as the focus of this chapter, are the factors that underlie the initial stages of substance use in early adolescence. The importance of this stage to understanding the etiology of SUDs has recently been underscored by the observation that the earlier an adolescent first tries alcohol the more likely he or she is to develop alcoholism in adulthood. In an analysis of 27,000 ever-drinking adult participants from the National Longitudinal Alcohol Epidemiologic Survey, Grant and Dawson (1997) reported that the lifetime rate of alcohol dependence was four

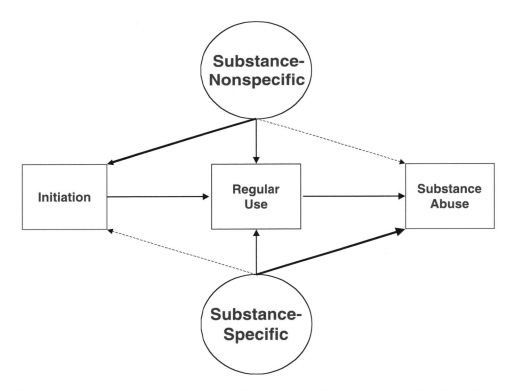

Figure 3.1. A heuristic model for the development of substance use disorders. Nonspecific risk factors (e.g., personality, mental health) are hypothesized to exert a greater influence on early as opposed to later transitions (bold versus dotted lines), whereas specific risk factors (e.g., pharmacological sensitivity) are hypothesized to exert a greater influence on later as opposed to early transitions.

times greater among those who first tried alcohol before age 15 as compared with those who first drank at age 20 or older. Others have also reported a strong association between age at first drink (AFD) and rate of alcoholism (Dewit, Adlaf, Offord, & Ogborne, 2000; Prescott & Kendler, 1999; York, 1999). Clearly, such an association has profound prevention implications. If nothing else, it suggests that some of the major risk factors for the development of adult alcoholism are already established by early adolescence. It may further suggest that delaying the age adolescents initially experiment with alcohol may prevent subsequent cases of alcoholism, but only if the association reflects a causal influence of AFD on alcoholism risk.

In this chapter, we review findings from our ongoing longitudinal study of adolescent twins to explore the nature of the association of AFD and SUDs. After introducing the research context, we address the following research questions:

1. Is early AFD a specific risk factor for alcoholism or is it associated with a broader array of substance use and mental health disorders?
2. Is the association between AFD and alcoholism better accounted for by a common vulnerability model or a causal model?
3. Is AFD familial and heritable?

The Minnesota Twin Family Study

In 1990, we initiated the Minnesota Twin Family Study (MTFS), a longitudinal study of approximately 1400 like-sex adolescent twin pairs and their parents. More than 5000 individuals have participated in the MTFS. Because a major focus of the MTFS is the investigation of the etiology of SUDs within a developmental, behavioral-genetic framework, assessments have been tied to major transitions in the twins' lives (Figure 3.2). Two MTFS cohorts are participating. The first, or "11-year-old," cohort was assessed initially when the twins were in fifth or sixth grade (ages 10 to 12), an age prior to when the vast majority of Minnesota youth have initiated substance use. This younger cohort was subsequently assessed at ages 14 to 15, when early initiation of substance use could be observed, and at ages 17 to 18, when they reached their senior year of high school and when many of the youths would have experienced a sharp increase in their substance-use behavior. We are engaged in the third follow-up of this cohort at ages 20 to 21, a life stage when substance abuse peaks for many individuals. Future plans include a follow-up at ages 24 to 25, when many will have moderated the heavy substance use patterns that characterized their college years. The second, or "17-year-old," cohort was assessed initially when they were seniors in high school (ages 16 to 18), and subsequently at both ages 20 to 21 and 24 to 25. We have initiated the ages 29 to 30 follow-up of this older cohort.

The intake MTFS assessment lasts a full day and includes a comprehensive assessment of SUDs and related clinical disorders, and an extensive battery of psychophysiological markers of risk (Iacono, Carlson, Taylor, Elkins, & McGue, 1999). There is also assessment for environmental risk, including characteristics of the peer group and parent–child relationship (Elkins, McGue, & Iacono, 1997), as well as attitudes and expectancies that

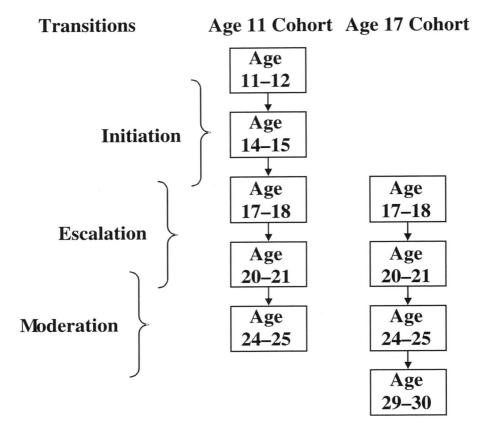

Figure 3.2. Completed and planned assessments of twins in the Minnesota Twin Family Study. The intake and first follow-up assessments are complete, and the second follow-up assessment is nearly complete.

might underlie adolescent substance use and other deviant behavior (Goldman, Brown, Christiansen, & Smith, 1991). Self-report measures of personality, academic achievement, gambling, and eating disorders (Klump, McGue, & Iacono, 2002; von Ranson, Iacono, & McGue, 2002) are also obtained. To maximize the longitudinal utility of our data, to the extent it is developmentally appropriate, every effort is made to ensure that follow-up assessments parallel those given at intake and that the assessments of the twins parallel those given to their parents.

Several features of the MTFS sampling framework are notable. First, twins are identified through Minnesota State birth records and thus constitute a community-based sample. In contrast with clinically ascertained samples, in which severe, comorbid cases are likely to be overrepresented (Kessler, Crum, & Warner, 1997; Kessler et al., 1996), community-based samples allow for more accurate characterization of clinical course and unbiased estimation of risk factor profile. Second, participating MTFS families are broadly representative of families with twins born in Minnesota for the birth cohorts sampled. The current addresses of more than 90% of twins born in Minnesota during the relevant birth years were identified using various public registries (e.g., telephone directories). Among families eligible to participate (i.e., live within a day's drive of our labs in Minneapolis, twins have no mental or physical disability that would prevent completion of our day-long assessment, and twins live with at least one biological parent), approximately 17% declined our invitation to participate. Important, however, is that more than 80% of nonparticipating families complete a brief telephone interview or self-report questionnaire. Comparison of participating with nonparticipating families revealed no significant differences in self-rated mental health of parents and twins and significant but modest differences in family socioeconomic status (e.g., parents in the participating families averaged approximately 0.2 to 0.3 years more education than parents in nonparticipating families). Iacono et al. (1999) provided additional details on the MTFS design and a detailed comparison of participating and nonparticipating families at intake.

A third distinctive feature of the MTFS is that assessments have been completed not only on the participating twins, but also on the vast majority of their biological, and, if different, rearing parents. Developmental psychopathologists have repeatedly criticized the field for failing to assess paternal psychopathology in studies on child development (Connell & Goodman, 2002; Phares, 1992). As a consequence, the impact of fathers on child functioning is poorly understood. In the MTFS, however, nearly 100% of biological mothers and 90% of biological fathers completed an intake assessment. Although participation rates among stepparents are understandably lower, the MTFS has also assessed more than 100 of the nonbiological, rearing parents of the twins.

A final notable feature of the MTFS sampling scheme is the relatively high rate of participation at follow-up assessments. We completed the first follow-up assessment of both cohorts. Participation rates at the first follow-up exceeded 90% for males and females in the younger cohort and for females in the older cohort and exceeded 80% for males in the older cohort. Comparison of follow-up nonparticipants with participants on intake psychopathology revealed few significant differences. The only significant differences observed among males were that, as compared to participants, nonparticipants had slightly higher rates of attention deficit-hyperactivity disorder (ADHD; $p = .03$) in the older cohort and slightly *lower* rates of conduct disorder (CD; $p = .04$) in the younger cohort. Among females, there were no significant differences in rates of clinical diagnoses between follow-up participants and nonparticipants in the younger cohort, although rates of conduct disorder (CD), antisocial personality disorder (ASPD), and drug abuse/dependence were significantly higher among nonparticipants as compared to participants in the older cohort. It is important to note that individuals who do not participate at a given assessment are not lost to subsequent follow-up. More than 50% of nonparticipants at the first follow-up have completed a second follow-up assessment.

In summary, the MTFS is a study of a large, community-based, and representative sample of families with twins born in Minnesota. The twins in these families are comprehensively assessed at regular intervals to chart the onset, escalation, and moderation of substance use and abuse in adolescence and early adulthood. Participation rates at follow-up are high and differences between participants and nonparticipants are generally minimal, making the MTFS an ideal study to explore the development of SUDs.

The Origins and Consequences of an Early Age at First Drink

Age at First Drink and Clinical Outcomes in MTFS Parents

To explore the implications of an early initiation of substance use, we investigated the correlates of AFD in a series of publications (Iacono, Malone, & McGue, 2003; McGue, Iacono, Legrand, & Elkins, 2001a, 2001b). As part of the MTFS assessment, we asked participating parents, "How old were you the first time you used alcohol (on your own; more than your parents allowed you to)?" Parents also completed a diagnostic clinical interview that included assessment of alcohol dependence, other drug abuse or dependence, and related mental health disorders. Diagnoses were made according to DSM-III-R criteria, the diagnostic system in place at the start of the MTFS, and were assigned at either a definite (all DSM criteria met) or probable (all but one symptom criterion met) level of certainty. Figure 3.3 contains rates of definite plus probable alcohol dependence in 2704 MTFS parents as a function of their AFD. In both the male and female samples, AFD was significantly and indeed substantially associated with alcohol dependence. Rates of alcohol dependence were three or more times greater among individuals who first tried alcohol

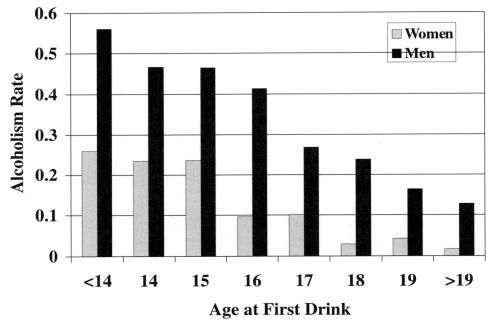

Figure 3.3. Rate of alcohol dependence in 1383 women and 1321 men as a function of age at first drink. Alcohol dependence is diagnosed using DSM-III-R criteria and based on a definite (all DSM criteria met) or probable (all except one DSM symptom criteria met) level of certainty. Data from "The Origins and Consequences of Age at First Drink. I. Associations With Substance-Use Disorders, Disinhibitory Behavior and Psychopathology, and P3 Amplitude," by M. McGue, W. G. Iacono, L. N. Legrand, and I. Elkins, 2001, *Alcoholism: Clinical and Experimental Research, 25,* pp. 1156–1165.

before age 15 than among those who first tried alcohol after age 19. We thus replicated with data from the MTFS parents the essential finding from the earlier Grant and Dawson (1997) study.

To understand the prevention implications of this finding, however, we must know further whether an early AFD is specifically associated with an increased risk of alcoholism or a broader array of mental health problems. The extensive clinical assessment of the parents in the MTFS allowed us to address this question. In McGue et al. (2001a), we showed that in both the MTFS mothers and fathers, an early AFD is associated not only with increased rates of alcohol dependence but also with increased rates of nicotine dependence, drug abuse/dependence, CD, and ASPD. Early AFD was also associated with the higher-order Constraint factor scale from the Multidimensional Personality Questionnaire (MPQ; Tellegen & Waller, in press; see Figure 3.4) and educational attainment. Although the magnitude of these latter associations are not strong, their existence demonstrates that an early AFD is not only associated with mental health indicators, but is also associated with normal-range psychological phenomena. In particular, the findings that early AFD is associated with lower scores on Constraint indicates that AFD is associated with normal range variation in disinhibited and undercontrolled behavior.

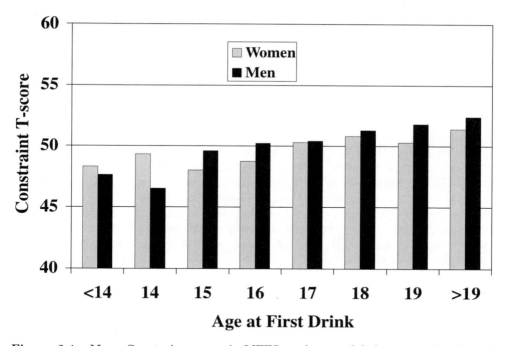

Figure 3.4. Mean Constraint scores in MTFS mothers and fathers as a function of age at first drink. Constraint scores were scaled to have a mean of 50 and a standard deviation of 10 in the overall sample (i.e., a T-score metric). Data from "The Origins and Consequences of Age at First Drink. I. Associations With Substance-Use Disorders, Disinhibitory Behavior and Psychopathology, and P3 Amplitude," by M. McGue, W. G. Iacono, L. N. Legrand, and I. Elkins, 2001, *Alcoholism: Clinical and Experimental Research, 25,* pp. 1156–1165.

The statistical significance of the associations with AFD was maintained even after we controlled for a diagnosis of alcohol dependence, indicating that the correlates of an early AFD are broader than alcoholism. Further insight into the nature of the AFD–alcoholism association can be gained by noting those characteristics that were not associated with AFD in the MTFS parent sample. AFD was not significantly associated with risk of major depressive disorder (MDD), and the MPQ higher-order scales of Positive Emotionality and Negative Emotionality. The most parsimonious explanation for this pattern of findings with the MTFS parents is that, rather than being a specific indicator of SUDs risk, an early AFD is a manifestation of generalized disinhibitory processes. This proposition gains additional support in analyses of data from the MTFS twins.

Age at First Drink in MTFS Twin Offspring

The findings discussed so far show that AFD is a nonspecific risk factor for a wide range of behavioral problems. However, the retrospective nature of the assessment severely limits our ability to infer the mechanisms that underlie these associations. Additional insight into the mechanisms of AFD risk is obtained through an analysis we completed with twins from the older MTFS cohort (McGue et al., 2001a). At intake, the 17-year-old twins completed an extensive assessment of psychophysiological markers of risk. Included in this battery was an assessment of the P3 component of the event-related potential (ERP) elicited using a standard visual oddball task. P3 amplitude corresponds to a positively oriented deflection of the averaged ERP waveform that occurs approximately 200 to 500 ms after stimulus onset and is thought to reflect processing of novel information. P3 is a well-established biological marker of risk for SUDs (Begleiter, Porjesz, Bihari, & Kissin, 1984) and general disinhibitory psychopathology (Iacono, Carlson, Malone, & McGue, 2002), with lower levels of P3 amplitude associated with greater risk for disinhibitory psychopathology and SUDs. P3 amplitude is also significantly associated with AFD in both the male ($n = 500$) and female ($n = 627$) 17-year-old twin samples (Figure 3.5), with lower P3 amplitude being associated with earlier age at first drink. Thus an early AFD is associated with a biological indicator of disinhibitory psychopathology (Iacono et al., 2002; Iacono et al., 2003), suggesting that biological (possibly genetic) factors may contribute to its association with SUDs risk.

   Analysis of early use of alcohol in the younger twin cohort further allowed us to sequence the onset of disinhibitory behavior relative to the onset of drinking (McGue et al., 2001a). Of the 1343 twins from the younger cohort who had not tried alcohol without parental permission at their intake assessment, 221 (34%) of the boys and 207 (30%) of the girls had reported trying alcohol by their first follow-up assessment at age 14. At intake, we had assessed various indicators of disinhibitory psychopathology including DSM-III-R diagnoses of ADHD, CD, oppositional defiant disorder (ODD), and teacher ratings of oppositional, hyperactive, and inattentive behavior and of grades. As with the parents, early use of alcohol was generally related to increased rates of disinhibitory behavior and psychopathology but was not related to internalizing

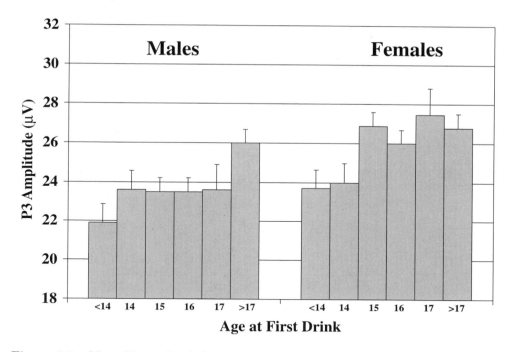

Figure 3.5. Mean P3 amplitude in 500 male and 627 17-year old twins as a function of age at first drink. The over-17 group includes twins who had not yet tried alcohol without parental permission by the time of their intake assessment. P3 amplitude is measured in microvolts (μV); error bars demarcate one standard error of the mean. Data from "The Origins and Consequences of Age at First Drink. I. Associations With Substance-Use Disorders, Disinhibitory Behavior and Psychopathology, and P3 Amplitude," by M. McGue, W. G. Iacono, L. N. Legrand, and I. Elkins, 2001, *Alcoholism: Clinical and Experimental Research, 25,* pp. 1156–1165.

psychopathology (e.g., MDD). For example, use of alcohol without parental permission by age 14 increased the odds of any externalizing disorder by 2.28 in boys (95% Confidence Interval of 1.60, 3.25) and 1.56 in girls (1.01, 2.42), and was associated with about a .2 to .5 standard deviation increase in teacher-rated hyperactivity/impulsivity. Because these observations of increased levels of disinhibition *preceded* the onset of alcohol use, we can unequivocally reject the hypothesis that the relationship of early alcohol use with the myriad of mental health factors with which it is associated inevitably reflects the causal impact of the former on the latter.

Age at First Drink in MTFS Twin Offspring

Consistent with this last finding, Prescott and Kendler (1999) hypothesized that the association of AFD with alcoholism reflects a common inherited vulnerability rather than a causal influence of the former on the latter. Support for this hypothesis comes from their analysis of data from nearly 9000 adult twins, showing that the association of AFD with alcoholism risk is genetically and not environmentally mediated. Using data from parents and twin offspring from the MTFS, we were able to further explore this common vulnerability hypothesis (McGue et al., 2001b).

Biological parents were classified as having either an early (age 14 or younger) versus late AFD, and this parental classification was then related to offspring substance use and psychopathology in the younger cohort. As expected, an early AFD runs in families. The sons and daughters of early-drinking mothers were significantly more likely to be early drinkers than the sons and daughters of late-drinking mothers. Somewhat unexpectedly, a similar significant effect was not observed with fathers' AFD. As with the within-person analyses presented previously, an early AFD in parents was not specifically associated with substance-use related outcomes but was rather associated with a broad range of offspring outcomes, at least among the boys. For example, early AFD by either mothers or fathers was significantly associated with increased symptoms of externalizing but not internalizing psychopathology in boys. As compared with boys whose parents had a late AFD, boys had on average 1.87 (SE of +.71) more externalizing symptoms when fathers but not mothers had an early AFD, 1.91 (± 0.81) more externalizing symptoms when mothers but not fathers had an early AFD, and 4.91 (± 1.42) more externalizing symptoms when both mothers and fathers had an early AFD. In contrast, early AFD in either mothers or fathers was not significantly related to either externalizing or internalizing psychopathology in girls.

These familial associations between parental AFD and offspring's early alcohol use and externalizing psychopathology may reflect common genetic or common environmental mechanisms, possibilities that can in principle be resolved through analysis of the twin data. Table 3.1 contains the monozygotic (MZ) and dizygotic (DZ) twin tetrachoric correlations for early alcohol use estimated separately in the male and female samples. Also in the table are the proportions of early use liability variance associated with additive genetic (a^2), shared environmental (c^2), and nonshared environmental (e^2) factors, estimated using standard biometrical methods (Neale, Boker, Xie, & Maes, 1999; Neale & Cardon, 1992).

The MZ twin correlation for early alcohol use was substantial in both the male ($r = .76$) and female ($r = .76$) samples. In the male sample, the DZ correlation was approximately half that of the corresponding MZ value ($r = .36$), implicating genetic factors. In the female sample, however, the DZ correlation was only slightly lower than the MZ value ($r = .67$), implicating shared envi-

Table 3.1. Twin Correlations and Variance Component Estimates for Early Alcohol Use

	MZ	DZ	a^2	c^2	e^2
Boys	.76	.36	.55	.20	.25
	(.36, .69)	(.12, .60)	(.24, .75)	(.03, .51)	(.18, .32)
Girls	.76	.67	.11	.65	.25
	(.70, .82)	(.55, .79)	(.01, .36)	(.42, .78)	(.18, .31)

Note. MZ = monozygotic, DZ = dizygotic. Number of twin pairs are: 215 MZ and 103 DZ in the male sample and 201 MZ and 122 DZ in the female sample.

ronmental effects. The biometric variance component estimates, which differed significantly by gender, are consistent with this interpretation. Genetic factors appear to be more important in boys than girls ($a^2 = .55$ vs. .11), but shared environmental factors appear to be more important in girls than boys ($c^2 = .65$ vs .20). Thus, an early AFD is heritable, although only modestly so in girls. Some twin studies of alcoholism (McGue, Pickens, & Svikis, 1992) and adolescent substance use (Han, McGue, & Iacono, 1999) also suggest weaker heritable effects in women than in men. Nonetheless, the hypothesis of gender differences in heritability has received inconsistent support, and based on the most recent evidence (Heath et al., 1997; Kendler et al., 1992), most have concluded that genetic factors exert an equal effect on alcoholism risk in men and women. Our finding of differential heritable effects on AFD suggests that it may be worthwhile to reassess the differential heritability hypothesis.

Early Initiation of Other Problem Behaviors

Further support for the proposition that an early AFD is an indicator of generalized disinhibitory processes comes from the observation that early use of alcohol is associated with early involvement in a wide range of adolescent problem behaviors (Jessor & Jessor, 1977). Adolescents who drink early also tend to use other drugs, get into problems with authority figures, and engage in sexual behavior early. Iacono et al. (2003) recently explored the importance of early involvement in adolescent problem behavior using data from the intake assessment of the older MTFS twin cohort. As expected, early use of alcohol (prior to age 15), early smoking (prior to age 15), and early sexual intercourse (by the time of the age-17 assessment) were all substantially intercorrelated, justifying the creation of a four-point index of early problem behavior that ranged from 0 (no early problem behaviors) to 3 (early engagement in all three problem behaviors). Among boys, 39% had an index score of 0, and 11% had an index score of 3. The comparable percentages among girls were 48% and 9%, respectively. There is clearly substantial variability in the degree of involvement in early problem behavior in these adolescents.

Iacono et al. (2003) reported a significant association of P3 amplitude with each individual problem behavior indicator as well as with scores on the summary index. The greater the number of early adolescent problem behaviors, the lower the mean P3 amplitude. For example, in girls, the mean P3 amplitude was 3.2 ($\pm$1.3) μV smaller among those with an index score of 3 versus those with an index score of 0. The comparable difference in boys was 4.0 ($\pm$1.1) μV. Early initiation into a range of adolescent problem behaviors thus appears to be associated with biological indicators of disinhibitory processes.

Are scores on the early adolescent problem index associated with clinical outcomes? Figure 3.6 reports rates of DSM-III-R Alcohol Dependence or Alcohol Abuse at intake for the 17-year-old MTFS twins as a function of their early problem index score. Diagnoses of Alcohol Dependence are made at either a definite or probable level of certainty, whereas diagnoses of Alcohol

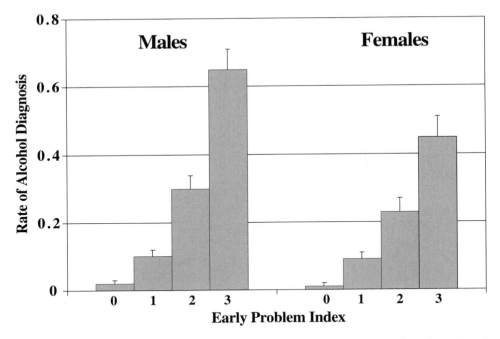

Figure 3.6. Rate of DSM-III-R alcohol dependence or abuse as a function of early problem behavior index in the 571 male and 667 female twins from the 17-year-old MTFS cohort. Diagnoses were at the definite or probable level of certainty for Alcohol Dependence, but at only the definite level of certainty for Alcohol Abuse, because the latter only requires a single symptom. The Early Problem Index was computed as the number of the following: smoking prior to age 15, alcohol use prior to age 15, and sexual intercourse by the time of the age-17 assessment. Error bars demarcate one standard error of the proportion.

Abuse are made only at a definite level of certainty because a DSM-III-R diagnosis of substance abuse only requires one symptom. As is apparent, early problem behavior is substantially associated with increased risk of alcohol abuse or dependence. Although not reported in this chapter, we have also found that the early problem index is significantly associated with other substance use (e.g., nicotine dependence, illicit drug abuse or dependence) and disinhibitory psychopathology (e.g., ASPD).

Discussion

Our developmental model leads us to the expectation that an understanding of the etiology of substance use disorders (SUDs) will require the identification and characterization of the factors that influence key transitions in the initiation, escalation and moderation of substance use and abuse in adolescence and early adulthood. In this chapter, we have reviewed findings from the Minnesota Twin Family Study (MTFS) as they relate to the very initial stages of the etiology of substance use disorders: the age at which an individual first tries alcohol (AFD). There are marked individual differences in AFD, and researchers have found that AFD is substantially associated with risk of alcoholism in adulthood (Grant & Dawson, 1997). Although there is little if any disagreement over the prognostic significance of an early AFD, there is debate about the basis for the association between AFD and alcoholism. An early AFD may exert a causal influence on risk of alcoholism and other SUDs by, for example, disrupting normal developmental processes in adolescence (Dewit et al., 2000). Alternatively, the association between AFD and alcoholism may arise because both are indicators of a common underlying construct (Prescott & Kendler, 1999).

In this chapter, we have presented findings from the MTFS that support the common vulnerability hypothesis for the association of AFD and alcoholism risk. Specifically, we have shown that (a) an early AFD is not specifically associated with alcoholism but rather is associated with a range of disinhibitory psychopathology and behavior as well as with reduced P3 amplitude, a promising biological marker of disinhibition; (b) indicators of behavioral psychopathology and behavior predate alcohol use onset in adolescence, ruling out the possibility that an early AFD causes at least these forms of disinhibitory psychopathology; (c) early AFD is associated with early involvement in other problematic adolescent behaviors, and these problem behaviors individually and collectively are associated with reduced P3 amplitude and increased risk for substance use and related mental health disorders; (d) the offspring of parents who have an early AFD are more likely to have an early AFD (both sons and daughters) and elevated rates of externalizing but not internalizing psychopathology (sons but not daughters) than the offspring of parents who do not have an early AFD; and (e) AFD is moderately heritable in boys but only modestly heritable in girls.

These findings converge on the conclusion that early AFD is a reflection of disinhibitory processes that underlie SUD risk. A substantial body of research has unequivocally established a link between SUDs and disinhibitory processes. For example, as compared with individuals who do not have SUDs, individuals with SUDs score higher on personality measures of behavioral undercontrol both concurrently (McGue, Slutske, & Iacono, 1999; McGue, Slutske, Taylor, & Iacono, 1997; Sher & Trull, 1994), and prospectively (Sher, Bartholow, & Wood, 2000) as early as age 3 (Caspi, Henry, McGee, Moffitt, & Silva, 1995). SUDs are also strongly associated with indicators of disinhibitory psychopathology, including ADHD and CD in adolescence and ASPD in adulthood (Sher & Trull, 1994). Our findings with AFD, as well as the contributions of others (Cloninger, 1987), suggest that disinhibitory processes may be especially important in early onset SUDs.

The fact that AFD is familial and modestly (in girls) to moderately (in boys) heritable is consistent with behavioral genetic research indicating that the commonalities among multiple indicators of behavioral disinhibition appear to reflect in part shared genetic mechanisms. There is a strong genetic association between CD and alcoholism (Slutske et al., 1997) and between both of these disorders and the personality dimension of behavioral undercontrol (Slutske et al., 2002). Furthermore, a highly heritable (approximately 80%) latent dimension of disinhibition appears to account for the phenotypic associations among externalizing psychopathology, the use and abuse of and dependence on both licit and illicit substances, and extreme scores on personality measures of behavioral undercontrol (Krueger, Hicks, Iacono, & McGue, 2002; Young, Stallings, Corley, Krauter, & Hewitt, 2000). This highly heritable latent dimension of disinhibition may also help account for another of the more salient clinical features of SUDs: their substantial comorbidity (Anthony, Warner, & Kessler, 1994). Although the coaggregation of some SUDs likely reflects common pharmacological factors, especially for alcohol and tobacco (Madden, Bucholz, Martin, & Heath, 2000), large-scale family (Bierut, Schuckit, Hesselbrock, & Reich, 2000; Merikangas et al., 1998) and twin studies (Madden et al., 2000; True et al., 1999; Tsuang et al., 1998) implicate shared, as well as specific, genetic mechanisms.

This research leads us to reject simple explanations for the association between AFD and SUDs risk, but it fails to fully explicate the basis for this important and perplexing association. It is remarkable that simply knowing the age at which adolescents first sample alcohol without parental permission has profound implications for their lifelong risk for SUDs and other mental health problems. This observation has profound implications for prevention efforts, directing our attention to the factors that exist in early adolescence that already establish an individual's level of risk. Effective interventions, however, will require understanding the mechanisms underlying the AFD-SUD association. Concluding that an early AFD is another indicator of a common vulnerability to disinhibitory psychopathology is not equivalent to concluding that an early AFD has *no* influence on risk for SUDs and other mental health problems. Rather, it may be that an early AFD is both an indicator of and contributor to disinhibitory psychopathology. Resolving the complexities of reciprocal associations like these will require longitudinal observations like those made in the MTFS.

References

Anthony, J. C., Warner, L. A., & Kessler, R. C. (1994). Comparative epidemiology of dependence on tobacco, alcohol, controlled substances, and inhalants: Basic findings from the National Comorbidity Survey. *Experimental and Clinical Psychopharmacology, 2,* 244–268.

Bachman, J. G., Johnston, L. D., O'Malley, P. M., & Schulenberg, J. E. (1996). Transitions in alcohol and other drug use and abuse during late adolescence and young adulthood. In J. A. Graber, J. Brooks-Gunn, & A. C. Petersen (Eds.), *Transitions through adolescence: Interpersonal domains and contexts.* Hillsdale, NJ: Erlbaum.

Ball, D., & Collier, D. (2002). Substance misuse. In P. McGuffin, M. J. Owen, & I. I. Gottesman (Eds.), *Psychiatric genetics and genomics* (pp. 267–302). Oxford: Oxford University Press.

Begleiter, H., Porjesz, B., Bihari, B., & Kissin, B. (1984). Event-related brain potentials in boys at risk for alcoholism. *Science, 225,* 1493–1496.

Bierut, L. J., Schuckit, M. A., Hesselbrock, V., & Reich, T. (2000). Co-occurring risk factors for alcohol dependence and habitual smoking. *Alcohol Health and Research World, 24,* 233–241.

Caspi, A., Henry, B., McGee, R. O., Moffitt, T. E., & Silva, P. A. (1995). Temperamental origins of child and adolescent behavior problems: From age three to age fifteen. *Child Development, 66*(1), 55–68.

Cloninger, C. R. (1987). Neurogenetic adaptive mechanisms in alcoholism. *Science, 236,* 410–416.

Colder, C. R., Campbell, R. T., Ruel, E., Richardson, J. L., & Flay, B. R. (2002). A finite mixture model of growth trajectories of adolescent alcohol use: Predictors and consequences. *Journal of Consulting and Clinical Psychology, 70,* 976–985.

Connell, A. M., & Goodman, S. H. (2002). The association between psychopathology in fathers versus mothers and children's externalizing behavior problems: A meta-analysis. *Psychological Bulletin, 128,* 746–773.

Dewit, D. J., Adlaf, E. M., Offord, D. R., & Ogborne, A. C. (2000). Age at first alcohol use: A risk factor for the development of alcohol disorders. *American Journal of Psychiatry, 157,* 745–750.

Elkins, I. J., McGue, M., & Iacono, W. G. (1997). Genetic and environmental influences on parent–son relationships: evidence for increasing genetic influence during adolescence. *Developmental Psychology, 33*(2), 351–363.

Goldman, M. S., Brown, S. A., Christiansen, B. A., & Smith, G. T. (1991). Alcoholism and memory: Broadening the scope of alcohol expectancy research. *Psychological Bulletin, 110,* 137–146.

Grant, B. F., & Dawson, D. A. (1997). Age at onset of alcohol use and its association with DSM-IV alcohol abuse and dependence: Results from the National Longitudinal Alcohol Epidemiologic Survey. *Journal of Substance Abuse, 9,* 103–110.

Han, C., McGue, M. K., & Iacono, W. G. (1999). Lifetime tobacco, alcohol, and other substance use in adolescent Minnesota twins: Univariate and multivariate behavioral genetic analyses. *Addiction, 7,* 981–993.

Heath, A., C., & Madden, P. A. F. (1995). Genetic influences on smoking behavior. In J. R. Turner, L. R. Cardon, & J. K. Hewitt (Eds.), *Behavior genetic approaches in behavioral medicine* (pp. 45–66). New York: Plenum.

Heath, A. C., Slutske, W. S., & Madden, P. A. F. (1997). Gender differences in the genetic contribution to alcoholism risk and to alcohol consumption patterns. In R. W. Wilsnack & S. C. Wilsnack (Eds.), *Gender and alcohol: Individual and social perspectives* (pp. 114–149). New Brunswick, NJ: Rutgers Center of Alcohol Studies.

Iacono, W. G., Carlson, S. R., Malone, S. M., & McGue, M. (2002). P3 event-related potential amplitude and the risk for disinhibitory disorders in adolescent boys. *Archives of General Psychiatry, 59*(8), 750–757.

Iacono, W. G., Carlson, S. R., Taylor, J., Elkins, I. J., & McGue, M. (1999). Behavioral disinhibition and the development of substance use disorders: Findings from the Minnesota Twin Family Study. *Development and Psychopathology, 11,* 869–900.

Iacono, W. G., Malone, S. M., & McGue, M. (2003). Substance use disorders, externalizing psychopathology, and P300 event related potential amplitude. *International Journal of Psychophysiology, 48,* 147–178.

Jessor, R., & Jessor, S. L. (1977). *Problem behavior and psychosocial development: A longitudinal study of youth.* New York: Academic Press.

Kendler, K. S., Heath, A. C., Neale, M. C., Kessler, R. C., & Eaves, L. J. (1992). A population-based twin study of alcoholism in women. *JAMA, 268*(14), 1877–1882.

Kendler, K. S., Neale, M. C., Sullivan, P., Corey, L. A., Gardner, C. O., & Prescott, C. A. (1999). A population-based twin study in women of smoking initiation and nicotine dependence. *Psychological Medicine, 29*(2), 299–308.

Kendler, K. S., & Prescott, C. A. (1998). Cannabis use, abuse, and dependence in a population-based sample of female twins. *American Journal of Psychiatry, 155*(8), 1016–1022.

Kessler, R. C., Crum, R. M., & Warner, L. A. (1997). Lifetime co-occurence of DSM-III-R alcohol abuse and dependence with other psychiatric disorders in the National Comorbidity Survey. *Archives of General Psychiatry, 54,* 313–321.

Kessler, R. C., Nelson, C. B., McGonagle, K. A., Edlund, M. J., Frank, R. G., & Leaf, P. J. (1996). The epidemiology of co-occurring addictive and mental disorders: Implications for prevention and service utilization. *American Journal of Orthopsychiatry, 66*(1), 17–31.

Klump, K. L., McGue, M., & Iacono, W. G. (2002). Genetic relationships between personality and disordered eating. *Journal of Abnormal Psychology, 111,* 380–389.

Krueger, R. F., Hicks, B. M., Iacono, W. G., & McGue, M. (2002). Etiologic correlations among substance dependence, antisocial behavior, and personality: Modeling the externalizing spectrum. *Journal of Abnormal Psychology, 111,* 411–424.

Lynskey, M. T., Heath, A. C., Nelson, E. C., Bucholz, K. K., Madden, P. A. F., Slutske, W. S., et al. (2002). Genetic and environmental contributions to cannabis dependence in a national young adult twin sample. *Psychological Medicine, 32,* 195–207.

Madden, P. A. F., Bucholz, K., Martin, N. G., & Heath, A. C. (2000). Smoking and the genetic contribution to alcohol-dependence risk. *Alcohol Research and Health, 24,* 209–214.

McGue, M. (1999). Behavioral genetic models of alcoholism and drinking. In K. E. Leonard & H. T. Blane (Eds.), *Psychological theories of drinking and alcoholism* (pp. 372–421). New York: Guilford Publications.

McGue, M., Elkins, I., & Iacono, W. G. (2000). Genetic and environmental influences on adolescent substance use and abuse. *American Journal of Medical Genetics (Neuropsychiatric Genetics), 96,* 671–677.

McGue, M., Iacono, W. G., Legrand, L. N., & Elkins, I. (2001a). The origins and consequences of age at first drink. I. Associations with substance-use disorders, disinhibitory behavior and psychopathology, and P3 amplitude. *Alcoholism: Clinical and Experimental Research, 25,* 1156–1165.

McGue, M., Iacono, W. G., Legrand, L. N., & Elkins, I. (2001b). Origins and consequences of age at first drink. II. Familial risk and heritability. *Alcoholism: Clinical and Experimental Research, 25,* 1166–1173.

McGue, M., Pickens, R. W., & Svikis, D. S. (1992). Sex and age effects on the inheritance of alcohol problems: A twin study. *Journal of Abnormal Psychology, 101*(1), 3–17.

McGue, M., Slutske, W., & Iacono, W. G. (1999). Personality and substance use disorders: II. Alcoholism versus drug use disorders. *Journal of Consulting and Clinical Psychology, 67*(3), 394–404.

McGue, M., Slutske, W., Taylor, J., & Iacono, W. G. (1997). Personality and substance use disorders: I. Effects of gender and alcoholism subtype. *Alcoholism: Clinical and Experimental Research, 21,* 513–520.

Merikangas, K. R., Stolar, M., Stevens, D. E., Goulet, J., Preisig, M. A., Fenton, B., et al. (1998). Familial transmission of substance use disorders. *Archives of General Psychiatry, 55,* 973–979.

Neale, M. C., Boker, S. M., Xie, G., & Maes, H. H. (1999). *Mx: Statistical modeling* (5th ed.). Richmond, VA: Department of Psychiatry, Medical College of Virginia.

Neale, M. C., & Cardon, L. R. (1992). *Methodology for genetic studies of twins and families.* Dordrecht, The Netherlands: Kluwer.

Phares, V. (1992). Where's poppa? The relative lack of attention to the role of fathers in child and adolescent psychopathology. *American Psychologist, 47,* 656–664.

Prescott, C. A., Aggen, S. H., & Kendler, K. S. (1999). Sex differences in the sources of genetic liability to alcohol abuse and dependence in a population-based sample of U.S. twins. *Alcoholism: Clinical and Experimental Research, 23*(7), 1136–1144.

Prescott, C. A., & Kendler, K. S. (1999). Age at first drink and risk for alcoholism: A noncausal association. *Alcoholism: Clinical and Experimental Research, 23,* 101–107.

Rutter, M., Pickles, A., Murray, R., & Eaves, L. J. (2001). Testing hypotheses on specific causal effects on behavior. *Psychological Bulletin, 127,* 291–324.

Sher, K. J., Bartholow, B. D., & Wood, M. D. (2000). Personality and substance use disorders. *Journal of Consulting and Clinical Psychology, 68,* 818–829.

Sher, K. J., & Trull, T. J. (1994). Personality and disinhibitory psychopathology: Alcoholism and antisocial personality disorder. *Journal of Abnormal Psychology, 103,* 92–102.

Sher, K. J., Trull, T. J., Bartholow, B. D., & Vieth, A. (1999). Personality theory and research. In K. E. Leonard & H. T. Blane (Eds.), *Psychological theories of drinking and alcoholism* (2nd ed., pp. 54–105). New York: Guilford Press.

Slutske, W. S., Heath, A. C., Dinwiddie, S. H., Madden, P. A. F., Bucholz, K. K., Dunne, M. P., et al. (1997). Modeling genetic and environmental influences in the etiology of conduct disorder: A study of 2,682 adult twin pairs. *Journal of Abnormal Psychology, 106,* 266–279.

Slutske, W. S., Heath, A. C., Madden, P. A. F., Bucholz, K., Statham, D. J., & Martin, N. G. (2002). Personality and the genetic risk for alcohol dependence. *Journal of Abnormal Psychology, 111,* 124–133.

Tarter, R. E., & Vanyukov, M. (1994). Alcoholism: A developmental disorder. *Journal of Consulting and Clinical Psychology, 62,* 1096–1107.

Tellegen, A., & Waller, N. G. (Eds.). (in press). *Exploring personality through test construction: Development of the Multidimensional Personality Questionnaire.* Greenwich, CT: JAI Press.

True, W. R., Xian, H., Scherrer, J. F., Madden, P. A. F., Bucholz, K. K., Heath, A. C., et al. (1999). Common genetic vulnerability for nicotine and alcohol dependence in men. *Archives of General Psychiatry, 56,* 655–661.

Tsuang, M. T., Lyons, M. J., Meyer, J. M., Doyle, T., Eisen, S. A., Goldberg, J., et al. (1998). Co-occurrence of abuse of different drugs in men: The role of drug-specific and shared vulnerabilities. *Archives of General Psychiatry, 55*(11), 967–972.

von Ranson, K. M., Iacono, W. G., & McGue, M. (2002). Disordered eating and substance use in an epidemiological sample: I. Associations within individuals. *International Journal of Eating Disorders, 31*(4), 389–403.

White, H. R., Pandina, R. J., & Chen, P. H. (2002). Developmental trajectories of cigarette use from early adolescence into young adulthood. *Drug and Alcohol Dependence, 65,* 167–178.

Windle, M., & Davies, P. T. (1999). Developmental theory and research. In K. E. Leonard & H. T. Blane (Eds.), *Psychological theories of drinking and alcoholism* (pp. 164–202). New York: Guilford.

York, J. L. (1999). Clinical significance of alcohol intake parameters at initiation of drinking. *Alcohol, 19,* 97–99.

Young, S. E., Stallings, M. C., Corley, R. P., Krauter, K. S., & Hewitt, J. K. (2000). Genetic and environmental influences on behavioral disinhibition. *American Journal of Medical Genetics, 96*(5), 684–695.

Zucker, R. A., Boyd, G., & Howard, J. (1994). *The development of alcohol problems: Exploring biopsychosocial matrix of risk.* Rockville, MD: National Institute on Alcohol Abuse and Alcoholism Research Monograph.

4

Middle Age, Marriage, and Health Habits of America's Greatest Generation: Twins as Tools for Causal Analysis

Susan L. Trumbetta

Introduction

Dr. Irving I. Gottesman's innovative use of twin designs to help resolve questions of etiology has long been a part of his genius. One notable example is his study with Bertelsen (Gottesman & Bertelsen, 1989) of the offspring of twins discordant for schizophrenia. The authors' elegant design provided dramatic evidence of the importance of genetic factors and the relative unimportance of environmental factors in the familial transmission of schizophrenia.

It was a privilege to work with Dr. Gottesman on my dissertation, a twin study of marital status and psychological disorders. More recently, we began to explore questions about marriage and physical health. This chapter uses a novel variation on traditional univariate twin designs to test the hypothesis that marriage buffers individuals against health risks. Of course, any health benefits of marriage may apply equally to other committed, domestic partnerships, but because the 1972 World War II Twin Registry questionnaires did not ascertain nonmarital domestic partnerships, we limited this investigation to the health benefits of marriage.

Health and Marital Status

Epidemiological and clinical studies show that married men enjoy better mental and physical health, on average, than bachelors or divorcés do. Three

The author acknowledges with appreciation the National Heart, Lung, and Blood Institute for underwriting the expenses of Questionnaires 2 and 7, and the staff of the National Academy of Sciences, who have maintained this database. The author is especially grateful to the participants in the World War II Veteran Twin Registry for their generous cooperation over many years. Vassar College students Katie Doyon and Jonathan Inerfeld also provided invaluable assistance. And of course, far more than thanks belong to Irv Gottesman for his incredibly generous mentoring.

sets of causal hypotheses may explain this phenomenon: (a) hospitalization or utilization, (b) social causation, and (c) social selection. Hospitalization and utilization hypotheses state that, without spouses, individuals will more often rely on hospitalization or some other nonspousal, nonfamilial support when ill. Therefore, clinical samples will overrepresent nonmarried individuals, and some observed relationships between marriage and health reflect ascertainment artifacts. One can easily test this possibility directly by comparing clinical samples to representative community samples for illness rates by marital status. Also, if nonmarried individuals were to receive professional services at lower symptom levels than were married individuals, then that, too, would be consistent with a hospitalization or utilization ascertainment bias.

Social causation and social selection hypotheses both assert nonartifactual, causal relationships between marital status and health. Social causation hypotheses assert that marital status influences health. One popular form is the stressor model, in which bad marriages, divorce, widowhood, and bachelorhood all adversely affect health. A second form is the "marriage as buffer" model, in which marriage diminishes health risks. Social selection hypotheses, on the other hand, assert that health influences marital outcomes. In stressor terms, social selection maintains that bad health either selects individuals out of marriage or strains existing marriages to the point of dissolution. In protective terms, social selection asserts that good health increases the likelihood of marriage and adds to the vitality, enjoyment, and endurance of existing marriages. Of course, social causation and social selection are not mutually exclusive, but two aspects of complex bidirectional influences. Nevertheless, it may help to evaluate the importance of social causation and/or social selection in specific instances of associations between marriage and health.

Empirical tests of social causation and social selection present some difficulties. Statistical ambiguities abound: Under social selection, for example, the range of possible patterns of association between marriage rates and illness rates is so wide that it may be difficult to determine if observed patterns of association between health and marriage better fit those predicted by social selection or by social causation hypotheses (Goldman, 1993, 1994), at least in genetically uninformative samples. In fact, mathematical simulations of social causation or social selection may produce, within either separate model, varying and sometimes unexpected patterns of illness relative to marital status (Goldman, 1993). One way to disentangle social causation from social selection might be to assume that causality will be reflected in temporal priority, but the exact beginnings and endings of illnesses and relationships can elude demarcation. Declines in marital satisfaction and in physical health can be so gradual that one cannot easily discern whether a decline in health led to marital dissatisfaction or a decline in marital satisfaction led to a decline in health. True experiments are unethical and impossible: We cannot assign individuals randomly to good or bad marriages or to good or ill health. Nevertheless, evidence that marital conflict may suppress immune function (Kiecolt-Glaser, Glaser, Cacioppo, & Malarkey, 1998) as well as evidence that some individuals experience spikes in blood pressure that are slow to abate following marital conflict (Gottman & Levenson, 1992) are consistent with stressor-focused social causation. Evidence that the presence of a supportive partner may enhance immunity (Spiegel, Sephton, Terr, & Stites, 1998), reduce cardiovascular responses to stress (Glynn, Christenfeld, & Gerin, 1999), and contribute to healthier behaviors (Roski, Schmid, & Lando, 1996) are all consistent with the social causation model of marriage as buffer. Evidence that individuals with higher levels of well-being are more likely to marry than their counterparts (Hope, Rodgers, & Power, 1999; Mastekaasa, 1992) supports social selection, as does evolutionary theory, which suggests that humans select mates according to health and likelihood of successful reproduction.

Marriage actually may be less strongly related to general physical health than to specific health-related behaviors. For example, physical characteristics generally associated with poorer health (such as obesity) are not significantly related to divorce risk, whereas risk behaviors for poor health (such as smoking) confer a higher risk for divorce (Fu & Goldman, 2000). In addition, marriage may improve health-related behaviors, not simply health status. Many of the additional health benefits enjoyed by the married appear to be related to health behaviors (Joung, Stronks, van de Mheen, & Mackenbach, 1995). Marriage seems to affect at least one known health behavior, that of seeking health care. Men were 2.7 times more likely than women and married individuals were 2.4 times more likely than nonmarried individuals to be influenced by a member of the opposite sex to seek health care (Norcross, Ramirez, & Palinkas, 1996).

Finally, although social causation models can generally take either a protective focus or a stressor focus, the literature suggests that, for health behaviors, marriage may buffer men against health risk behaviors such as smoking (Mermelstein, Cohen, Lichtenstein, Baer, & Karmack, 1986) and also may provide support for men's health promotion behaviors, such as regular physician checkups (Norcross et al., 1996). When marriage buffers against health risk, cross-sectional studies will show that married individuals, on average, will exhibit lower levels of health risk than nonmarried individuals. This observation could reflect either the buffering influences of marriage or the selection of healthier individuals into marriage, however. A twin design can begin to disentangle these possibilities.

This chapter applies twin data to one specific social causation hypothesis: that marriage serves as a buffer against health risk behaviors. Most cross-sectional data cannot illuminate such causal relationships, but because of the presumed causality of genetic and environmental influences on phenotype, genetically informative, cross-sectional data, like those found in twin studies, provide means by which to test causal hypotheses, such as the hypotheses that marriage buffers against health risks. Neale and Cardon (1992) initially described a novel twin design for the study of marriage as a buffer, an approach later elaborated by Heath and colleagues (Heath, Eaves, & Martin, 1998). This approach assumes that, if marriage provides a buffer against a particular disorder, then marriage will mute the phenotypic expression of any genetic vulnerability to that disorder. In their examination of marriage and depression, Heath et al. predicted that, if marriage buffered against depression, then the heritability of depression among twin pairs concordant for marriage ought to be lower than either the heritability of depression among concordant, nonmarried twin pairs or among marriage-discordant twin pairs.

Indeed, this is what Heath et al. (1998) found among female twins in the Australian Twin Registry. Twin pairs concordant for marriage showed a lower heritability for depression than did concordant nonmarried pairs. This approach did not consider the heritability of marital status but simply tested whether the heritability of depression varied by marital group.

Of course, such an approach begins with the assumption that there is no evidence for social selection. This means that there should be no evidence that the cotwins of healthy individuals are more likely to be married than the cotwins of less healthy twins. In the Australian sample, there was no evidence of social selection out of marriage among individuals at risk for depression, because no significant correlations existed either between Twin A's marital status and Twin B's depression or between Twin B's marital status and Twin A's depression, even though marriage and depression were negatively correlated within-twin. This twin model may be helpful in testing the role of marriage as a buffer against health risk behaviors. It may also prove helpful in considering health promotion behaviors in that, if marriage encourages healthier behaviors than one might normally pursue, then we would expect to see patterns of heritability similar to those observed when marriage buffers against health risk.

Method

Sample

The NAS-NRC World War II Veteran Twin Registry was based on the records of live, Caucasian male multiple births from 40 states during the years 1917 to 1927. The records were matched to names in Master Index of the Veterans Administration in 1958 to 1959, yielding 15,924 pairs of twins in which both had served in the U.S. Armed Forces. In 1965, 8747 complete pairs responded to the first registry questionnaire. Subsequent questionnaires and telephone interviews assessed various aspects of participants' health and social behaviors. The current study uses data from mailed health questionnaires completed in 1972, when participants were between 45 and 55 years of age.

Measures

In 1972, 4740 complete pairs provided current marital status as either single, married, remarried, divorced or separated, or widowed. For this study, marital status was recoded simply as either currently married or currently not married. Self-reported health behaviors included exercise, dietary information, alcohol consumption, and smoking. The first of these items asked, "How much physical exercise (outside of work) have you had after 35 years of age?" with possible responses of "hardly any," "light exercise" (e.g., regular walks, light gardening), "minor sports," and "hard physical training." The second asked, "How often do you usually eat fruits and vegetables?" with possible responses of "daily or almost daily," "once or twice a week," "once or twice a month," and "less often." Responses to fruit and vegetable consumption were transformed into frequency of consumption per week, up to a maximum of seven times, for purposes of comparing mean differences by marital status.

Because the number of categories was small, however, this variable was treated as an ordinal scale for correlational analyses. The smoking item simply asked for the number of cigarettes smoked per day.

Questions about alcohol consumption covered three categories of alcohol: beer, wine, and liquor. Two questions assessed consumption in each category, the first of which asked about frequency, "How often do you drink [beer, wine, liquor]?" with possible responses of "daily," "once or twice a week," "once or twice a month," "once or twice a year," or "less often." The second question assessed quantity: "On a day when you drink [beer, wine, liquor], how much do you usually drink?" with responses appropriate to each beverage (number of bottles for beer, number of glasses to "one bottle or more" for wine, and number of shots to "more than one pint" for liquor). Responses to items about frequency and quantity of consumption were transformed into measures of total annual alcohol consumption by taking the average alcohol content for each type of drink and multiplying it by the average frequency and quantity, then summing the annual alcohol consumed across all types of beverages.

Preliminary Analyses

Preliminary analyses examined whether or not healthier behaviors were associated with marriage. Mean differences in health behaviors between all married and all nonmarried twins in the sample, regardless of cotwin ascertainment, were tested using independent samples t-tests. Although exercise intensity was an ordinal scale, it was treated as continuous for this analysis to obtain a rough idea of whether or not it varied by marital status.

Health behaviors were ascertained from a population-based sample, so hospitalization/utilization hypotheses were irrelevant. Before examination of the social causation "marriage as buffer" hypothesis could be tested, we had to rule out social selection processes, in which health behaviors influence marital status. To the extent that health behaviors are influenced by genetics and/or shared family environments, any evidence of a significant association between twin health behavior and cotwin marital status would be consistent with social selection processes, in which familial predispositions toward health behaviors are associated with the probability of marriage. Cross-twin cross-trait correlations were examined and compared with within-twin cross-trait correlations to help rule out possible social selection effects before testing the "marriage as buffer" hypothesis. Because the data variously included binary, ordinal, and continuous measures, polychoric, polyserial, and Pearson's correlations as well as covariance matrices were computed, as appropriate. We used SPSS 10.0 to calculate the covariance and Pearson's correlation matrices (SPSS Inc., 1999) and Prelis 2.30 for the polychoric and polyserial correlation matrices (Joreskog & Sorbom, 1999).

Univariate Biometric Analyses

Marital status and health behavior data were each fitted to univariate biometric models for the entire sample using Lisrel 8.30 (Joreskog & Sorbom, 1999) maximum likelihood methods for continuous data and weighted least

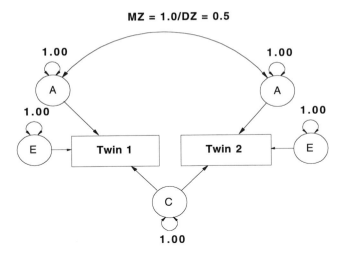

Figure 4.1. Biometric decomposition of phenotypic twin variance into its additive genetic (A), common environmental (C), and nonshared environmental (E) sources.

squares for ordinal data. Figure 4. 1 presents the basic ACE model, in which phenotypic variance is partitioned into variance explained by additive genetic factors (A), common environmental factors (C), and nonshared environmental factors combined with measurement error (E; see also chapter 1). Parameters associated with these three components of the model are h^2 (heritability), c^2 (variance caused by shared environments), and e^2 (variance caused by nonshared environments and measurement error). The ACE model and its submodels of AE and CE were tested. Although it is also possible to model nonadditive genetic effects using an ADE model, comparisons between models of additive and of nonadditive effects are not entirely feasible because ADE models are not fully nested within ACE models. Furthermore, nonadditive effects may be heterogeneous, including either genetic dominance or epistasis, or both, so for the sake of clarity, ACE models and submodels were used. Biometric models for each variable were compared for parsimony and goodness-of-fit using Akaike's Information Criterion (AIC) for the best fitting model. Then the sample was divided into three groups: concordant nonmarried, concordant married, and maritally discordant twin pairs, and the health behavior data were fitted by group to the full biometric model for each phenotype. We then compared heritability among concordant married, concordant nonmarried, and maritally discordant twin pair groups for any evidence of the buffering effects of marriage (cf., Neale & Cardon, 1992; Heath et al., 1998).

Results

PRELIMINARY UNIVARIATE ANALYSES OF MARITAL STATUS AND HEALTH BEHAVIORS. Tetrachoric correlations for current marital status, construed dichotomously as either married or not married, were .51 for MZ and .23 for

Table 4.1. Chi-Square, Akaike's Information Criterion (AIC), Parameter Estimates, and Confidence Intervals for Best-Fitting Biometric Models of Health Promotion and Risk Behaviors: Full 1972 Sample

Health behavior	Model	χ^2	AIC	h^2 (c.i.)	c^2 (c.i.)	e^2 (c.i.)
Annual alcohol consumption	ACE	0.00	0.00	.32 (.23, .43)	.06 (.01, .17)	.61 (.56, .64)
Cigarettes smoked daily	AE	2.37	0.37	.43 (.40, .47)		.57 (.53, .60)
Exercise intensity	AE	2.30	0.30	.30 (.25, .34)		.70 (.66, .75)
Frequency of fruit and vegetable consumption	AE	0.15	−1.85	.30 (.23, .39)		.70 (.62, .78)

DZ twin pairs, suggesting that genetic factors account for approximately 50% of variability in marriage. As can be seen in Table 4.1, the best fitting models for health behavior variables generally included additive genetic and non-shared environmental sources of variance. Heritability for both health promotion variables was approximately .30, despite fruit and vegetable consumption showing limited variability and a highly skewed distribution. (These archival data provided a history lesson. In the current era of campaigns to "strive for five" servings of fruits and vegetables per day, the high end of the 1972 scale, "at least one serving daily of fruits and vegetables," seems quite low.) Heritability of alcohol consumption fell in a similar range, but with some evidence for effects of common environment. Number of cigarettes smoked showed somewhat higher heritability.

TESTS OF MARITAL STATUS DIFFERENCES IN HEALTH-RELATED BEHAVIORS. Table 4.2 presents means and standard deviations for health behaviors for

Table 4.2. Means and Standard Deviations for Health Variables by Marital Status

	Twin A		Twin B	
	N	M (SD)	N	M (SD)
Exercise intensity				
Nonmarried	654	3.59 (1.72)	639	3.46 (1.69)
Married	6321	3.60 (1.53)	6171	3.59 (1.53)
Fruits and vegetables per week				
Nonmarried	594	5.63 (2.68)*	585	5.60 (2.70)*
Married	6047	6.16 (2.20)	5965	6.12 (2.24)
Alcohol (kg per year)				
Nonmarried	610	8.26 (10.87)*	636	8.55 (11.57)*
Married	5936	5.64 (8.41)	6148	5.90 (8.56)
Cigarettes per day				
Nonmarried	653	14.73 (16.85)*	639	14.21 (16.21)*
Married	6268	12.34 (15.90)	6171	12.19 (15.81)

*$p < .001$ for t-test between married and nonmarried within subsamples of Twins A or B.

Table 4.3. Within-Twin Cross-Trait and Cross-Twin Cross-Trait Correlations for Marital Status (MS) and Health Promotion and Risk Behaviors for All Complete Twin Pairs of Known Zygosity, 1972

Health behavior		N pairs	MS Twin A, Health Twin A	MS Twin B, Health Twin B	MS Twin A, Health Twin B	MS Twin B, Health Twin A
Exercise	MZ	2269	−0.007	0.072	0.041	0.054 PC[a]
intensity	DZ	2384	−0.016	−0.009	0.044	−0.003 PC
Frequency	MZ	2096	0.113	0.203	0.017	−0.014 PC
of fruits and vegetables per week	DZ	2198	0.094	0.118	0.070	−0.027 PC
Kilograms	MZ	2128	−0.148	−0.158	−0.127	−0.041 PS[b]
alcohol per year	DZ	1763	−0.180	−0.090	−0.059	0.029 PS
Cigarettes	MZ	2231	−0.025	−0.018	0.012	−0.002 PS
per day	DZ	2369	−0.123	−0.073	−0.044	−0.026 PS

[a]PC = Polychoric correlation
[b]PS = Polyserial correlation

married and nonmarried twins. Across both Twin A and Twin B subsamples and across all variables except exercise, married men's behaviors were significantly healthier than those of their nonmarried counterparts. For exercise alone, there was no significant difference between married and nonmarried men's behavior.

WITHIN-TWIN CROSS-TRAIT AND CROSS-TWIN CROSS-TRAIT CORRELATIONS. Table 4.3 contains within-twin cross-trait and cross-trait cross-twin correlations for marital status and health behaviors. Within-twins marital status correlated slightly positively with frequency of fruit and vegetable consumption, slightly negatively with annual alcohol consumption, even more slightly negatively with number of cigarettes smoked, and virtually not at all with exercise intensity. Cross-twin cross-trait correlations provide modest evidence of selection out of marriage with greater alcohol consumption and negligible evidence of selection into marriage for diet but no evidence of marital selection for the other health protection or risk behaviors. This suggests that married men's lower rates of smoking may be attributable to social causation: Marriage may buffer against smoking. Their higher rates of fruit and vegetable consumption may caused in very small part by marital selection but may also be attributable in part to social causation in which marriage protects against the neglect of fruits and vegetables.

UNIVARIATE BIOMETRIC ANALYSES OF HEALTH BEHAVIORS BY MARITAL STATUS. Table 4.4 shows the MZ and DZ intrapair correlations for each of the health variables for concordant nonmarried, concordant married, and maritally discordant pairs. As expected, MZ correlations exceed DZ correla-

Table 4.4. Intrapair Correlations for Health Behaviors by Marital Group, 1972.

Health promotion		Exercise		Fruits & vegetables	
		n	r (polychoric)	n	r (polychoric)
Nonmarried pairs	MZ	64	0.45	64	0.36
	DZ	37	−0.21	33	0.21
Married pairs	MZ	1935	0.30	1798	0.18
	DZ	2002	0.02	1862	0.12
Discordant pairs	MZ	270	0.38	240	0.21
	DZ	347	0.12	304	0.19
Health risk		Alcohol consumption		N Cigarettes smoked	
		n	r (Pearson's)	n	r (Pearson's)
Nonmarried pairs	MZ	58	0.30	63	0.52
	DZ	33	−0.03	36	0.59
Married pairs	MZ	1819	0.38	1903	0.43
	DZ	1870	0.24	1988	0.20
Discordant pairs	MZ	251	0.45	265	0.52
	DZ	328	0.12	346	0.11

tions, but the magnitude of both MZ and DZ correlations varies by marital concordance status. Simple comparisons of MZ–DZ differences between concordant married and unmarried pairs suggest that marriage might moderate genetic predispositions along the dimensions of exercise, fruit and vegetable consumption, and alcohol consumption. For number of cigarettes smoked, however, the MZ–DZ differences are the opposite of what would be predicted by a buffering hypothesis for concordant married versus unmarried twin pairs. In addition, the large MZ–DZ differences in smoking among maritally discordant pairs reflect, primarily, a lower DZ correlation than the other two groups, which may indicate that DZ pairs discordant for marriage may also be more discordant for genotype than are maritally concordant pairs.

When twin models were fitted to the data by marital group, the relatively small numbers of concordant, unmarried twin pairs and of maritally discordant pairs resulted in large confidence intervals around estimates of genetic and environmental contributions to phenotypic variation for these groups, and confidence intervals for heritability overlapped between at least two marital status groups for each of the four phenotypes. Neither exercise intensity nor alcohol consumption showed any significant differences in heritability across marital groups. Parameters for the best fitting models for the other two behaviors by marital group are presented in Table 4.5. Both smoking and frequency of fruit and vegetable consumption showed significant heritability differences between concordant married and concordant unmarried pairs. However, under the "marriage as buffer" hypothesis, we had predicted that marital buffering would lower the heritability of a behavior among concordant married twin pairs compared with their concordant nonmarried or maritally discordant counterparts. In both the cases of fruit and vegetable consumption and of cigarette smoking, concordant married pairs and maritally discordant pairs showed no difference from each other in heritability, but both showed

Table 4.5. Parameter Estimates and Confidence Intervals for Best Fitting Models of Health-Related Behaviors for Concordant Nonmarried, Concordant Married, and Marriage-Discordant Twin Pairs, With AIC Comparisons for Full ACE Models

Health behavior	ACE χ^2	Best fitting model	χ^2	AIC	h^2 (c.i.)	c^2 (c.i.)	e^2 (c.i.)
Frequency of fruit and vegetable consumption							
Nonmarried	0.80	CE	0.80	−1.20		.29 (.14, .56)	.71 (.53, .91)
Married	0.13	AE	0.13	−1.87	.23 (.05, .56)		.77 (.52, .99)
Discordant	0.00	ACE	0.00	−2.00	.24 (.05, .59)	.14 (.00, .43)	.62 (.51, .73)
N cigarettes smoked daily							
Nonmarried	0.30	CE	0.29	−1.71		.55 (.44, .67)	.45 (.39, .52)
Married	0.44	AE	0.43	−1.57	.43 (.38, .46)		.57 (.54, .61)
Discordant	7.44	AE	7.43	5.43	.48 (.38, .60)		.52 (.46, .62)

Note. AIC for AE model of annual alcohol consumption for concordant married twins was 2.52 ($\chi^2 = 4.52$).

higher heritability for these health-related behaviors than did concordant non-married pairs. In fact, concordant nonmarried pairs showed no significant genetic influences on these behaviors, but sizeable effects of common environment. This suggests that marriage, rather than decreasing phenotypic expression of genetic propensities toward health-related behaviors, actually enhances or amplifies the expression of men's genetic propensities toward fruit and vegetable consumption and toward cigarette smoking. These findings, combined with a review of Table 4.4, also suggest that unmarried twins are more likely than married twins to resemble each other in their smoking and fruit and vegetable consumption, regardless of zygosity.

Discussion

Data from the World War II Veteran Twin Registry comparing married and unmarried men for health-related behaviors are consistent with most of the literature: Married men's habits were more protective of health than the habits of the nonmarried group of bachelors, divorcés, and widowers. Married men drank less, smoked less, and ate fruits and vegetables more regularly than their nonmarried counterparts. However, there was no significant difference in their level of exercise.

When marital status was considered solely in terms of currently married versus currently not married, the data also showed some evidence of marital selection against alcohol consumption. There was no evidence of marital buffering for any of the health behavior variables. Because married and nonmarried men did not differ in exercise intensity, the lack of marital buffering is understandable. Because alcohol consumption showed some evidence for social selection, it is also not surprising that it showed no evidence of marital buffering.

For cigarette smoking and for fruit and vegetable consumption, however, the data provide counterintuitive findings. Despite literature suggesting that marriage exerts a protective effect against smoking by providing social support by which smokers are more likely to quit (Mermelstein et al., 1986), these data suggest that marriage amplifies men's phenotypic expression of their genetic predisposition toward becoming a smoker or nonsmoker. In other words, either men whose genotype more strongly predisposes them toward smoking will smoke more if married than if not married or men who are genetically "smoking-neutral" or protected against smoking are likely to smoke less if married than if not married, or both. Positive marital assortment for smoking might explain this observation, as a similarly inclined spouse could reinforce either smoking or not smoking. Recent evidence shows significant marital concordance for smoking cessation in middle age (Franks, Pienta, & Wray, 2002), but it is not clear how strong the relative effects of marital assortment and of shared marital environments for smoking may be. Unfortunately, the World War II Twin Registry data did not include wives' smoking behaviors and therefore remain uninformative about marital assortment in our sample.

Another hypothesis is that unmarried twins may spend more time together and thereby share more common environments, which, in turn, may influence them to be more similar in their health habits. Unfortunately, the 1972 questionnaires did not ascertain degree of twins' intrapair contact. However, a 1985 questionnaire obtained data on frequency of in-person and telephone contact between twins in this sample and may provide some clues. In 1985, concordant unmarried twins reported significantly more frequent in-person and telephone contact with each other than did their concordant married counterparts. If nonmarried twin contact also exceeded married twin contact in 1972, then that would be consistent with a hypothesis of cotwin influence on health behaviors, at least for smoking and consumption of fruits and vegetables. A hypothesis of cotwin influence on phenotype, however, cannot be supported across all health-related behaviors: Unmarried twins were no more similar to each other than were married twins for alcohol consumption.

This study revealed no evidence of marital buffering either against health risk behaviors or against the neglect of health promotion behaviors. Instead, it demonstrated, counterintuitively, that marriage may actually amplify the expression of some genetic predispositions, whether to the benefit or detriment of health. This finding suggests a need to revise the traditional "marriage as buffer" construct, at least for smoking and some aspects of diet. Contrary to the assumption that spouses uniformly reinforce better health behaviors, it seems, instead, that spouses reinforce health-related behaviors either for better or for worse, depending, in part, on the genetic predisposition of their partners. Of course, under conditions of positive marital assortment, this genotype-syntonic influence would also reflect the spouse's predisposition. Quality of marriage may also play a role in degree and direction of marital influence. In the absence of a spouse, a man's family of origin, or at least his twin, may also influence some of his health behaviors.

Twin studies may illuminate epidemiological questions about the relative influences of health and social structures on each other. They can provide complementary and unique insights into the complex processes epidemiologists seek to describe. They also may present evidence that causes us to rethink hypotheses previously tested in the absence of genetically informative data. The thoughtful and creative use of twin studies remains one of Dr. Gottesman's many fine gifts to psychiatric genetics and genetic epidemiology.

References

Franks, M. M., Pienta, A. M., & Wray, L. A. (2002). It takes two: Marriage and smoking cessation in the middle years. *Journal of Aging and Health, 14*(3), 336–354.

Fu, H., & Goldman, N. (2000). The association between health-related behaviours and the risk of divorce in the USA. *Journal of Biosocial Science, 32*(1), 63–88.

Glynn, L. M., Christenfeld, N., & Gerin, W. (1999). Gender, social support, and cardiovascular responses to stress. *Psychosomatic Medicine, 61*(2), 234–242.

Goldman, N. (1993). Marriage selection and mortality patterns: Inferences and fallacies. *Demography, 30*(2), 189–208.

Goldman, N. (1994). Social factors and health: The causation-selection issue revisited. *Proceedings of the National Academy of Sciences of the United States of America, 91*(4), 1251–1255.

Gottesman, I. I., & Bertelsen, A. (1989). Confirming unexpressed genotypes for schizophrenia. Risks in the offspring of Fischer's Danish identical and fraternal discordant twins. *Archives of General Psychiatry, 46,* 867–872.

Gottman, J. M., & Levenson, R. W. (1992). Marital processes predictive of later dissolution: Behavior, physiology, and health. *Journal of Personality and Social Psychology, 63,* 221–233.

Heath, A. C., Eaves, L. J., & Martin, N. G. (1998). Interaction of marital status and genetic risk for symptoms of depression. *Twin Research, 1,* 119–122.

Hope, S., Rodgers, B., & Power, C. (1999). Marital status transitions and psychological distress: Longitudinal evidence from a national population sample. *Psychological Medicine, 29,* 381–389.

Joreskog, K. G., & Sorbom, D. (1999). *Lisrel 8.30 and Prelis 2.30.* Chicago: SSI Scientific Software International.

Joung, I. M., Stronks, K., van de Mheen, H., & Mackenbach, J. P. (1995). Health behaviours explain part of the differences in self reported health associated with partner/marital status in The Netherlands. *Journal of Epidemiology and Community Health, 49,* 482–488.

Kiecolt-Glaser, J. K., Glaser, R., Cacioppo, J. T., & Malarkey, W. B. (1998). Marital stress: Immunologic, neuroendocrine, and autonomic correlates. *Annals of the New York Academy of Sciences, 840,* 656–663.

Mastekaasa, A. (1992). Marriage and psychological well-being: Some evidence on selection into marriage. *Journal of Marriage and the Family, 54,* 901–911.

Mermelstein, R., Cohen, S., Lichtenstein, E., Baer, J. S., & Karmack, T. (1986). Social support, smoking cessation and maintenance. *Journal of Consulting and Clinical Psychology, 54,* 447–453.

Neale, M. C., & Cardon, L. R. (1992). *Methodology for genetic studies of twins and families.* Boston: Kluwer Academic Publishers.

Norcross, W. A., Ramirez, C., & Palinkas, L. A. (1996). The influence of women on the health care-seeking behavior of men. *The Journal of Family Practice, 43,* 475–480.

Roski, J., Schmid, L. A., & Lando, H. A. (1996). Long-term associations of helpful and harmful spousal behaviors with smoking cessation. *Addictive Behaviors, 21*(2), 173–185.

Spiegel, D., Sephton, S. E., Terr, A. I., & Stites, D. P. (1998). Effects of psychosocial treatment in prolonging cancer survival may be mediated by neuroimmune pathways. *Annals of the New York Academy of Sciences, 840,* 674–683.

SPSS, Inc. (1999). *SPSS for Windows, Release 10.0.5.* Chicago, IL: Author.

Part III

Personality and Genetics

5

Genetic Correlations as "Z" Variables: Evaluating Personality → Psychopathology Associations

David L. DiLalla and Gregory Carey

The purpose of this chapter is to summarize ongoing work regarding application of behavioral genetic models to associations among personality characteristics and psychopathology. In particular, we show that traditional causal models that focus on correlations between phenotypes may be misleading to the degree that they do not account for genetic correlations among the phenotypes. Genetic correlation (rG) reflects the degree to which characteristics correlate because of shared genetic influence on the traits; in general terms, it is assessed by comparing cross-twin cross-trait correlations. For example, if we were to consider monozygotic (MZ) and dizygotic (DZ) correlations for depression and neuroticism, genetic correlation would be indicated by a significantly higher MZ as compared with DZ correlation between one twin's depression score and the cotwin's neuroticism score. We illustrate these points using personality and antisocial behavior data drawn from the Washington University (WU) Twin Study of Psychopathology.

Associations Between Personality and Psychopathology

Interest in links between personality characteristics and mental distress and disorder has a long theoretical and empirical history (Widiger, Verheul, & van den Brink, 1999; Zuckerman, 1999). When individuals with existing psychopathology are assessed with personality trait measures, norm-deviant scores are typically obtained (e.g., Berenbaum & Fujita, 1994; Clark, Watson, & Mineka, 1994; Costa & McCrae, 1990; DiLalla, Gottesman, & Carey, 1993; Schroeder, Wormworth, & Livesley, 1994; Trull & Sher, 1994). Prospective

We wish to express our heartfelt gratitude to Dr. Irving I. Gottesman for his contributions to the Washington University Twin Study and for his friendship and mentorship over the years. We are grateful for support provided by USPHS grants MH-313032 and AA—03539 to the Washington University Department of Psychiatry. We also thank Dr. George Vogler for his contribution to the WU twin project.

longitudinal studies also show associations between personality and later expression of psychopathology (Kendler, Neale, Kessler, Heath, & Eaves, 1993; Krueger, 1999).

The nature of covariation between personality and psychopathology has been hotly debated, and there are several competing models (Clark et al., 1994; DiLalla, Gottesman, & Carey, 2000; Tellegen, 1985; Widiger et al., 1999). First, individual differences in personality might directly increase risk for developing psychopathology *(Personality Causes Psychopathology)*. Second, the presence of a psychological disorder might result in changes in personality characteristics *(Psychopathology Causes Personality)*. Third, personality might act as a potentiator or depotentiator for individuals at risk for developing psychopathology *(Triggering)*. Fourth, psychopathology and personality might reciprocally influence each other *(Reciprocity)*. Finally, personality characteristics and psychopathology might share a common underlying diathesis *(Continuity)*.

Continuity models have been supported by factor analytic work indicating generally invariant factor structures for personality inventories and psychopathology measures in unselected and clinical populations (DiLalla, Gottesman, Carey, & Vogler, 1993; O'Connor, 2002). Continuity between normal personality and psychopathology is also supported by recent genetic correlation research that parallels some of the work presented in this chapter. Jang and Livesley (1999) used twin methodology to investigate the etiology of comorbidity between normal personality traits (measured by the NEO-Five Factor Inventory [NEO-FFI]; Costa & McCrae, 1992) and personality disorder symptoms (measured by the Dimensional Assessment of Personality Problems—Basic Questionnaire [DAPP-BQ]; Livesley & Jackson, in press; Livesley, Jang, & Vernon, 1998). Moderate to large genetic correlations were found between NEO-FFI Neuroticism, Extraversion, Conscientiousness, and Agreeableness, and the personality disorder scales of the DAPP-BQ. Significantly smaller genetic correlations were found between DAPP-BQ scales and NEO-FFI Openness. This suggests overlap between genetic factors that contribute to scores on both scales and supports current conceptualizations of personality disorders as continuous with normal personality traits. Livesley and Jang also reported significant, albeit smaller, nonshared environmental correlations, demonstrating that unique environmental events may also contribute to phenotypic similarity between measures of normal and "disordered" personality.

Markon, Krueger, Bouchard, and Gottesman (2002) drew from the Minnesota Study of Twins Reared Apart (MISTRA) to further investigate underlying etiology of phenotypic correlations between normal and abnormal personality characteristics. Markon et al. conducted a series of bivariate Cholesky analyses on Multidimensional Personality Questionnaire (MPQ; Tellegen, 1982) and Minnesota Multiphasic Personality Inventory (MMPI; Hathaway & McKinley, 1983) scales and found substantial genetic and environmental correlations, particularly for pairs of the MPQ's negative affect scales and many of the MMPI's clinical scales. Related to the goals of the present chapter, Markon et al. found that phenotypic covariance between indicators of externalizing psychopathology (e.g., MMPI Ego Control, Family

Problems, Authority Conflict, and Pd scales) and disinhibitory personality traits (e.g., MPQ Control, Aggression, Harm Avoidance) were mediated by genetic factors. There was also a strong genetic correlation between MPQ Alienation and MMPI Pd, Family Problems, and Authority Conflict. In a related fashion, Mustanski, Viken, Kaprio, and Rose (2003) reported significant genetic correlations between personality traits (social deviance and excitement seeking) and alcohol problems. These findings are consistent with those we report in this chapter.

The research we describe extends the work done by Jang and Livesley (1999) and Markon and colleagues (Markon et al., 2002). Both groups focused principally on genetic mediation of correlations between normal and abnormal personality characteristics. Our work also echoes findings by others on genetic correlations between neuroticism and affective and anxiety disorders (Jardine, Martin, & Henderson, 1984; Kendler et al., 1993; Roberts & Kendler, 1999). Our interest is in assessing the degree to which shared genetic factors contribute to associations between normal personality traits and externally rated symptoms of psychopathology (including antisocial behavior and alcohol and substance abuse/dependence). Our approach applies a dimensional orientation to description of psychopathology and involves multiple methods, rather than relying solely on self reported personality characteristics.

General Methodological Concerns

A complicating factor for researchers interested in evaluating models for personality → psychopathology associations is that traditional phenotypically focused methodologies may ultimately be misleading. Consider the empirical observation that conduct problems in early childhood and adolescence are predictive of adult problems including problematic gambling (Slutske et al., 2001) and substance abuse (Kratzer & Hodgins, 1997; Lerner, Inui, Trupin, & Douglas, 1985; White, Xie, Thompson, Loeber, & Stouthamer-Loeber, 2001; Woodward & Fergusson, 1999). Temperament ratings in childhood and adolescence have also been found in longitudinal studies to be associated with later delinquency and antisocial behavior (Caspi, 2000; Loeber, Farrington, Stouthamer-Loeber, Moffitt, & Caspi, 1998; Moffitt & Caspi, 2001; Romero, Luengo, & Sobral, 2001), with some evidence that this covariation is influenced by genetic factors (Gjone & Stevenson, 1997). One hypothesis is that individual differences in temperament or personality variables such as impulsiveness, reward-dependence, sensation seeking, and obedience to authority figures mediate the association between juvenile and adult antisocial behavior. This implies that personality has a direct causal role in continuity of problem behavior.

Twin methodology allows for specification of mathematical models for evaluating such personality → psychopathology models. A purely phenotypic model (see Figure 5.1) applied to twin data shows personality characteristics for Twin 1 directly influencing expression of psychopathology in Twin 1. Likewise, personality for Twin 2 influences psychopathology in Twin 2. Among twins reared together, personality and psychopathology for each twin are

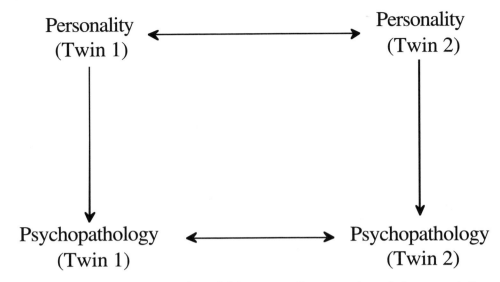

Figure 5.1.   General phenotypic model for personality → psychopathology association.

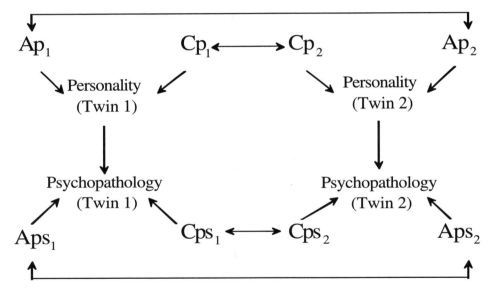

Figure 5.2.   General phenotypic model for personality → psychopathology association with genetic parameters. Ap = Additive genetic effect on personality phenotype; Aps = Additive genetic effect on psychopathology phenotype; Cp = Common environmental effect on personality phenotype; Cps = Common environmental effect on psychopathology phenotype. Subscripts 1 and 2 refer to Twin 1 and Twin 2.

assumed under the model to reciprocally influence each other. A somewhat more sophisticated model (see Figure 5.2) includes specification of genetic parameters. In this model, in addition to the phenotypic path from personality to psychopathology, there are additive genetic (Ap_1, Ap_2, Aps_1, Aps_2) and shared environmental influences specified for each twin for personality and for psychopathology (Cp_1, Cp_2, Cps_1, Cps_2) respectively.

We argue that causal models such as those described previously may be misspecified. It is instructive to recall Kenney's (1979, p. 4) admonition regarding causality: "The third and final condition for a causal relationship is nonspuriousness. For a relationship between X and Y to be *nonspurious*, there must *not* be a Z that causes both X and Y such that the relationship between X and Y vanishes once Z is controlled." Our general hypothesis is that genes function as "z variables" that may induce spurious correlations among phenotypes and result in failure of causal models that do not take into account genetic correlations between personality and psychopathology.

Washington University Twin Study of Psychopathology

We illustrate these points using antisocial behavior ratings and normal personality trait data drawn from the Washington University (WU) Twin Study of Psychopathology. The WU Twin sample included 295 twin probands consecutively admitted to inpatient or outpatient psychiatry departments or to an urban mental health center. Cotwins of these psychiatric probands (some of whom also had psychiatric disorders) also participated in the study, yielding a total sample of 590 individuals. There were 88 MZ twin pairs, 102 same-sex DZ pairs, and 101 opposite-sex DZ pairs (4 pairs were of unknown zygosity and were not included in genetic analyses). The sample was approximately 66% Caucasian and 33% African American. There were 254 men (43%) and 336 women (57%). Age at time of entry into the study varied considerably, ranging from 16 to 83 years ($M = 35.7$, $SD = 13$). Participants spanned a wide socioeconomic range. The samples described in this chapter for the present analyses are reduced from the full sample size as a result of missing data when measures were combined for analyses.

All probands (and as many cotwins as possible) underwent an evaluation that included extensive diagnostic interviewing. In terms of diagnoses, the sample was fairly typical of inpatient and outpatient psychiatric settings. Given the focus of this chapter, we do not present specific diagnostic breakdowns here. Information about diagnostic procedures and frequencies of diagnoses for the sample is presented by DiLalla, Gottesman, and Carey (1993).

Evaluation of Higher Order Personality Trait → Psychopathology Models

PSYCHOPATHOLOGY MEASURES. For antisocial behavior (ASB) and alcohol abuse/dependence (ALC), we developed continuous measures of psychopathology using two sources of information. The first was the number of relevant symptoms endorsed on the Diagnostic Interview Schedule (DIS; Helzer & Robins, 1988) and contained in a systematic review of previous medical records. The second consisted of diagnostic certainty ratings of case-history information. Confidence ratings were on an 8-point scale with anchor points ranging from "complete confidence in diagnosis" to "no confidence that diagnosis is present." Because the number of diagnostic raters for each twin varied, we averaged ratings on each individual across all judges, and then standardized to a mean of 0 and standard deviation of 1.0. These were then added to the standardized symptom counts from the DIS to arrive at the final score.

For drug abuse/dependence (DRG), we used diagnostic certainty ratings for drug abuse/dependence along with a scale developed by Gynther, Carey, Gottesman, and Vogler (1995). To parallel the approach used for the DIS, the Gynther et al. scale was scored as a total symptom count. Once again, the two sources of information were standardized before adding them together.

PERSONALITY MEASURE. The prepublication version of the MPQ (Tellegen, 1982) is a 300-item, factor-analytically derived normal personality trait measure. Test–retest correlations for the MPQ average .89 (range, $r = .82$ to .92) and alpha coefficients range from .76 to .89 for the 11 primary scales (Tellegen, 1982) indicating good reliability. Validation studies on the MPQ have converged on a similar interpretation of the higher order and primary factors (Church, 1994; DiLalla, Gottesman, Carey, & Vogler, 1993; Tellegen, 1982; Tellegen & Waller, in press). For the first set of analyses to be presented, we used the three second-order factor scales Positive Emotionality (PE), Negative Emotionality (NE), and Constraint (CN). In the group of analyses described in this chapter, we used five of the MPQ's primary factor scales (Alienation, Aggression, Control, Harm Avoidance, Traditionalism). Content summaries for these eight scales are in Table 5.1.

Because of potential effects of age and sex on the variables of interest, we adjusted all scores for sex, age, and age squared using the regression technique described by McGue and Bouchard (1984) and used the adjusted scores in all analyses.

STATISTICAL ANALYSIS OF MODELS. Three statistical models were evaluated using the Davidson-Fletcher-Powell (DFP) program, a maximum likelihood minimization routine developed by Carey (1989). The first was a *general model* specifying that the structure of associations between higher order MPQ personality traits and antisocial behavior scales was comparable for probands and cotwins. This was designed to provide a baseline for comparison with subsequently tested models. The *general model* assumed that proband correlations were equivalent to cotwin correlations (but with the potential for different standard deviations) and that the cross twin correlation matrix was symmetric. When this model was fit to the personality and psychopathology data, the χ^2 and AIC indicated that the fit was adequate (see Table 5.2).

The second model tested was a *Personality → Psychopathology Model*. The general structure of this model (without genetic parameters) is shown in Figure 5.3. There are causal paths from each twin's higher order personality traits (PE, NE, CN) to each of that twin's three antisocial behavior measures (ASB, ALC, DRG). There are also paths representing reciprocal influence between each twin's personality traits and the cotwin's personality traits and between each twin's antisocial behavior measures and those of the cotwin.

Table 5.1. Content Summary for Selected MPQ Scales

Scale	High score	Low score
	Primary factor scales	
Alienation (AL)	Is a victim of bad luck, feels mistreated, believes that others wish him or her harm.	Does not see self as victim, feels treated fairly, does not feel taken advantage of.
Aggression (AG)	Will hurt others for own advantage, is physically aggressive, is vindictive, likes to frighten and discomfit others, likes violent scenes.	Will not take advantage of others, is not violent, does not often seek revenge, does not like to witness physical aggression.
Control (CO)	Is reflective, cautious, careful, rational, and sensible; likes to anticipate events; likes to plan activities.	Is impulsive and spontaneous, can be reckless and careless, refers to "play things by ear."
Harm Avoidance (HA)	Does not enjoy the excitement of adventure and danger; prefers safer activities, even if they are tedious or aggravating.	Enjoys risky adventures and the excitement of an emergency; might expose self to possible injury.
Traditionalism (TR)	Has high moral standards, supports traditional religious values and institutions, deplores permissiveness, endorses strict child rearing practices.	Considers traditional religion outdated, questions authority, values freedom of expression, does not believe in punitive discipline.
	Secondary factor scales	
Positive Emotionality (PE)[a]	Is positively engaged in relationships and experiences positive mood states.	Lacks positive emotional engagements and may experience depressed mood.
Negative Emotionality (NE)[b]	Is negatively engaged in relationships and has high levels of anxiety, anger, and worry.	Less likely to experience negative mood states and to be stressed by daily life.
Constraint (CON)[c]	Tends to be timid, shy, avoidant, and compulsive.	Is adventurous, unconventional, impulsive.

Note. Primary scale descriptions (Tellegen, 1982) are based on a confirmed-perspective cluster analysis of item content sortings by 9–12 judges. From *Manual for the Multidimensional Personality Questionnaire* (pp. 7–8), by A. Tellegen, 1982. Unpublished manuscript. Adapted with permission.
[a]Indexed by high loadings for Well Being, Social Potency, and Achievement (Tellegen, 1982).
[b]Indexed by high loadings for Stress Reaction, Social Closeness (reversed), Alienation, and Aggression (Tellegen, 1982).
[c]Indexed by high loadings for Harm Avoidance, Control, and Traditionalism (Tellegen, 1982).

Table 5.2. Statistical Fit for Personality → Psychopathology Models

Model	df	χ^2	p	AIC	Decision
General/Baseline	87	88.9	.42	−85.1	Adequate
Personality → Psychopathology	105	137.0	.02	−73.0	Reject
Personality → Psychopathology with Genetic Parameters	117	151.8	.02	−82.2	Reject

When this model was fit to the data (see Table 5.2), the χ^2 and AIC indicated a poor fit, and the model was rejected.

Last, we tested a *Personality → Psychopathology Model with Genetic Parameters*. For the sake of visual clarity, we have not included a depiction of this rather "dense" path model. However, the model can be conceived as the same as Figure 5.3 with the additional specification of genetic factors (correlated .5 for DZ pairs and 1.0 for MZ pairs) and shared environmental factors (correlated 1.0 for MZ and DZ pairs) for each psychopathology and personality variable. This model also yielded a poor fit (see Table 5.2).

Why do these models fail to fit the data? We suggest that it occurs because such models fail to account for genetic correlations between personality and psychopathology. Table 5.3 presents heritability estimates for the personality and psychopathology variables in this study, as well as genetic correlation estimates

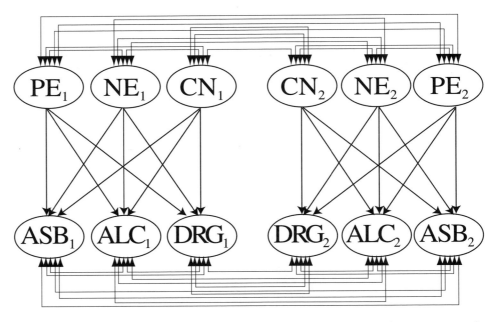

Figure 5.3. Personality → psychopathology model without genetic parameters for MPQ higher order traits and antisocial behavior scales. PE = Positive Emotionality; NE = Negative Emotionality; CN = Constraint; ASB = Antisocial Behavior Rating; ALC = Alcohol Abuse/Dependence Rating; DRG = Drug Abuse/Dependence Rating. Subscripts 1 and 2 refer to Twin 1 and Twin 2.

Table 5.3. Heritability Estimates (h^2) and Genetic Correlations Between Personality and Psychopathology Measures

| | h^2 | Genetic Correlations | | |
		Antisocial	Alcohol	Drug
Positive Emotionality	.51	.29	.22	.29
Negative Emotionality	.34	.53	.53	.46
Constraint	.48	−.66	−.41	−.72
Antisocial behavior	.63			
Alcohol abuse or dependence	.55			
Drug abuse or dependence	.30			

between personality and psychopathology. These estimates were obtained separately from bivariate genetic models of pairs of the personality and psychopathology variables. The heritability estimates are similar to those reported previously for the MPQ (Tellegen et al., 1988) and for antisocial behavior (Carey & Goldman, 1997; DiLalla, Carey, Gottesman, & Bouchard, 1996; McGuffin & Thapar, 1998). There are moderate genetic correlations between Positive Emotionality and antisocial behavior, strong positive genetic correlations between Negative Emotionality and antisocial behavior, and strong negative genetic correlations between Constraint and antisocial behavior. This suggests that rather than personality functioning as a mediator or filter through which externalizing psychopathology is expressed, there are shared genetic factors that contribute both to personality characteristics and psychopathology. In other words, our findings support *continuity* between personality and externalizing psychopathology.

In summary, this first set of results demonstrates that statistical models of personality → psychopathology associations may not fit the data well when they focus on phenotypic links among constructs. Rather, it is essential to model these relationships in a more complex way by allowing for the influence of genetic factors that contribute to the covariation between personality and psychopathology. At the same time, we recognize that phenotypic causal models such as these may also fit poorly because of error associated with the manifest variables included in the model. A cleaner test of the model would include multiple indicators of each latent trait. It should be noted that although genetic correlation is the focus of this particular illustration, environmental correlations (shared environmental influences that affect both personality and psychopathology) could function in an analogous manner.

Genetic Correlations Between Primary Personality Traits and Antisocial Behavior

To follow up the results presented previously, we were interested in the degree to which similar effects could be demonstrated for primary personality traits. To investigate this, we again analyzed antisocial behavior and personality trait data from the WU twin study (DiLalla, 2001). This time, we focused on factor-analytically derived dimensions of antisocial behavior and 5 of the 11 primary factor scales of the MPQ. The relatively small sample size for this analysis was 38 MZ twin pairs and 44 same-sex DZ twin pairs, representing the individuals who had valid MPQ protocols (see Tellegen, 1982) and complete data for the antisocial behavior rating scale.

Measures

We selected MPQ primary scales that were associated with antisocial behavior in prior research (DiLalla, Gottesman, & Carey, 1993). These included Control, Harm Avoidance, and Traditionalism—the three scales that define the higher order Constraint factor—as well as Alienation and Aggression, two scales associated with the Negative Emotionality domain. To create dimensional measures of antisocial behavior, we factor analyzed the items on the DIS-based antisocial behavior rating scale described previously. All individuals from the full sample of 522 diagnosed twins were used for this principal factor analysis. Evaluation of the scree plot suggested a three-factor model accounting for 31% of the variance. Varimax rotation yielded the factor loadings that appear in Table 5.4. Factor 1 was largely defined by conduct problems and aggression that occurred during youth. Factor 2 was defined by items of content similar to those of Factor 1, although the behaviors were exhibited during adulthood. Factor 3 had high loadings on rating scale items related to adult "irresponsibility," for example, work problems and failure to honor financial obligations. Unit weighted scales were created using a factor loading of .40 as the criterion for significant association of an item with a

Table 5.4. Varimax Rotated Factor Loadings for Antisocial Behavior Factors ($N = 522$)

	Factor 1	Factor 2	Factor 3
Frequent misbehavior in school	.63		
Skipped school at least 2×/year	.59		
Lied a lot in childhood or teens	.53		
Expelled or suspended from school	.49		
Started fights before age 18	.45		
Destroyed property before age 18	.44		
Fighting at school before age 18	.42		
Use of weapon after age 18		.65	
Convicted of felony		.49	
Arrested after age 18		.49	
Hitting or throwing at spouse/partner		.42	
Fighting outside school before age 18	.40	.40	
Fired from more than 1 job			.59
Travel more than 1 month without plan			.53
3 or more jobs in 5-year period			.53
Late or absent to work > 3 times since age 18			.50
Quit job ≥ 3 times without having another job			.48
Period of ≥ 1 month with no regular place to live			.47

Note. Factor loadings < .4 omitted.

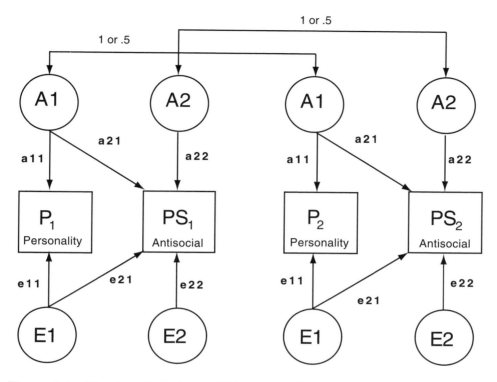

Figure 5.4. Bivariate Cholesky model for personality and psychopathology data. P_1= personality phenotype for Twin 1, PS_1= psychopathology (antisocial behavior) phenotype for Twin 1. P_2= personality phenotype for Twin 2; PS_2 = psychopathology (antisocial behavior) phenotype for Twin 2. A1 and A2 = additive genetic effects. E1 and E2 = unique environmental effects.

factor. All scores were adjusted for the effects of age and age squared, and the residuals were standardized prior to analysis.

Estimation of Genetic Correlations

We estimated genetic correlations between primary personality traits and the three antisocial behavior dimensions using a bivariate Cholesky decomposition (see Neale & Cardon, 1992.). This approach analyzes pairs of variables, in this case, pairs of personality traits and antisocial behavior dimensions. In Figure 5.4, measured variables appear in boxes, and latent variables are represented by circles. For example, P_1 and PS_1 represent personality and psychopathology scores for Twin 1; P_2 and PS_2 represent the same scores for Twin 2. A1 reflects an additive genetic factor that influences the personality trait and the antisocial behavior dimension, and A2 represents an additive genetic effect specific to the psychopathology factor. The twin correlation between A1 and A2 is 1.0 for MZ twin pairs and 0.5 for MZ twin pairs. Latent variables E1 and E2 represent nonshared environmental effects. The genetic correlation (rG) between personality trait and psychopathology dimension equals the genetic covariance (product of the coefficients of paths a11 and a21) divided by the square root of the product of the genetic variance estimate for the personality trait and the genetic variance component for the psychopathology dimension. Unique environmental correlations (rE) were calculated analogously. Common environment effects (C) were not estimated in this model (i.e., in the terminology typically used in the field we evaluated an AE model rather than an ACE model). This was because of concerns regarding power to estimate small effects given the sample size coupled with the empirical observation that common environmental pathways can be typically dropped from such analyses (e.g., Jang & Livesley, 1999) without significantly worsening the fit of the model.

Separate Cholesky analyses were conducted for each of the possible pairs of five personality traits with the three psychopathology dimensions. Parameters were estimated by the LISREL 8 computer program (Joreskog & Sorbom, 1993). The AE model, specifying additive genetic and unique environmental effects, fit the data adequately for most pairs of scales as indexed by nonsignificant overall model chi-square tests. For MPQ Aggression and Antisocial Behavior Factor 2 (adult conduct problems and aggression) the AE model fit was poor (χ^2 (14) = 32.4, p < .01) and for Alienation and adult conduct problems the fit was marginal (χ^2 (14) = 13.8, p < .10). Genetic and environmental correlations derived from the analyses are presented in Table 5.5. Genetic correlations were of moderate magnitude. For example, there was a consistent finding of significant genetic "overlap" between traits tapping one's tendency to engage in thrill-seeking, harm-avoidant (reverse), undercontrolled behavior and a range of antisocial behaviors in childhood and adulthood. This suggests a broader genetic influence on disinhibition that is reflected in both personality characteristics and antisocial behavior. The results for trait aggression were not so clear. There was evidence of genetic overlap between trait aggression and childhood conduct problems and adult irresponsibility, but the model did not fit well for adult conduct problems as noted above. For the trait Alienation—related to a worldview that others are likely to take advantage or hurt you if they can—there was evidence of a genetic association with child and adult conduct problems, although the genetic correlation estimate for child-

Table 5.5. Genetic (rG) and Environmental (rE) Correlation Estimates for MPQ Scales and Antisocial Behavior Factor Scales

| | Antisocial Behavior Factor Scales | | | | | |
| | ASB1 | | ASB2 | | ASB3 | |
MPQ Scales	rG	rE	rG	rE	rG	rE
Alienation	.99	.12	.53	.31*	.11	.17
Aggression	.72	.23	.55	.17**	.69	.09
Control	−.69	−.07	−.82	−.04	−.40	.05
Harm avoidance	−.67	.00	−.54	−.05	−.65	.00
Traditionalism	−.07	.02	.30	−.15	−.74	−.28

Note. ASB1 = Childhood behavior problems and aggression; ASB2 = Adult behavior problems and aggression; ASB3 = Adult Irresponsibility; rG = Genetic Correlation; rE = Environmental Correlation.
* Reflects marginally fitting model (1.0 > p > .05)
**Reflects poor fitting model

hood conduct problems seems a clear overestimate, probably as a result of the small sample size. This is reminiscent of recent research and theory regarding the role of hostile attribution bias in the etiology of aggression (Crick & Dodge, 1996; Crick, Grotpeter, & Bigbee, 2002) and suggests that common genetic mechanisms may mediate this association.

Conclusion

Although the analyses described in this chapter were conducted on a small, selected sample (resulting in fairly large standard errors for parameter estimates), they suggest that genes contributing to externalizing psychopathology, including antisocial behavior and drug and alcohol abuse/dependence, overlap with genes that influence personality traits often shown to be correlated with such psychopathology. The results, although not a specific focus of this chapter, also suggest the possibility that nonshared environmental effects on personality may overlap with those that contribute to externalizing psychopathology.

The pattern of genetic correlations also suggests some specificity regarding subdomains of antisocial behavior. We previously reported (DiLalla, Gottesman, & Carey, 1993) higher Alienation and Aggression scores among individuals with Antisocial Personality Disorder. The present results suggest that the genetic influences on Alienation overlap to a moderate degree with genetic influences on childhood and adulthood antisocial behavior and aggression but that there is a much smaller degree of genetic overlap between Alienation and adult irresponsibility. Likewise, the MPQ's Traditionalism scale shows little genetic overlap with the childhood and adulthood antisocial behavior scales but a high degree of overlap with adult irresponsibility. These associations would not be evident if we were to focus only on higher level personality domains such as Negative Affectivity and Constraint or on global conceptualizations of antisocial behavior.

In terms of the debate regarding the most reasonable way to conceptualize personality → psychopathology associations, our findings support a Continuity model that harkens back to Paul Meehl's (1962, 1989) theory of schizotaxia and highlights the complexity of genetic and environmental influences on personality and psychopathology (Sherman et al., 1997). Despite popular press reports that sporadically trumpet the discovery of specific genes "for" particular personality traits, it bears repeating that genetic influences on personality and psychopathology are likely to be multifactorial rather than Mendelian (Eaves, Eysenck, & Martin, 1989; Gottesman, 1991, 2002; Loehlin, 1992) and may be nonadditive (Finkel & McGue, 1997). Moreover, each gene in a multifactorial system codes for a polypeptide chain that contributes to synthesis of biological molecules. These subsequently enter biochemical pathways with multiple interacting feedback loops. Hence, the path from gene to behavior is indirect and multifaceted. At the same time, we believe that by focusing on genetic influences on homogenous subdomains of the phenotypes of interest—as opposed to looking for genetic influences on the global phenotype—we may be better positioned to uncover major genes of effect in these systems. Although not our principal focus here, we believe a similar approach would yield fruit in a search for major environmental effects on complex phenotypes such as psychopathology.

References

Berenbaum, H., & Fujita, F. (1994). Schizophrenia and personality: Exploring the boundaries and connections between vulnerability and outcome. *Journal of Abnormal Psychology, 103,* 148–158.

Carey, G. (1989). DFP minimization routine. Unpublished computer software. University of Colorado, Boulder.

Carey, G., & Goldman, D. (1997). The genetics of antisocial behavior. In D. F. Stoff, J. Brilling, & J. D. Maser (Eds.), *Handbook of antisocial behavior* (pp. 243–254). New York: Wiley.

Caspi, A. (2000). The child is the father of the man: Personality continuities from childhood to adulthood. *Journal of Personality and Social Psychology, 78,* 158–172.

Church, A. (1994). Relating the Tellegen and Five-Factor Models of personality structure. *Journal of Personality and Social Psychology, 67,* 898–909.

Clark, L. A., Watson, D., & Mineka, S. (1994). Temperament, personality and the mood and anxiety disorders. *Journal of Abnormal Psychology, 103,* 103–116.

Costa, P. T., & McCrae, R. R. (1990). Personality disorders and the five-factor model of personality. *Journal of Personality Disorders, 4,* 362–371.

Costa, P. T., & McCrae, R. R. (1992). *Revised NEO personality inventory (NEO-PI-R) and the NEO five-factor inventory (NEO-FFI) professional manual.* Odessa, FL: Psychological Assessment Resources.

Crick, N. R., & Dodge, K. A. (1996). Social information–processing mechanisms on reactive and proactive aggression. *Child Development, 67,* 993–1002.

Crick, N. R., Grotpeter, J. K., & Bigbee, M. A. (2002). Relationally and physically aggressive children's intent attributions and feelings of distress for relational and instrumental peer provocations. *Child Development, 73,* 1134–1142.

DiLalla, D. L. (2001, November). *Genetic correlations between normal personality traits and disinhibitory psychopathology.* Paper presented at Society for Research in Psychopathology, Madison, WI.

DiLalla, D. L., Carey, G., Gottesman, I. I. & Bouchard, T. J., Jr. (1996). Heritability of MMPI personality indicators of psychopathology in twins reared apart. *Journal of Abnormal Psychology, 105,* 491–499

DiLalla, D. L., Gottesman, I. I., & Carey, G. (1993). Assessment of normal personality traits in an abnormal sample: Dimensions and categories. In L. Chapman, J. Chapman, & D. Fowles (Eds.), *Progress in Experimental Personality and Psychopathology Research* (Vol. 16, pp. 137–162). New York: Springer.

DiLalla, D. L., Gottesman, I. I., & Carey, G. (2000). Madness beyond the threshold? Associations between personality and psychopathology. In V. J. Molfese & D. L. Molfese (Eds.), *Temperament and personality across the lifespan.* Mahwah, NJ: Erlbaum.

DiLalla, D. L., Gottesman, I. I., Carey, G. C., & Vogler, G. V. (1993). Joint factor analysis of the Multidimensional Personality Questionnaire and the MMPI in a psychiatric and high-risk sample. *Psychological Assessment, 5,* 207–215.

Eaves, L. J., Eysenck, H. J., & Martin, N. G. (1989). *Genes, culture and personality: An empirical approach.* San Diego, CA: Academic Press.

Finkel, D., & McGue, M. (1997). Sex differences and nonadditivity in heritability of the Multidimensional Personality Questionnaire Scales. *Journal of Personality and Social Psychology, 72,* 929–938.

Gjone, H., & Stevenson, J. (1997). A longitudinal twin study of temperament and behavior problems: Common genetic or environmental influences? *Journal of Abnormal Child Psychology, 25,* 277–286.

Gottesman, I. I. (1991). *Schizophrenia genesis: The origins of madness.* New York: W. H. Freeman.

Gottesman, I. I. (2002). Forward: Genetic transmission of temperament and personality—Past and prospect. In J. Benjamin, R. P. Ebstein, & R. H. Belmaker (Eds.), *Molecular genetics and human personality* (pp. xiii–xx). Washington, DC: American Psychiatric Press.

Gynther, L., Carey, G., Gottesman, I. I., & Vogler, G. P. (1995). A twin study of non-alcohol substance abuse. *Psychiatry Research, 56,* 213–220.

Hathaway, S. R., & McKinley, J. C. (1983). *Manual for administration and scoring of the MMPI.* Minneapolis: National Computer Systems.

Helzer, J. E., & Robins, L. N. (1988). The diagnostic interview schedule: Its development and use. *Social Psychiatry and Psychiatric Epidemiology, 23,* 6–16.

Jang, K. L., & Livesley, W. J. (1999). Why do measures of normal and disordered personality correlate? A study of genetic comorbidity. *Journal of Personality Disorders, 13,* 10–17

Jardine, R., Martin, N. G., & Henderson, A. S. (1984). Genetic covariation between neuroticism and the symptoms of anxiety and depression. *Genetic Epidemiology, 1,* 89–107.

Joreskog, K. G., & Sorbom, D. (1993). *LISREL 8: Structural equation modeling with the SIMPLIS command language.* Hillsdale, NJ: Erlbaum.

Kendler, K. S., Neale, M. C., Kessler, R. C., Heath, A. C., & Eaves, L. J. (1993). A longitudinal twin study of personality and major depression in women. *Archives of General Psychiatry, 50,* 853–862.

Kenney, D. A. (1979) *Correlation and causality.* New York: Wiley.

Kratzer, L., & Hodgins, S. (1997). Adult outcomes of child conduct problems: A cohort study. *Journal of Abnormal Child Psychology, 25,* 65–81.

Krueger, R. F. (1999). Personality traits in late adolescence predict mental disorders in early adulthood: A prospective-epidemiological study. *Journal of Personality, 67,* 39–65.

Lerner, J. A., Inui, T. S., Trupin, E. W., & Douglas, E. (1985). Preschool behavior can predict future psychiatric disorders. *Journal of the American Academy of Child Psychiatry, 24,* 42–48.

Livesley, W. J., & Jackson, D. N. (in press). *Manual for the dimensional assessment of personality problems—Basic questionnaire.* Port Huron, MI: Sigma.

Livesley, W. J., Jang, K. L., & Vernon, P. A. (1998). Phenotypic and genetic structure of traits delineating personality disorder. *Archives of General Psychiatry, 55,* 941–948.

Loeber, R., Farrington, D. P., Stouthamer-Loeber, M., Moffitt, T. E., & Caspi, A. (1998). The development of male offending: Key findings from the first decade of the Pittsburgh Youth Study. *Studies on Crime and Crime Prevention, 7,* 141–171.

Loehlin, J. C. (1992). *Genes and environment in personality development.* Newbury Park, CA: Sage.

Markon, K. E., Krueger, R. F., Bouchard, T. J., Jr., & Gottesman, I. I. (2002). Normal and abnormal personality traits: Evidence for genetic and environmental relationships in the Minnesota study of twins reared apart. *Journal of Personality, 70,* 661–693.

McGue, M., & Bouchard, T. J., Jr. (1984). Adjustment of twin data for the effects of age and sex. *Behavior Genetics, 14,* 325–343.

McGuffin, P., & Thapar, A. (1998). Genetics and antisocial behavior. In T. Millon & E. Simonsen (Eds.), *Psychopathy: Antisocial, criminal and violent behavior* (pp. 215–230). New York: Guilford Press.

Meehl, P. E. (1962). Schizotaxia, schizotypy, and schizophrenia. *American Psychologist, 17,* 827–838.

Meehl, P. E. (1989). Schizotaxia revisited. *Archives of General Psychiatry, 46,* 935–944.

Moffitt, T. E., & Caspi, A. (2001). Childhood predictors differentiate life-course persistent and adolescence-limited antisocial pathways among males and females. *Development & Psychopathology, 13,* 355–375.

Mustanski, B. S., Viken, R. J., Kaprio, J., & Rose, R. J. (2003). Genetic influences on the association between personality risk factors and alcohol use and abuse. *Journal of Abnormal Psychology, 112,* 282–289.

Neale, M. C., & Cardon, L. R. (1992). *Methodology for genetic studies of twins and families.* Boston: Kluwer Academic Press.

O'Connor, B. (2002). The search for dimensional structure differences between normality and abnormality: A statistical review of published data on personality and psychopathology. *Journal of Personality and Social Psychology, 83,* 962–982.

Roberts, S. B., & Kendler, K. S. (1999). Neuroticism and self-esteem as indices of the vulnerability to major depression in women. *Psychological Medicine, 29,* 1101–1109.

Romero, E., Luengo, M. A., & Sobral, J. (2001). Personality and antisocial behaviour: Study of temperamental dimensions. *Personality & Individual Differences, 31,* 329–334.

Schroeder, M. L., Wormworth, J. A., & Livesley, W. J. (1994). Dimensions of personality disorder and their relationships to the big five dimensions of personality. In P. T. Costa & T. A. Widiger (Eds.), *Personality disorders and the five-factor model of personality* (pp. 117–127). Washington, DC: American Psychological Association.

Sherman, S. L., DeFries, J. C., Gottesman, I. I., Loehlin, J., Meyer, J. M., Pelias, M. Z., et al. (1997). Recent developments in human behavioral genetics: Past accomplishments and future directions. *American Journal of Human Genetics, 60,* 1265—1275.

Slutske, W. S., Eisen, S., Xian, H., True, W. R., Lyons, M. J., Goldberg, J., et al. (2001). A twin study of the association between pathological gambling and antisocial personality disorder. *Journal of Abnormal Psychology, 110,* 297–308.

Tellegen, A. (1982). *Manual for the Multidimensional Personality Questionnaire.* Unpublished manuscript.

Tellegen, A. (1985). Structures of mood and personality and their relevance to assessing anxiety, with an emphasis on self report. In A. H. Tuma & J. D. Maser (Eds.), *Anxiety and the anxiety disorders* (pp. 681–706). Hillsdale, NJ: Erlbaum.

Tellegen, A., Lykken, D. T., Bouchard, T. J., Jr., Wilcox, K. J., Segal, N. L., & Rich, S. (1988). Personality similarity in twins reared apart and together. *Journal of Personality and Social Psychology, 54,* 1031–1039.

Tellegen, A., & Waller, N. (in press). Exploring personality through test construction: Development of the Multidimensional Personality Questionnaire. In S. R. Briggs & J. M. Cheek (Eds.), *Personality measures: Development and evaluation* (Vol. 1). Greenwich, CT: JAI Press.

Trull, T. J., & Sher, K. J. (1994). Relationship between the five-factor model of personality and axis I disorders in a nonclinical sample. *Journal of Abnormal Psychology, 103,* 350–360.

White, H., Xie, M., Thompson, W., Loeber, R., & Stouthamer-Loeber, M. (2001). Psychopathology as a predictor of adolescent drug use trajectories. *Psychology of Addictive Behaviors, 15,* 210–218.

Widiger, T. A., Verheul, R., & van den Brink, W. (1999). Personality and psychopathology. In L. A. Pervin & O. P. John (Eds.) *Handbook of personality: Theory and research* (2nd ed., pp. 347–366). New York: Guilford.

Woodward, L. J., & Fergusson, D. M. (1999). Childhood peer relationship problems and psychosocial adjustment in late adolescence. *Journal of Abnormal Child Psychology, 27,* 87–104.

Zuckerman, M. (1999). *Vulnerability to psychopathology: A biosocial model.* Washington, DC: American Psychological Association.

6

Genetic Influence on Social Attitudes: Another Challenge to Psychology From Behavior Genetics

Thomas J. Bouchard Jr., Nancy L. Segal,
Auke Tellegen, Matt McGue, Margaret Keyes,
and Robert Krueger

Introduction

The idea that genes influence attitudes is likely to meet with considerable resistance. Such resistance is easily understood. We all bring strong presumptions to our work and outlook on life, and most psychologists are of the opinion that individual differences in attitudes are largely shaped by family influence and schooling, with cultural factors determining the content and level (Adorno, Frenkel-Brunswick, Levinson, & Sanford, 1950; B. Altemeyer, 1981, 1988; R. Altemeyer, 1996; Olson & Zanna, 1993; Tesser & Schaffer, 1990). Nevertheless, even social psychologists have begun to take the behavior-genetic findings in this domain seriously. Eagly and Chaiken (1993) specifically did not exclude genetic influence in their definition of attitudes. Tesser and his colleagues (Crelia & Tesser, 1996) have carried out a research program exploring the role of "degree of genetic influence" as an independent variable.

In 1986, in response to a seminal paper published in the *Proceedings of the National Academy of Science* (Martin et al., 1986) the Minnesota Study of Twins Reared Apart (MISTRA) incorporated a version of the Wilson–Patterson Conservatism Scale (W–P), developed for the Virginia Twin Study, into the MISTRA test battery. At about the same time, David Lykken was in communication with Bob Altemeyer regarding the Right-Wing Authoritarianism Scale (RWA; B. Altemeyer, 1981, 1988; R. Altemeyer, 1996), a copy of which he sent out to a large sample of monozygotic and dizygotic twins reared together from the Minnesota Twin Registry (MTR; Lykken, Bouchard, McGue, & Tellegen, 1990). We also sent out the W–P and the RWA, with a number of other questionnaires, to the MISTRA twins who had completed the assessment and whom we felt confident would complete it reliably. In addition, we began to administer these instruments to twins newly participating in our assessment program. Shortly thereafter, we turned to our first study of a clearly "attitude-like" variable, specifically religiousness (Waller, Kojetin, Bouchard, Lykken, &

Tellegen, 1990). In this chapter, we update and summarize some of our findings.

A Digression on Methodology

Before turning to our findings and placing them in context, we would like to make a brief methodological digression to explain the logic of the standard twin and twin reared apart design for readers unfamiliar with behavior genetic models. The easiest way to introduce these designs is via the Hoyt (1941) or Parallel Test reliability coefficient. The path model for the Hoyt reliability coefficient is shown as (a) in the upper left-hand part of Figure 6.1. A and B are parallel tests (scores are shown as boxes, latent traits are shown in circles). The paths with the path coefficients (*t*s) indicate that the cause (arrows pointing to the test scores) of the correlation between the two tests results from the latent trait, in this instance the "true score." Following the rules of path analysis, the path coefficients connecting the scores are multiplied. In this instance, there is only one path connecting the two sets of scores, thus $r_{ab} = t * t = t^2$.

This correlation coefficient is computed via analysis of variance and is an intraclass correlation as opposed to an interclass correlation. The standard interpretation of the Hoyt reliability is that it indexes the amount of variance accounted for by the latent trait. Note that the correlation coefficient is not squared; it directly assesses the proportion of variance caused by the latent trait. The correlation between Monozygotic Twins Reared Apart (MZAs) is exactly parallel. The twins are parallel forms, and the cause of the correlation is their genes, which as we know from genetic theory are the same. Consequently, this common genetic latent trait is linked by a path indicating a correlation of 1.00 as shown in (b) in the upper right-hand part of Figure 6. 1. Again the correlation is computed via analysis of variance and the correlation is interpreted directly; it is not squared. Under this model, the correlation between monozygotic twins reared apart is a direct estimate of the proportion of variance caused by genetic factors. The correlation for Dizygotic Twins Reared Apart (DZAs) is represented by simply setting the correlation between the genetic influences (Gs) at .50 in place of 1.00, because we know from genetic theory that they share, on average, half the genes on which they vary. The path diagram is shown as (c) in Figure 6.1. The correlation for Monozygotic Twins Reared Together (MZT) must include environmental factors that may make them alike; thus an additional latent trait, common environment (C), must be added to the model. This model is shown as (d) in Figure 6.1. The correlation for Dizygotic Twins Reared Together (DZT) involves simply adding C to the DZA diagram and is not shown. Diagram (e) shows the correlation between unrelated individuals reared together. They are similar because they share environmental influences, called shared or common environmental factors. The final diagram (f) shows the correlation between unrelated individuals reared in correlated environments. These last two models are, of course, environmental designs rather than genetic ones. We return to the last figure shortly. The fundamental reason we can interpret these correlations as "causal" is because they

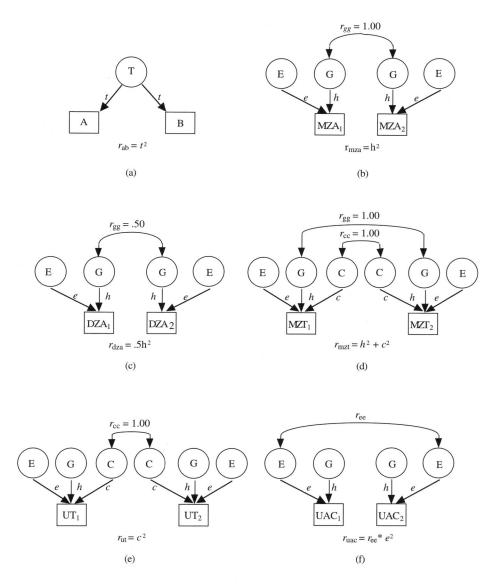

Figure 6.1. Path model for (a) the Hoyt Parallel Form Reliability, (b) Monozygotic Twins Reared Apart, (c) Dizygotic Twins Reared Apart, (d) Monozygotic Twins Reared Together, (e) Unrelated Individuals Reared Together, and (f) Unrelated Individuals Reared in Correlated Environments.

are derived from experiments. The MZ and DZ twins are "experiments of nature" (individuals with precisely two different doses of genes) and the rearing together and apart treatment (adoption vs. rearing in one's biological family) is an "experiment of society."

Genetic Influence on Measures of Religiousness

In our initial study (Waller et al., 1990), we reported the MZA and DZA findings for the MMPI Wiggins Religious Fundamentalism Scale (WRF), the Strong–Campbell Interest Inventory Religious Activities Scales (SCII-RA), and the Allport–Vernon–Lindzey Religious Values Scale (AVL-RV). In addition, we reported MZA, DZA, MZT, and DZT (four group design) findings for the Minnesota Interest Inventory Religious Occupational Interest Scale (MII-ROI) and the Minnesota Leisure Time Inventory Religious Leisure Time Interests Scale (MLTI-RLT). A considerable number of additional twins reared apart have participated in our studies since that time. We also included the WRF items as part of a group of 80 personality items, a Job Satisfaction Questionnaire, a Work Attitude Questionnaire, and an Organizational Questionnaire sent to a sample of twins reared together. The sampling procedure and the results from the Job Satisfaction Questionnaire have been reported (Arvey, McCall, Bouchard, & Taubman, 1994). Unfortunately, because of a typing error, one MMPI item from the WRF was left off the questionnaire. We also dropped one item that loaded poorly on the general factor. As a consequence, we have a slightly shorter scale for this follow-up sample than for the one reported in our earlier work. We call this revised WRF scale the WRF10 to indicate that it is made up of 10 items. The 10 items are given in Table 6.1 with their loadings on the first principal component in the two samples.

The coefficient alpha for the MISTRA sample was .83 ($N = 438$). For the new twin-reared-together sample, it was .82 ($N = 353$). In each case, the first principal component accounted for 41% of the variance. The intraclass correlations for the WRF10, MII-ROI, and MLI-RLT (scales on which we have four-group data) are shown in Table 6.2.

There is little variation in the correlations from measure to measure within kinships, so their weighted mean is a good representation of the data.

Table 6.1. Minnesota Multiphasic Personality Inventory Religious Items and Loadings on the First Principal Component for the MISTRA and New Twin Samples

| | Loading on 1st PC | |
| | MISTRA | New Twin Sample |
Item	(N=438)	(N=348)
I believe in the second coming of Christ.	.77	.77
I pray several times each week.	.76	.63
I believe there is a Devil and a Hell in afterlife.	.68	.71
I go to church almost every week.	.66	.58
I read in the Bible several times a week.	.66	.43
Christ performed miracles such as changing water into wine.	.63	.79
I am very religious (more than most people).	.61	.50
I believe in a life hereafter.	.59	.73
I believe there is a God.	.54	.69
I feel sure there is only one true religion.	.44	.39

Table 6.2. Intraclass Correlations and Sample Sizes (Number of Pairs) for the Various Religiousness Measures for the Samples of Monozygotic and Dizygotic Twins Reared Together and Reared Apart

Scale (# of items)	Twin Type			
	MZA	MZT	DZA	DZT
Wiggins Religious Fundamentalism (10) (WRF10)	.55 (78)	.56 (95)	.01 (56)	.23 (79)
Religious Occupational Interests (4) (MII-ROI)	.55 (65)	.43 (511)	.09 (50)	.23 (393)
Religious Leisure Time Interests (6) (MLI-RLT)	.50 (64)	.58 (519)	.12 (49)	.28 (403)
Weighted Mean	.53	.51	.07	.25

The MZA and MZT means are essentially the same and suggest a heritability of about .50 with no shared environmental influence because there is no difference between the two correlations. The MZT and DZT data taken together lead to the same conclusion. The DZA data are discrepant, suggesting a heritability of no more than .14. The DZA sample size is, however, modest, and sampling variation may be the explanation. This is nicely shown by the fact that the 95% Confidence Interval for the DZA correlation of .01 for WRF10 is −.25 to +.27.

When we try to fit a simple E model, it yields a large and statistically significant chi-square as well as a large Akaike Information Statistic (AIC), indicating a very poor fit. The best fitting model (most parsimonious taking into account both the chi-square and AIC values) is the AE model for all measures. For the WRF10, h^2 = .54 (95% CI = .43–.64); for Religious Occupational Interests, h^2 = .44 (95% CI = .38–.50); and for Religious Leisure Time Interests, h^2 = .57 (95% CI = .51–61).

The intraclass correlations for the Religious Activities Scale of the Strong–Campbell Interest Inventory were MZA = .42 (N = 78) and DZA=.32 (N = 56) and for the Religious Values Scale of the Allport–Vernon–Lindzey test, they were MZA = .50 (N = 65) and DZA =.13 (N = 50). With regard to model fitting, the environmental model is easily rejected in each instance. For the SCII-Religious Activities Scale, the best fitting model was an AE model, h^2 = .43 (95% CI = .26–.58). For the AVL Religious Values Scale, the AE and DE models fit equally well, h^2 = .46 (95% CI = .26–.61).

The Intrinsic–Extrinsic Religiousness Scale

Because these initial findings were so interesting and it seemed reasonable that there should be better measures of religiousness available, we searched for a better instrument. We turned up a revision of the Allport Intrinsic–Extrinsic Religiousness measure called the Age Universal Religious Orientation Scale (AUROS; Gorsuch, 1988). We chose to use the AUROS version of the I–E scale is because it is usable with both children (fifth grade and above) and adults, and our sample included a very broad range of educational backgrounds. We slightly revised some of the items to refer to religions other than those in the Judeo-Christian tradition. We also modified the response format to be consistent with other instruments in our battery in order to simplify the task for our respondents. This item set is known to generate two factors, and that is what we found. Our factor scores correlated .97 (Intrinsic Religiousness, henceforth IR) and .93 (Extrinsic Religiousness, henceforth ER) with the standard scoring scheme, so we chose to analyze the standard scales.

The correlation between the IR and ER scales is .04, and the coefficient Alphas are .88 and .66, respectively. Clearly ER is not as good a scale as IR, and IR is the one we are most interested in. The correlation between the IR and the full Wiggins Religious Fundamentalism scale is .67 ($N = 200$), whereas the correlation between ER and the Wiggins Religious Fundamentalism scale is $-.22$. This is superb convergent and discriminant validity and strongly supports the use of the WRF as a measure of religiousness.

The MZA and DZA intraclass correlations for IR are .37 ($N = 35$, 95% CI $= .04–.64$) and .20 ($N = 37$, 95% CI $= -.13–.43$). The IR MZA and DZA correlations are highly consistent with a simple additive genetic model, with the DZA correlation being very close to half the MZA correlation. The purely environmental model is easily rejected. Model fitting the variance–covariance matrix yields a heritability estimate of .43 (95% CI $= .15–.64$). These results converge very nicely with the estimates for other religiousness measures reported previously. The MZA and DZA intraclass correlations for ER were .24 (95% CI $= -.10–.53$) and .38 (95% CI $= .06–.63$). The findings for ER are anomalous, with the DZA correlation higher than the MZA correlation. Nevertheless, given these sample sizes, a simple additive model does fit the data, with a model-fitting heritability estimate of .39 (95% CI $= .09–.61$). The 95% confidence intervals on the correlations and variance estimates are very wide and should make it clear that a replication study based on a very large sample of twins reared together would be highly desirable.

Some critics have asserted that these findings simply reflect the repeated finding in the domain of personality of a heritability between .40 and .50 for most personality traits. In other words, religiousness is simply a facet of the standard array of personality traits and not a unique trait in its own right. That is simply not the case, as we demonstrated by correlating IR and ER with the Multidimensional Personality Inventory and the California Psychological Inventory (Bouchard, McGue, Lykken, & Tellegen, 1999).

One possible explanation for the MZA and DZA correlations for religiousness, apart from genetic influence, is placement bias. Might it be the case that the adopted twins were placed in homes with similar levels of religious upbringing? In order to test placement hypotheses, we included the Family Environment Scale (Moos & Moos, 1994) in our assessment battery. One of the 10 scales that can be scored from this instrument is the Moral Religious Emphasis Scale (MRE). We indeed do find considerable placement on this variable. Among our MZA twins, the correlation is $r =.32$ ($N= 68$ pairs). Does this mean that placement explains much of the similarity between the MZA twins and thus the heritability? Critics of adoption studies often leave the reader with the impression that placement "wipes out" much of the genetic effect. This argument is highly misleading because it ignores a crucial piece of what is essentially a quantitative argument. Placement alone is insufficient to explain anything. The variable on which placement occurs must be shown to be "causal." One could plausibly argue that the moral religious orientation of one's rearing family is "causally relevant" to the trait of religiousness. Such an argument, however, is just that, "an argument." It does not constitute evidence. It may well be that families who provide a strong moral religious orientation for their children are made up of parents who are, on average, strongly religious in their beliefs, and in biological families, they pass this trait on to their children through both their genes and the environment they provide, whereas in adoptive families, they provide only environmental transmission. The hypothesis that there is "causally relevant" environmental influence on religiousness can be tested and quantified. One can compute the correlation between moral religious orientation of a family and the IR scores of adult biological offspring reared in such families. This correlation alone is ambiguous because it may be caused by genetic factors, environmental factors or both. It gains interpretability, however, when it is compared with the same correlation computed on the members of adoptive families, families in which genetic influence is not transmitted. This allows us to estimate the "trait relevance" of the supported environmental factor. Because MISTRA also includes the spouses of its twins, we have access to both adoptive and biological families and we can compute these correlations. As would be expected by many social scientists, the correlation between the reported moral religious orientation of families and scores on the IR scale is .53 ($N = 54$). This is a substantial correlation and on the surface provides construct validity for both of the measures. Nevertheless, the correlation in adoptive families is only .10 ($N = 127$). The biological correlation is 5.3 times larger than the adoptive correlation. If we return to the path diagram for unrelated individuals reared together in Figure 6.1, we can see how this information might be used to quantify placement effects on twin similarity. The placement coefficient (r_{ee}) is .32 and the trait-relevant causal influence is .10. Thus $.32 * .10^2 = .003$. This is the degree of similarity expected for unrelated individuals reared in a correlated environment with this degree of "causal influence." Virtually none of the MZA similarity can be explained by placement in homes similar in moral religious orientation.

Authoritarianism

Although we were pushed into the domain of genetic influence on attitudes by Martin et al.'s (1986) work with the W–P Conservatism scale, the first attitude-like measure on which we published data was the Multidimensional Personality Questionnaire (MPQ) Traditionalism scale (Tellegen et al., 1988). At that time, we reported the heritability of Traditionalism based on a four-group design. Since then, Finkel and McGue (1997) have published the results of a 12-group design (4300 pairs) that does not include twins reared apart. The mean heritability for Traditionalism across both sexes is .54. The MZA twin correlation for our full sample who completed the MPQ ($N = 74$ pairs) is .52. It is worth noting that the MZT correlation for Traditionalism is .54 ($N = 626$, adult sample). Finkel and McGue concluded that there is little if any shared environmental influence on Traditionalism, and the contrast between the MZT and MZA correlations leads to the same conclusion. As with most personality traits, one can infer a good estimate of the heritability of Traditionalism from the MZT correlation alone (Bouchard & Loehlin, 2001).

One of the major criticisms of the original measure of authoritarianism (the Fascism or F-scale) generated by the research program on the Authoritarian Personality (Adorno et al., 1950) was that it had much too high a correlation with IQ and socioeconomic status (SES; Christie & Jahoda, 1954). The RWA (Right-Wing Authoritarianism) Scale was developed by Altemeyer (1981; 1988; R. Altemeyer, 1996; Christie, 1991) as a modern replacement for the F-scale. Because we had the relevant data, we thought we would check on whether RWA was highly correlated with IQ and SES. As mentioned previously, correspondence between Bob Altemeyer and David Lykken led to the inclusion of the RWA Scale in both the MISTRA and the MTR. The correlations among RWA, education, and SES for MTR are −.37 and −.30. For the MISTRA study, they are −.36 and −.40. In addition, MISTRA included a measure of General Cognitive Ability (GCA), for which the correlation was −.37.

The RWA Scale correlated nearly as highly with IQ and SES as the scale it is supposed to replace. This is a threat to the validity of the RWA Scale, and it posed a problem for any genetic analysis because IQ is known to be highly heritable (Bouchard, 1998). Indeed, Sandra Scarr and Richard Weinberg (1981) had already shown that although it appeared to be genetic, the transmission of authoritarianism, as measured by the F-scale, could be accounted for, in part, by verbal ability. Nevertheless, IQ could not account for the twin similarity in the MISTRA sample. The MISTRA MZA and DZA intraclass correlations without GCA partialled out are .69 and .00. With GCA partialled out they are .59 and −.09. The MZT and DZT correlations are .63 and .42. Again we encounter a very low DZA correlation in contrast to a sizeable DZT correlation. It is worth noting that the simple Falconer heritability computed from the twins reared together, 2(rMZT − rDZT), would be .41. Model-fitting the variance–covariance matrices shows that a simple environmental model can easily be rejected. In addition, because the DZA sample size is so modest, it is possible to achieve an acceptable fit to a simple model (additive genetic variance = .50, shared environmental variance = .16, specific environmental variance plus error = .34). Because the spouse correlation is .62 (.56 controlling for GCA), we fit a number of models that included an assortative mating parameter (AM). A model with assortative mating (with AM = .40) fit the data as well as the simple model (additive genetic + assortative mating variance = .64, specific environmental variance = .36). These findings are interesting because they match the findings for the Australian twin study of Conservatism discussed later. In that study, the inclusion of an assortative mating parameter made the inclusion of a common environmental parameter unnecessary. Assortative mating on a trait heavily influenced by additive genetic variance increases the similarity of first-degree relatives (DZ twins). The fact that the DZT correlation is somewhat higher than half the MZT correlation is thus accounted for. The very low DZA correlation is still difficult to account for. We note, however, that there is reason to believe that assortment among individuals who do not marry (the parents of most of our reared-apart twins) is much less than among pairs of individuals who do marry. See McCourt, Bouchard, Lykken, Tellegren, and Keyes (1999) for a discussion of this point.

In this study, placement was again unable to explain the MZA twin similarity. Four scales from the Moos Family Environment Scale (retrospective reports of home rearing) correlated with RWA in the nonadoptee sample but did not reach significance in the adoptee sample. Those results are shown in Table 6.3. As expected, the Moral Religious Emphasis Scale yielded the highest correlation, but in the nonadoptee sample only.

The Wilson–Patterson Conservatism Scale

The instructions for the Wilson–Patterson Conservatism Scale (W–P) are as follows: Here is a list of various topics. Please indicate whether or not you agree with each topic by circling Yes or No as appropriate. If you are uncertain please circle "?"; again the best answer is usually the one that comes to mind first, so just give us your first reaction and don't spend too long on any one topic.

The topics mentioned in the instructions just given are shown in Table 6.4. This "catch phrase" format strikes many psychologists as inadequate and of doubtful validity. We concurred with this judgment, but because of the scale's brevity and the strong genetic influence on the Conservatism score derived from this instrument reported by Martin et al. (1986), we incorporated it into the MISTRA assessment.

Using twins from the Virginia Twin Registry, Eaves and his colleagues (1997) have shown that the heritability of conservatism is age-dependent. The MZ and DZ correlations do not diverge until after age 20. The lack of early divergence is probably caused by at least two factors: (a) lack of salience of the items in younger samples because variance in the first principal component is very low at the younger ages and (b) the continuing impact of common family environment while the younger samples are still at home. Once these factors are overcome, genetic influence manifests itself. These age effects are consistent with the findings of no genetic influence on religious attitudes in the National Merit Scholarship Twins (NMST) as reported by Loehlin and Nichols

Table 6.3. Correlations Between Right-Wing Authoritarianism and Four Family Environment Scale Measures in the Nonadoptee ($N = 69$, Mostly Spouses of Twins) and Adoptee ($N = 139$) Samples

Measure of Rearing Environment	Nonadoptees	Adoptees
Moral Religious Emphasis	.35*	.10
Organization	.28*	.08
Control	.26*	.13
Achievement Orientation	.22*	.07

*p<.01

Table 6.4. Factor Loadings for the First Principal Component and the Factors of a Three-Factor Varimax Solution for the W–P Scale Items ($N = 348$)

Items	First Principal Component	Factors		
		Sexual Conservatism	Social Conservatism	Militarism
Abortion	.63	**.76**	.06	−.08
Living Together	.60	**.72**	.07	−.08
X-Rated Movies	.41	**.64**	−.14	−.06
Divorce	.51	**.61**	.16	.10
Gay Rights	.68	**.51**	.40	−.20
Women's Lib.	.47	**.43**	.28	.04
Censorship	−.16	**−.41**	.28	.10
Modern Art	.38	**.34**	.28	.14
Capitalism	.12	**.26**	−.05	.14
Astrology	.20	**.25**	.11	.20
Democrats	.46	.18	**.61**	.13
Pacifism	.35	.00	**−.56**	−.07
Unions	.27	−.08	**.54**	−.00
Liberals	.59	.38	**.53**	.06
Socialism	.56	.25	**.51**	−.22
Foreign Aid	.28	−.02	**.51**	.06
Immigration	.24	−.02	**.42**	−.01
Death Penalty	−.29	.10	**−.41**	.40
Federal Housing	.26	.04	**.39**	.03
Busing	.18	.05	**.24**	−.01
Military Drill	−.38	−.19	−.04	**.73**
The Military Draft	−.36	−.12	−.11	**.69**
Republicans	−.05	.12	.04	**.58**
School Prayer	−.45	−.38	−.05	**.46**
Nuclear Power	−.23	.13	−.31	**.44**
Moral Majority	−.25	−.23	.08	**.43**
Property Tax	.05	.08	.06	**.17**
Segregation	.00	.05	.02	**.16**
% Variance Accounted for	—	14.6	8.3	7.9

(1976). The NMST sample is of high school age, and the MZ and DZ correlations for belief in God were .60 and .58 and for involvement in religious affairs they were .56 and .67, mimicking the results presented by Eaves et al. (1997). The heritabilities of religiousness and conservatism are clearly age dependent.

We have previously reported the results of a twin analysis of the total score used by the Virginia group from whom we obtained this version of the W–P (Bouchard et al., 2003). Here we report the results for a slightly refined total score and three underlying factors. The Virginia W–P (VW–P) items were subjected to a principal component analysis with Varimax rotation. The analysis suggested four factors (scree test). The fourth factor was difficult to interpret. A repeat of the analysis by sex showed that the fourth factor was quite different for males and females, whereas the first three factors were similar though not identical. A comparison of the factor results of the American sample ($N = 150$)

versus the British, New Zealander, and Australian participants ($N = 168$) also suggested that three factors would provide the most comparability across these different groups and allow us to carry out a meaningful twin analysis. The results of the factor analysis are shown in Table 6.4.

Based on the loadings, we have named the three factors Sexual Conservatism, Social Conservatism, and Militarism. As shown in column 2, most of the items have a significant loading on the first principal component, suggesting a large general factor. The sum of the 25 highest loading items (with appropriate reflections) constitutes our overall Conservatism measure. The coefficient alpha was .75, exactly the same as the frequency-weighted mean internal consistency reliability derived from a meta-analysis of the Big Five personality factors (Viswesvaran & Ones, 2000). Taking into account the factor loadings and the coefficient alphas, we chose for the respective scales the first eight items loading on the Sexual Conservatism factor (alpha =.73), all items loading on the Social Conservatism factor (alpha =.66), and the first six items loading on the Militarism factor (alpha =.63). Eaves et al. (1999) reported finding five oblique factors (Sex, Tax, Militarism, Political Preference, and Religious Fundamentalism) in their analysis of the VW–P, based on the Virginia 30,000 (Eaves et al., 1999), although they do not report details of their analysis. When we scored our sample for these factors, the alpha coefficients for Tax, Political Preference, and Religious Fundamentalism were very poor (.16, .25 and .39). Our measures of Sex and Militarism are similar to theirs (rs of .99 and .77 with their measures).

The correlations between the Total Conservatism Score and the three W–P scales we developed (Sexual Conservatism, Social Conservatism, and Militarism) and the MPQ, RWA, and WAIS IQ (convergent and discriminant validity coefficients) are given in Table 6.5.

With regard to personality, Conservatism correlates highly only with the MPQ Traditionalism Scale (.60). The subscale correlations with Traditionalism are somewhat less: .54 with Sexual Conservatism, .34 with Social Conservatism, and .38 with Militarism. All four scales have a more modest correlation with the Constraint factor, reflecting the fact that Traditionalism is only one component of Constraint. Conservatism correlates .73 with RWA. The subscale correlations with RWA are .62 with Sexual Conservatism, .42 with Social Conservatism, and .51 with Militarism. IQ correlates only modestly with Conservatism, (–.21) and even less with the subscales.

These results clearly show that the W–P reflects a basic underlying attitudinal dimension of conservatism as suggested by Wilson (1970, 1985). It demonstrates both convergent and discriminant validity. It correlates .73 with RWA, a scale that has been extensively validated (B. Altemeyer, 1981; 1988; R. Altemeyer, 1996) and that is considered by some to be "the best current measure of what the authors of *The Authoritarian Personality* were attempting to measure" (Christie, 1991, p. 552). In addition, it correlates .60 with the MPQ Traditionalism Scale, a personality measure of adherence to traditional values. Furthermore, it does not correlate very highly (above .14) with any other MPQ scale. Because the MPQ broadly samples the personality domain at an intermediate level of generality, it is unlikely that the Conservatism measure can be subsumed by other personality constructs. The same can be said for the three underlying facets of this particular measure of conservatism.

Table 6.5. Correlations Between the Minnesota Study of Twins Reared Apart Conservatism Score, the Three Subscale Scores, the Multidimensional Personality Questionnaire Scales ($N = 345$), the Altemeyer Right-Wing Authoritarianism Scale ($N = 208$) and WAIS Full-Scale IQ ($N = 338$)

	Wilson–Patterson Scales			
Scales	Total Conservatism Score	Sexual Conservatism	Social Conservatism	Militarism
MPQ Primary Scales				
Well-Being	−.04	−.07	−.07	.08
Social Potency	−.04	−.14	.07	.05
Achievement	.04	−.02	.08	.08
Social Closeness	−.03	.03	−.09	−.03
Stress Reaction	.04	.02	.10	−.01
Alienation	.14	.07	.16	.08
Aggression	−.03	−.19	.18	−.04
Control	.14	.17	.02	.08
Harm Avoidance	.07	.17	−.06	−.01
Traditionalism	.60	.54	.34	.38
Absorption	−.13	−.12	−.06	−.08
MPQ Factors				
Positive Emotionality	−.01	−.08	.02	.07
Negative Emotionality	.13	.03	.21	.06
Constraint	.38	.40	.15	.22
Right-Wing Authoritarianism	.73	.62	.42	.51
WAIS Full-Scale IQ	−.21	−.16	−.14	-.18

In an unpublished memo, Goldberg, Tucker, Altemeyer, Dawes, and Rothbart (1984) reported a correlation of .85 ($N = 111$) between a different version of the W–P Scale (24 items) and the 1981 RWA Scale (24 items). The coefficient alphas were .85 and .90, respectively. Thus, in spite of quite different item content, response format, and differences in control for response set, the correlation between the two measures in both studies is very high. Goldberg also reported that the RWA Scale correlated −.36 and −.27 with the Quick Word Test Level 1 and The Quick Word Test Level 2, whereas the Conservatism scale correlated −.15 and −.12 with the same tests. The Quick Word Tests each consist of 100 vocabulary words, normed for persons with high school and college educations, respectively. Because these data are based on college samples with restriction of range on IQ and perhaps RWA, the correlations for the population in general are underestimated. In the MISTRA database, which includes people of diverse educational backgrounds, RWA correlates −.37 with IQ whereas Conservatism correlates only −.21. Thus in both studies, the W–P measure had a much lower correlation with IQ than did RWA. The RWA scale and the W–P Conservatism scale appear to measure a very similar underlying construct in spite of dramatic differences in question wording and format. In addition, the Conservatism scale appears to be significantly less confounded by IQ. This is not a minor matter, as pointed out previously; the original measure of authoritarianism (the F-Scale) was discredited in part because of its correlation with IQ. The correlation between the F-Scale and IQ is estimated to be between −.40 and −.50 in large representative samples (Christie, 1991; Christie & Jahoda, 1954). Scarr (Scarr & Weinberg, 1981) reported a correlation of −.35 between the F-Scale and an IQ measure made up of four WAIS subtests. Her sample ($N = 914$) consisted of the participants in a large adoption study. In spite of efforts to avoid a strong correlation with IQ, the RWA Scale, like the F-Scale before it, shares a significant amount of variance with IQ. The modest correlation between the VW–P scale and IQ shows that high correlations with IQ are not a necessary feature of social attitude measures of Conservatism. We note here that the correlation between the MPQ Traditionalism Scale and WAIS Full Scale IQ in our sample ($N = 520$) is −.26. In sum, the evidence suggests that the Conservatism scale, used in this study and the Virginia 30,000 study, reflects a valid and robust attitudinal construct that is distinct from the standard array of personality traits as well as general cognitive ability.

Table 6.6 contains the MISTRA intraclass correlations and the assortative mating coefficients for the MISTRA scales. All scales are corrected for age, sex and age * sex (McGue & Bouchard, 1984).

All the MISTRA MZA scale correlations are larger than the DZA correlations, suggesting genetic influence. For Conservatism, the DZA correlation is very close to half the MZA correlation. Thus, in spite of the high assortative mating coefficient in this sample (.60), the data suggest that a simple additive model fits the data. The one deviant correlation is the DZA correlation for Militarism (−.05). The results of model fitting the variance–covariance matrices for the corrected scores are shown in Table 6.7.

A purely environmental effects model could be rejected for all. The AE model fit total Conservatism, Sexual Conservatism, and Social Conservatism with estimates of additive genetic variance of .60, .49 and .52, respectively. Because of the slightly negative DZA correlation for Militarism, dropping dominance resulted in a poorer fit than the ADE model (zero estimate for A), but the change in χ^2 is not significantly worse. Estimates for both models are given in Table 6.7.

The discrepancy between the results of the factor analysis in the MISTRA and the Virginia study deserves comment. The MISTRA sample is composed of two somewhat different populations, a group from the United States and a group from the British Isles, New Zealand, and Australia. These two groups have grown up in societies that experience somewhat different economic and political structures, and this may be why the factor analysis produces somewhat

Table 6.6. Intraclass Correlations for Monozygotic and Dizygotic Twins Reared Apart and Spouse Interclass Correlations and their 95% Confidence Intervals on the MISTRA Wilson–Patterson Scales

Scales	MZA ($N = 54$)	DZA ($N = 46$)	Spouses ($N = 93$)
Conservatism (Total score)	.62 (.43–.76)	.29 (.00–.53)	.60 (.45–.72)
Sexual Conservatism	.51 (.28–.68)	.13 (−.16–.40)	.41 (.23–.57)
Social Conservatism	.52 (.30–.69)	.35 (.07–.58)	.53 (.37–.66)
Militarism	.55 (.33–.71)	−.05 (−.33–.24)	.57 (.41–.69)

Table 6.7. Model-Fitting Results for the MISTRA Wilson–Patterson Scales: The Standardized Maximum-Likelihood Variance Estimates and Their 95% Confidence Intervals, the χ^2 Values and the Probability Estimates and Akaike Information Statistic for the Best Fitting Model and Alternative Models (in Italics) When Model Fits Are Close

Scales	Variance Estimates			Fit Indices			
	A	D	E	χ^2	df	p	AIC
MISTRA Scales							
Conservatism	.60 (.43–.73)	—	.40 (.27–.57)	1.74	4	.78	−6.26
Sexual Conservatism	.49 (.28–.65)	—	.51 (.35–.72)	1.69	4	.79	−6.31
Social Conservatism	.52 (.33–.67)	—	.48 (.33–.67)	5.22	4	.27	−2.78
Militarism	—	*.51 (.00–.67)*	*.49 (.33–.79)*	*2.66*	*4*	*.45*	*−3.34*
Militarism	*.47 (.25–.64)*	—	*.53 (.36–.75)*	*5.13*	*4*	*.27*	*−2.87*

different subscales—some items clearly have more salience for the U.S. sample than for the non–U.S. sample. Consider the Political Preferences scale (two items: Democrats and Republicans scored in opposite directions). The spouse correlation for the United States sample is .39, whereas it is essentially zero for the full sample. School Prayers, Moral Majority, and Segregation are items that appear in the Religious Fundamentalism scale and are unlikely to be very salient for the non–U.S. sample, thus producing low alpha coefficients.

The MZA correlation for the MISTRA measure suggests a heritability of .62 for the Conservatism score. The estimate derived from model-fitting the MZA and DZA covariance matrices is .60. The heritability estimate for the full scale in the Eaves et al. (1999) study of the Virginia 30,000 (mean of males and females) is .55. As mentioned in the introduction, Martin et al. (1986) had predicted a correlation of .62 for MZA twins based on the results of the Australian twin study. Our results clearly confirm that prediction and closely approximate the Virginia findings. There are, however, differences in the details of the various studies. Our DZA correlations (.29 and .21 for the abbreviated and full length scales, respectively) are lower than the DZT correlations in Virginia (.37) and in Australia (.44), which are larger than half the MZ correlations. In both of those studies, assortative mating variance is included in the models to accommodate this fact. We found no need to incorporate assortative mating variance into our model because the DZA correlations were at or somewhat below half the MZA correlations. We were able to demonstrate that there is assortative mating in our sample (.61.) a figure similar to that reported by Eaves et al. (.62; 1999) and Feather (.68; 1978). The question therefore arises, Why was this effect absent from our data? The answer may well be sampling error, because the DZA sample is quite small. There may also be unknown biases in both the MZA and DZA samples, because they are not random samples. It may be the case, as previously mentioned for the RWA Scale, that the biological parents of adopted children are less similar on Conservatism than biological parents who marry or remain together. That is, there is much less assortative mating in the parental genera-tion of our twins who are mostly adoptees.

The heritabilities of .49, .52, and about .51 for the three subscales are not surprising given the results for the total score. We have no explanation for the essentially zero DZA correlation for Militarism except to note that the DZT and Sibling correlations for Militarism are the lowest (.23 and .20) of all the attitude measures in the Eaves et al. (1999) study as well.

In summary, we have demonstrated that the Conservatism scale measures a highly salient and valid attitudinal construct. In addition, using twins reared apart, we have replicated the general finding, based on twins in the Australian study and based on multiple kinships in the Virginia study, that the construct is significantly influenced by genetic factors.

Conclusion

The findings reported in this chapter strongly support the conclusion that well-developed and construct-valid measures of social attitudes are significantly and substantively influenced by genetic factors. Initial findings from MISTRA of genetic influence on the MMPI WRF Scale have been confirmed with data collected on MZT and DZT twins. Increased MZA sample sizes for the original measures of religiousness continue to support the hypothesis of genetic influ-ence. The subsequent inclusion in MISTRA of the Intrinsic–Extrinsic Reli-giousness Scale, which also has been shown to be influenced by genetic factors, strongly supports the construct validity of the MMPI WRF scale. We have also been able to show that the RWA and Conservatism scales are strongly influ-enced by genetic factors. Our findings with the Conservatism scale clearly replicate both the findings from the Australian Twin Registry and the huge Virginia study of 30,000 twins and their relatives.

References

Adorno, T. W., Frenkel-Brunswick, E., Levinson, D. J., & Sanford, R. N. (1950). *The authoritarian personality*. New York: Harper.

Altemeyer, B. (1981). *Right-wing authoritarianism*. Winnipeg, Canada: University of Manitoba Press.

Altemeyer, B. (1988). *Enemies of freedom*. San Francisco: Jossey-Bass.

Altemeyer, R. (1996). *The authoritarian specter*. Cambridge, MA: Harvard University Press.

Arvey, R. D., McCall, B., Bouchard, T. J., Jr., & Taubman, P. (1994). Genetic influence on job sat-isfaction and work values. *Personality and Individual Differences, 17,* 21–33.

Bouchard, T. J., Jr. (1998). Genetic and environmental influences on adult intelligence and special mental abilities. *Human Biology, 70,* 257–279.

Bouchard, T. J., Jr., & Loehlin, J. C. (2001). Genes, personality and evolution. *Behavior Genetics, 31,* 243–273.

Bouchard, T. J., Jr., McGue, M., Lykken, D. T., & Tellegen, A. (1999). Intrinsic and extrinsic religiousness: Genetic and environmental influences and personality correlates. *Twin Research, 2,* 88–98.

Bouchard, T. J., Jr., Segal, N. L., Tellegen, A., McGue, M., Keyes, M., & Krueger, R. F. (2003). Evidence for the construct validity and heritability of the Wilson–Patterson conservatism scale: A reared-apart twins study of social attitudes. *Personality and Individual Differences, 34,* 959–969.

Christie, R. (1991). Authoritarianism and related constructs. In J. P. Robinson, P. R. Shaver, & L. S. Wrightsman (Eds.), *Measures of personality and social psychological attitudes*. San Diego, CA: Academic Press.

Christie, R., & Jahoda, M. (Eds.). (1954). *Studies in the scope and method of "The authoritarian personality."* New York: Free Press.

Crelia, R. A., & Tesser, A. (1996). Attitude heritability and attitude reinforcement: A replication. *Personality and Individual Differences, 21,* 803–808.

Eagly, A. H., & Chaiken, S. (1993). *The psychology of attitudes.* San Diego, CA: Harcourt Brace Jovanovich.

Eaves, L. J., Heath, A. C., Martin, N. G., Maes, H. H., Neale, M. C., Kendler, K. S., et al. (1999). Comparing the biological and cultural inheritance of personality and social attitudes in the Virginia 30,000 study of twins and their relatives. *Twin Research, 2,* 62–80.

Eaves, L. J., Martin, N. G., Heath, A. C., Schieken, R., Meyer, J., Silberg, J., et al. (1997). Age changes in the causes of individual differences in conservatism. *Behavior Genetics, 27,* 121–124.

Feather, N. (1978). Family resemblance in conservatism: Are daughters more similar to parents than sons? *Journal of Personality, 46,* 260–278.

Finkel, D., & McGue, M. (1997). Sex differences and nonadditivity in heritability of the Multidimensional Personality Questionnaire scales. *Journal of Personality and Social Psychology, 72,* 929–938.

Goldberg, L., Tucker, D., Altemeyer, B., Dawes, R., & Rothbart, M. (1984). *The Tucker hypothesis that Liberalism/Conservatism is related to individual differences in the strength of the fundamental attribution error.* Unpublished manuscript. University of Oregon, Eugene.

Gorsuch, R. L. (1988). Psychology of religion. In M. R. Rosensweig & L. W. Porter (Eds.), *Annual Review of Psychology: Vol. 39* (pp. 201–221). Palo Alto, CA: Annual Reviews, Inc.

Hoyt, C. (1941). The reliability estimated by analysis of variance. *Psychometrika, 6,* 153–160.

Loehlin, J. C., & Nichols, R. C. (1976). *Heredity, environment, and personality: A study of 850 sets of twins.* Austin: University of Texas Press.

Lykken, D. T., Bouchard, T. J., Jr., McGue, M., & Tellegen, A. (1990). The Minnesota twin family registry: Some initial findings. *Acta Geneticae Medicae et Gemellologiae, 39,* 35–70.

Martin, N. G., Eaves, L. J., Heath, A. C., Jardine, R., Feingold, L. M., & Eysenck, H. J. (1986). Transmission of social attitudes. *Proceedings of the National Academy of Sciences USA, 83,* 4364–4368.

McCourt, K., Bouchard, T. J., Jr., Lykken, D. T., Tellegen, A., & Keyes, M. (1999). Authoritarianism revisited: Genetic and environmental influence examined in twins reared apart and together. *Personality and Individual Differences, 27,* 985–1014.

McGue, M., & Bouchard, T. J., Jr. (1984). Adjustment of twin data for the effects of age and sex. *Behavior Genetics, 14,* 325–343.

Moos, R. H., & Moos, B. S. (1994). *Family environment scale: Manual* (3rd ed.). Palo Alto, CA: Consulting Psychologists Press.

Olson, J. M., & Zanna, M. P. (1993). Attitude and attitude change. *Annual Review of Psychology, 44,* 117–154.

Scarr, S., & Weinberg, R. (1981). The transmission of authoritarianism in families: Genetic resemblance in social–political attitudes. In S. Scarr (Ed.), *Race, social class, and individual differences* (pp. 399–427). Hillsdale, NJ: Erlbaum.

Tellegen, A., Lykken, D. T., Bouchard, T. J., Jr., Wilcox, K. J., Segal, N. L., & Rich, S. (1988). Personality similarity in twins reared apart and together. *Journal of Personality and Social Psychology, 54,* 1031–1039.

Tesser, A., & Schaffer, D. (1990). Attitudes and attitude change. *Annual Review of Psychology,* 479–523.

Viswesvaran, C., & Ones, D. S. (2000). Measurement error in "Big Five Factors" personality assessment: Reliability generalization across studies and measures. *Educational and Psychological Measurement, 60,* 224–235.

Waller, N. G., Kojetin, B. A., Bouchard, T. J., Jr., Lykken, D. T., & Tellegen, A. (1990). Genetic and environmental influences on religious interests, attitudes, and values: A study of twins reared apart and together. *Psychological Science, 1,* 138–142.

Wilson, G. D. (1970). Is there a general factor in social attitudes? Evidence from a factor analysis of the Conservatism scale. *British Journal of Social and Clinical Psychology, 9,* 101–107.

Wilson, G. D. (1985). The "catch phrase" approach to attitude measurement. *Personality and Individual Differences, 6,* 31–37.

Part IV

Genetic Influences on Psychopathology

7

Bad Luck and Bad Genes in Depression

Anne Farmer

Introduction

Major technological advances have ensured that molecular genetics has dominated research activity in psychiatric disorders and behavioral traits over the past 2 decades. Some researchers have focused all their attention on "genes" and seem to regard "the environment" as that proportion of the variance in liability (to develop a particular disorder or trait) that is "left over" in calculations of the contribution of genetic risk factors and therefore as something that can be "ignored." One reason for this lack of interest is that for the most part, environmental risk factors for many disorders and traits are unknown. Also, those that are recognized make relatively small contributions to the variance compared with genetic risk factors (Jablensky & Eaton, 1995). In contrast to those who ignore the environment, Dr. Irving I. Gottesman, whose life's work we are celebrating, has always emphasized the importance of environmental risk factors and their interaction and coaction with genes in relation to both disorders and behavioral traits (Gottesman, 1991). Dr. Gottesman was among those first to point out that trying to establish the psychosocial and physical–environmental risk factors for disorders such as schizophrenia is more problematic than determining genetic risk factors. He pointed out that environmental effects do not impact as single identifiable "events" but instead act cumulatively. Although the casual observer might just see a single event as "the straw that broke the camel's back," the way in which that event affects an individual depends on several other factors. These include how the event is perceived by the individual, what events have preceded it, and the individual's vulnerability at the time the event occurred. This sequence of "evolving transactions" has been termed "epigenetic" (Gottesman & Shields, 1982; Singer & Wynne, 1965). The term *epigenetic* is defined as the "changes over time in a person's constitution (the sum total of his or her physical self) associated with the turning on and off of genes in response to changes in external and/or internal environments" (Gottesman, 1991).

In recognition of Dr. Gottesman's major contribution to research in this area, I discuss recent studies examining both genetic and environmental risk factors in major depression, where the causal role of certain types of life events is well recognized (Brown & Harris, 1978). By way of illustration, I discuss the findings from two studies that have examined life events and familiality in depression: the Camberwell Depression Study, undertaken in the mid-1980s (Bebbington et al., 1988; McGuffin, Katz, & Bebbington, 1988), and the Cardiff Depression Study, completed between 1995 and 1998 (Farmer et al., 2000). Unlike some twin studies (Kendler, Neale, Kessler, Heath, & Eaves, 1994), in which a self-report checklist method has been used to assess whether particular events have occurred, in both the Camberwell and Cardiff studies, life events were recorded following a detailed interview, the Life Events and Difficulties Schedule (LEDS; Brown & Harris, 1978), and independently rated for context by an expert panel (Brown & Harris, 1978). In addition, aspects of personality and cognitive and attributional style were examined in both studies.

Definitions of Depression

Depressive symptoms such as low mood; poor sleep, concentration, and memory; and a diminished appetite are relatively common in the general population. Fortunately, for the majority, these symptoms are transient and a full recovery occurs without a need for medical intervention (Goldberg & Huxley, 1992). When depressive symptoms cluster together or are more severe and longer lasting, it is less likely that recovery will be spontaneous and medical intervention is usually necessary. Depressive symptom clusters of sufficient severity and duration to warrant medical treatment (i.e., medication, psychotherapy, or both) are defined operationally according to DSM-IV or ICD-10 criteria as an episode of Major Depressive Disorder (MDD). The National Comorbidity Study undertaken in the United States during the early 1990s has suggested that prevalence rates of MDD in the general U.S. population were around 30% (Kessler et al., 1994); this figure is somewhat higher than figures from epidemiological studies undertaken elsewhere in the world, where rates of major depression range between 4% and 12%, depending on the definition. This suggests that the National Comorbidity Study included as cases of depression rather broader, less severe disorders than did studies undertaken elsewhere. Indeed, this discrepancy has been commented on (Regier et al., 1998) as one that could cause major problems for service organizations in the United States. Throughout his working life, Dr. Gottesman noted the importance of careful definition of the phenotype, in relation to schizophrenia in particular. Irrespective of the purpose of making a diagnosis (in this case of schizophrenia), the greater latitude provided by the use of operational criteria for assigning a diagnosis is "extremely troubling" (Gottesman, 1991, p. 34). Diagnoses based on too broad or too narrow a definition give the least useful results, especially for genetic studies. This was illustrated very clearly in a study of 120 twin subjects with schizophrenia undertaken before the era of operational definitions (Gottesman & Shields, 1972). These were assigned a diagnostic category by six diagnosticians of different persuasions ranging in their diagnostic practice from the strict to the liberal. The study showed that the most genetically informative definitions were those that were neither too strict nor too broad but rather were "middle of the road" (Gottesman & Shields, 1972). Despite these issues being pointed out in the 1970s, the problems caused by the adoption of very broad definitions of depression that have led to very high prevalence rates for the disorder are only now being addressed in the United States (Regier et al., 1998).

In the two studies, depression was (fairly narrowly) defined as follows: In the Camberwell study, depression was defined according the CATEGO computerized scoring program of the Present State Examination, version 9 (PSE-9; Wing, Cooper, & Sartorius, 1974), which employed a diagnostic system based on ICD-8 descriptions for depression. In the Cardiff study, depression was operationally defined according to ICD-10 and DSM-IV operational criteria via the use of a semistructured interview, the Schedules for the Clinical Assessment of Neuropsychiatry (SCAN; Wing et al.,1990). SCAN incorporates the most recent version of the PSE, PSE-10. Both studies also employed a severity rating system for determining the "caseness" level of depression incorporated in the CATEGO scoring algorithms of PSE-9 (and PSE-10), called the Index of Definition (ID). ID consists of eight severity levels ranging from 1, representing only minor severity, up to 8, for the most severe disorders. For both studies, caseness was determined by an ID level of 5 or greater. This represents the severity of disorder that would receive treatment from primary care physicians or psychiatrists in the UK (Wing, Mann, & Leff, 1978).

Bad Genes, Bad Luck, and Depression

There is now a considerable body of research evidence showing that genetic risk factors confer a susceptibility to develop depression when other environmental risk factors are present. Recent twin studies have shown that between 48% and 75% of the variance in liability to develop depression is contributed to by genetic risk factors (McGuffin, Katz, Watkins, & Rutherford, 1996). The remaining variance is almost all attributable to nonshared environmental factors (Kendler et al., 1994). Unlike other psychiatric disorders, one type of environmental risk factor for depression is well recognized, namely, that certain types of severe and threatening life events are causally related to episode onsets. Early research into the role of life events as precipitants of depressive episodes emphasized the impact of severe, threatening, and "independent" events, that is, the "bolt from the blue" that is unforeseen (Brown & Harris, 1978). An example of such an event is losing a job because the factory suddenly closes. However, such events are probably comparatively rare, and many of the events that trigger episodes of depression are in some way "dependent" on the individual's actions. An example of a dependent event is losing a job because one had an argument with the supervisor.

Consequently, although it is possible to attribute excess life events to simple "bad luck," there are also occasions when the individual is at least in part responsible for the events that occur. Also, as Dr. Gottesman has reminded us in his use of the term *epigenetic* (Gottesman, 1991; *vide supra*), other factors operate to enhance or diminish the impact of an event for an individual. For example, certain personality traits such as extraversion or sensation seeking could lead to an excess of life events because of the outgoing nature of such an individual. Extraverts are more likely to be attracted to risky sports, where they are more likely to be injured. It has been suggested that such individuals could be described as having "hazard-prone" personality characteristics (McGuffin et al., 1988; Farmer et al., 2000).

Experiencing a deprived or abusive upbringing or loss during childhood can also affect the way individuals views the world or their attributional style (Beck, Ward, Mendelson, Mock, & Erbaugh, 1961). This in turn determines the way bad events are interpreted and dealt with (coping style). Such past experiences can interact with personality characteristics such as neuroticism (Eysenck & Eysenck, 1975), leading to excessive concern and an inability to deal with bad events appropriately when they occur. Such individuals may also exaggerate the impact of an event and have been described as "threat perceiving" (McGuffin et al., 1988; Farmer et al., 2000).

The possibility that an individual may either exaggerate or diminish the impact of an event was recognized by the authors of the LEDS (Brown & Harris, 1978). The LEDS approach to rating events includes the decision of an independent expert panel, which rates each reported event according to "context," that is, the threat and severity of the event to "the average person." Consequently, all events rated on LEDS are scored for severity and threat according to both subjective report by the subject and the expert panel contextual consensus.

Interaction Between Genes and Adversity in Causing Depression

The interaction between genes and environmental risk factors cannot be considered as simplistic as that represented by the equation *genes + life events = depression* (Gottesman, 1991; *vide supra*). Rather, the genetic component of the etiology of depression may be operating directly in causing depression or indirectly in causing personality characteristics more likely to lead to excess, severe threatening life events. Similarly, environmental risk factors can operate both directly in precipitating an episode of depression or indirectly by influencing attributional style and coping strategies. This building up of genetic and environmental assets and liabilities has been described in relation to schizophrenia (Gottesman, 1991). Because major depression is also a polygenic multifactoral disorder, the same model can be applied. Dr. Gottesman postulated that there are a number of different types of genes and environments that pose a risk for the development of a disorder such as depression, and these he has termed genetic and environmental "liabilities." In addition, it is also possible to postulate that there may be protective genes and environments, or "assets." Because the liability to develop depression can be considered normally distributed within the general population, a "balance sheet" of genetic and environmental assets and liabilities can be drawn up.

The contributions to the different types of liability and assets have been assigned different weights to give the idea of different values of a "currency of liability." Only those individuals whose sum of assets and liabilities exceeds a threshold will manifest the signs and symptoms of the disorder (Gottesman, 1991). The Camberwell Depression Study was among the first to attempt to separate the roles of life events and family history in the etiology of depression.

The Camberwell Depression Study

The Camberwell Depression Study (CDS) examined life events, as measured using the LEDS interview approach (Brown & Harris, 1978), and family history of depression in 83 families identified via a depressed proband. The probands and their first-degree relatives were compared with a community sample for number and type of life events (Bebbington et al., 1988). As described in this chapter, all the family members included in the study were interviewed using the PSE-9 (Wing et al., 1974) and assigned to an ICD-8 diagnostic category corresponding to the categorization by the CATEGO computerized scoring program (Bebbington et al., 1988). Depressed probands were a consecutive series of depressed individuals living in the Camberwell area of south London who recently had been admitted to Maudsley Hospital for the treatment of depression. All fulfilled CATEGO-derived ICD-8 diagnostic categories for (major) depression ($N = 296$). Their ID severity rating scores ranged from 5 to 8 *(vide supra),* and all had experienced the onset of a depressive episode just prior to the interview. The community comparison group had been collected as part of a previous study (Bebbington et al., 1988) to provide rates of life events in the general population.

Depression as defined in the CDS was substantially familial, with rates in first-degree relatives of depressed probands of about 25% for the broadest definition (McGuffin et al., 1988). This compares with other studies that have demonstrated a threefold increased risk for first-degree relatives of depressed participants compared with the general population (McGuffin & Katz, 1986).

Depressed participants had experienced significantly more recent threatening life events compared with the community sample. However, the CDS also somewhat surprisingly showed that there were more severe and threatening life events even in the nondepressed relatives of the depressed participants compared with the community sample (Bebbington et al., 1988; McGuffin et al., 1988). Also, within families, exposure to life events showed only a weak association with depression. That life events are familial and are also in part genetically determined has also been shown by other authors (Plomin & Bergeman, 1991; Thapar & McGuffin, 1996). The authors of the CDS concluded that part of the association between life events and depression resulted from familial factors, which influenced both. They suggested two possible explanations: First of these was that in the families of depressed probands there is an excess of threat-perceiving personality traits. Such individuals would view the world as being a threatening and hostile place and would tend to overreact, for example by making "mountains out of mole hills" when bad things happen. Such threat-perceiving personality traits would include measures of dysfunctional attitudes (Beck, 1987; Power et al., 1994) and neuroticism (Farmer et al., 2000; McGuffin et al., 1988).

The alternative explanation of the findings of the CDS was that the excess of life events running in the families of individuals with depression was attributable to their engaging in "hazard-prone" behaviors. As discussed previously, hazard proneness would be associated with extraverted and sensation-seeking behaviors; indulgence in certain risky activities or hobbies associated with these personality characteristics are more likely to cause injury or accidents. The Cardiff Depression Study (CARDEP; Farmer et al., 2000) undertaken in Cardiff, Wales, UK, attempted to replicate the CDS and explore these issues further.

The Cardiff Depression Study

The CARDEP Study was undertaken between 1995 and 1998 and was a sibling-pair study of life events and familiality in major depression. The aims of the study were to further explore the familiality of measures of environmental adversity such as life events and to try to replicate the CDS findings of the cofamiliality of life events and depression.

Unlike the CDS, in which all first-degree relatives were interviewed, the CARDEP Study only examined pairs of siblings. The study compared 108 depressed probands (D-probands) and their nearest-aged siblings (D-sib) with 105 healthy control probands (C-proband) and their nearest-aged sibling (C-sib). Another methodological difference between the CDS and the CARDEP Study was that CARDEP D-probands were not necessarily interviewed close in time to the onset of their episode of depression. Although all D-probands were depressed at the time of interview, most were several weeks or months into an episode or had been chronically depressed for some time. However, all D-probands fulfilled ICD-10 criteria for unipolar depression (F32 and F33). They were recruited from community mental health teams, day hospitals, and inpatient psychiatric facilities in the Newport and Cardiff area of South Wales. D-probands were also recruited from among those receiving repeated antidepressant medication prescriptions from two general practitioner lists in Cardiff. The main inclusion criterion was that D-probands had to have a sibling willing to participate in the study. Depressed participants with no siblings or unwilling siblings were excluded from further study.

Age- and sex-matched C-probands were recruited via the orthopedic and dental outpatient clinics and from among employees of the University Hospital of Wales National Health Service Trust. The Trust employees were invited to participate via a request included in their pay slips. All potential control participants were screened for mental health disorders and were excluded if they had experienced current or past episodes of depression or if they did not have a sibling willing to participate. Only 65% of the D-probands were able to recruit their nearest aged sibling compared with 75% of the C-probands. This difference was statistically significant ($\chi^2 = 5.33$, $df = 1$, $p = .02$).

All participants were interviewed with SCAN and LEDS and completed a number of self-report questionnaires, including the Beck Depression Inventory (BDI; Beck et al., 1961), the Dysfunctional Attitudes Scale (DAS; Power et al., 1994), and the Sensation Seeking Questionnaire (SSQ; Zuckerman, Eysenck, & Eysenck, 1978).

The results showed that all D-probands and 20 D-sibs fulfilled ICD-10 criteria for lifetime-ever major depression (although 28 D-sibs *reported* a history of depression). Two of the C-sibs also fulfilled ICD-10 criteria for lifetime-ever depression (whereas 5 reported past depression). The relative risk (λs) of being affected for D-sibs compared with C-sibs is 9.70 (95% Confidence Interval [CI] 2.34, 40.01). This indicates that ICD-10 operationally defined depression is substantially familial (Farmer et al., 2000).

D-probands also had significantly more severe threatening life events compared with the other three participant groups, both at 3 and 12 months prior to illness onset (12 months: Analysis of variance [ANOVA] $F[3, 422 = 10.52, p < .001]$; 3 months: ANOVA $F[3,422 = 12.02, p < .001]$). The percentage of participants in each group who had experienced at least one severe and threatening event in 12 months and 3 months is also shown in Table 7.1. Significantly more D-probands had experienced at least one such event in the 12 months and 3 months prior to illness onset compared with the three other groups (12 months: Pearson's $\chi^2 = 17. 81, df = 3, p < .001$. 3 months: Pearson's $\chi^2 = 28.77, df = 3, p < .001$).

There was also a significant association between life events in the 3 months prior to illness onset and current depression in D-sibs compared with D-sibs who were not depressed. Of D-sibs who were depressed at the time of interview, 37.5% had experienced at least one severe event in the 3 months prior to illness onset compared with 7% of D-sibs who were not depressed (Yates $\chi^2 = 4.9, df = 1, p = .013$ one tailed), suggesting that prior events may precipitate depression (Farmer et al., 2000). However, there were no differences in the percentage of D-sibs who had experienced a severe threatening event compared with C-sibs, suggesting no familiality effect for experiencing these events.

There was significant familiality for life events across sibling pairs for 12- and 3-month periods (12 months: $r = .32, p < .001$; 3 months: $r = .19, p < .005$). However these significant correlations disappeared when events shared by both siblings were excluded from the analyses.

The CARDEP Study has shown that ICD-10 operationally defined depression is substantially familial and that the relative risk of the disorder in siblings of depressed probands is somewhat higher than was shown in previous studies (Tsuang & Faraone, 1990). However, the relative risk in D-sibs could be artificially inflated because of the comparatively low rate of depression in the C-sibs (Farmer et al., 2000), who had been ascertained via C-probands selected for mental health. In addition, the CARDEP Study has not confirmed the CDS findings of the familiality of life events that are only weakly associated with depression (McGuffin et al., 1988). The probable reasons for this failure to confirm the CDS findings have to do with the methodological differences between the two studies *(vide supra)*, and with the removal of obligatorily shared sibling events from the analyses in the CARDEP study (Farmer et al., 2000).

Table 7.1. Mean Number of Severe Threatening, Contextually Rated Life Events and the Percentage of Participants Experiencing at Least One Such Event in 3- and 12-Month Time Frames* for Each Participant Group

	12 months prior	12 months prior	3 months prior	3 months prior
	Mean number (SEM)	% subjects with at least event	Mean number *(SEM)*	% subjects with at least 1 event
D-probands	1.04 (0.14)**	51***	0.45 (0.07)**	31***
D-sibs	0.52 (0.09)	31	0.17 (0.05)	12
C-probands	0.36 (0.06)	29	0.10 (0.03)	9
C-sibs	0.41 (0.08)	27	0.10 (0.03)	10

Note. D-probands-depressed probands; D-sibs-siblings of depressed probands; C-probands-control probands; C-sibs-siblings of control probands; SEM-standard error of the mean. Data from "The Cardiff Depression Study: A Sib-Pair Study of Dysfunctional Attitudes in Depressed Probands and Healthy Control Subjects," by A. E. Farmer, T. Harris, K. Redman, S. Sadler, M. Mahmood, and P. McGuffin, 2000, *British Journal of Psychiatry, 176,* pp. 150–156.

*Life events were rated for the 12 months and 3 months prior to illness onset for all participants (D-probands and D-sibs) who were depressed at the time of interview, after carefully determining the timing of onset for the current episode. For all other participants, life events were rated for the 12 months and 3 months prior to interview

**D-probands experienced significantly more events for both time periods compared to the other 3 groups: 12 months: Analysis of Variance (ANOVA) $F(3, 422 = 10.52, p <.001)$. Tukey post hoc test: D-probands > D-sibs, C-probands, C-sibs; 3 months: ANOVA $F(3\ 422 = 2.05, p < .001)$. Tukey post hoc test: D-probands > D-sibs, C-probands, C-sibs.

***More D-probands had experienced at least one severe threatening contextually rated event in the 12 and 3 months prior to illness onset compared with the other three groups: 12 months: Pearson's χ^2 test $= 17.81, df = 3, p <.001$; 3 months: Pearson's χ^2 test $= 28.77, df = 3, p < .001$.

The main question that was addressed in the CARDEP Study was whether there are any personality or cognitive style measures that enhance or diminish the impact of life events in precipitating an episode of depression. An exploration of the role of different personality and cognitive style measures as possible mediating factors between the occurrence of a life event and the onset of depression will be considered next.

Threat Perceiving or Hazard Prone

The CDS findings led the authors to conclude that the relationship between life events and depression could be mediated by personality or cognitive style, leading to hazard-prone behavior or a threat-perceiving view of the world (McGuffin et al., 1988). As mentioned previously, this was further explored in the CARDEP Study. Although a number of self-report measures of personality and cognitive and attributional style were employed, in this chapter the focus is on the results for the Dysfunctional Attitudes Scale (DAS; Farmer, Harris, et al., 2001; Power et al., 1994) and the Sensation Seeking Questionnaire (SSQ; Farmer, Redman, et al., 2001; Zuckerman et al., 1978). The DAS was originally designed to measure the attitudes and beliefs underpinning a depressed cognitive style (Beck, 1987). The constructs underlying the scale are believed to indicate the vulnerability traits that interact with environmental stressors that lead to the development of depression. A shortened version the DAS-24 (Power et al., 1994) has been shown to be reliable in clinical populations and stable over time (Power et al., 1994).

The SSQ (Zuckerman et al., 1978) provides one method for measuring the risk-taking personality traits that may be associated with excess adverse events. Several versions of the SSQ are available; the version used in the CARDEP Study was version 5. It can be argued that the DAS provides a measure of threat perception, whereas the SSQ measures those aspects of personality likely to lead to hazard-prone behaviors. Both questionnaires consist of a number of subscales that are added to provide a total score. In this chapter, only the findings for the total scores on both questionnaires are considered. The Beck Depression Inventory (BDI) scores are used as the measure of mood at the time of interview, and two life-event measures are also presented in the analyses, namely, the number of severe and threatening life events (N12c) as well as the number of less severe events (N34c) contextually rated over a 12-month time frame. The mean scores on these measures for the four groups of subjects are shown in Table 7.2.

The table shows that the D-probands had significantly higher DAS scores and significantly lower SSQ scores compared with the other three groups (DAS: ANOVA $F[3\ 422 = 51.53, p < .001]$; SSQ: ANOVA $F[3\ 421] = 10.04, p < .001$). As also noted in Table 7.1, D-probands also had experienced significantly more severe and threatening life events compared with the other three groups. They had also had fewer of the less severe nonthreatening events, but there were no statistically significant differences between the participant groups for these events.

In addition, although the SSQ showed significant age and sex differences, there were no age or sex differences for DAS scores. Mean SSQ score for 140 male participants was 17.79 (95% CI 16.52, 19.06) and for 286 female participants was 13.33 (95% CI 12.54, 14.13; $t = 6.09$, $df = 424$, $p < .001$). Age was significantly negatively correlated with SSQ scores (Pearson's correlation coefficient $r = -.49$, $p < .001$). The correlations of the DAS and SSQ scores with other variables, namely BDI, N12c, and N34c, as well as across sib pairs, are shown in Table 7.3.

The table shows that the DAS is highly significantly correlated with current mood as measured by BDI and with the number of severe threatening life events over 12 months. DAS scores are not familial, however, nor are they correlated with less severe events. SSQ scores are negatively correlated with BDI score as well as positively correlated with the number of less severe rather than severe and threatening events. SSQ scores are also significantly familial.

If DAS or SSQ scores are representing traits rather than merely reflecting mood state, it would be expected that D-sibs who share genes in common with their depressed siblings would have significantly different scores from C-sibs who are related to participants (C-probands) selected for good mental health. Consequently, it might be predicted that DAS and SSQ scores in the 80 D-sibs who reported having never been depressed would be significantly different from the 100 never-depressed C-sibs. Although there

Table 7.2. Means Scores and 95% Confidence Intervals (95% CI) for Each Subject Group for Beck Depression Inventory (BDI), Dysfunctional Attitudes Scale Total Score (DASTOT), Sensation Seeking Questionnaire Total Score (SSQ), the Number of Severe Threatening (N12c), and Less Severe Life Events (N34c) Contextually Rated Over a 12-Month Time Frame

	D-probands	D-sibs	C-probands	C-sibs
Mean BDI	29.87*	7.56	4.62	5.00
(95%CI)	(27.17,32.57)	(5.77,9.36)	(3.95,5.67)	(4.03,5.97)
Mean DASTOT	102.94**	76.38	72.23	73.52
(95%CI)	(98.40,107.49)	(72.31,80.45)	(68.41,76.04)	(69.90,77.14)
Mean SSQ	12.07***	14.21	15.84	17.18
(95%CI)	(10.90,13.24)	(12.89,15.52)	(14.46,17.21)	(15.55,18.81)
N12c	1.04****	0.52	0.36	0.41
(95% CI)	(0.76,1.31)	(0.34,0.69)	(0.24,0.48)	(0.26,0.56)
N34c	1.95	2.20	2.46	2.26
(95%CI)	(1.59,2.31)	(1.88,2.53)	(2.08,2.83)	(1.86,2.66)

Note. Mean score and Confidence Interval data from "An Inventory for Measuring Depression," by A. T. Beck, C. H. Ward, M. Mendelson, J. Mock, and J. Erbaugh, 1961, *Archives of General Psychiatry, 4.* DASTOT data from "Dysfunctional Attitude Scale (DAS). A Comparison of Forms A and B and Proposals for a New Sub-Scale Version," by M. J. Power, R. Katz, P. McGuffin, C. F. Duggan, F. Lam, and A. T. Beck, 1994, *Journal of Research in Personality, 28.* SSQ data from "Sensation Seeking in England and America: Cross Cultural, Age and Sex Comparisons," by M. Zuckerman, S. Eysenck, and H. J. Eysenck, 1978, *Journal of Consulting and Clinical Psychology, 46.*

*D-probands have significantly higher BDI scores compared to the other three groups. One-way analysis of variance (ANOVA) $F(3, 418 = 183.66, p < .001)$. Tukey post hoc test: D-probands > D-sibs, C-probands, C-sibs.

**D-probands have significantly higher DASTOT scores compared to the other three groups. ANOVA: $F(3, 422 = 51.53, p < .001)$ Tukey post hoc test: D-probands > D-sibs, C-probands, C-sibs.

***D-proband have significantly lower SSQ scores compared to the C-probands and C-sibs. ANOVA: $F(3, 421) = 10.04, p < 0.001)$. Tukey post hoc test: D-probands, D-sibs < C-probands, C-sibs.

****D-probands have significantly more severe threatening life events (in 12 months) compared with the other 3 groups. ANOVA: $F(3, 422) = 10.52, p < 0.001)$. Tukey post hoc test: D-probands > D-sibs, C-probands, C-sibs.

Table 7.3. Pearson Correlation Coefficients (r) for Beck Depression Inventory (BDI) Scores, the Number of Severe Threatening (N12c) and Less Severe Nonthreatening Events (N34c) in 12 Months, and Sib Pair Correlations for the Dysfunctional Attitudes Scale (DAS) and the Sensation Seeking Questionnaire (SSQ)

	BDI	N12c	N34c	Sib pair
DAS	**.68**	**.26**	−.06	−.09
SSQ	−.22	−.01	**.20**	**.28**

Note. Correlations shown in bold are statistically significant at $p < 0.001$ (two-tailed). DAS data are from "Dysfunctional Attitude Scale (DAS). A Comparison of Forms A and B and Proposals for a New Sub-Scale Version," by M. J. Power, R. Katz, P. McGuffin, C. F. Duggan, F. Lam, and A. T. Beck, 1994, *Journal of Research in Personality, 28,* pp. 263–276. SSQ data are from "Sensation Seeking in England and America: Cross Cultural, Age and Sex Comparisons," by M. Zuckerman, S. Eysenck, and H. J. Eysenck, 1978, *Journal of Consulting and Clinical Psychology, 46,* pp. 139–149.

were no significant differences between these groups for DAS ($t = 0.47$, $df = 163.54$; Farmer, Harris, et al., 2001), never-depressed C-sibs had significantly higher SSQ scores compared with never-depressed D-sibs. Mean SSQ scores for never-depressed D-sibs = 14.20 (95% CI = 12.69, 15.70). Mean SSQ scores for never-depressed C-sibs = 17.31 (95% CI = 15.66, 18.96; $t = 2.72$, $df = 188$, $p = .007$).

These findings suggest that threat perception measures such as the DAS are more important in linking the impact of severe threatening events and depression rather than hazard-prone measures such as SSQ scores (Farmer, Harris, et al., 2001; Farmer, Redman, et al., 2001). DAS scores are not familial, however, nor are they highly significantly correlated with BDI current depression scores or significantly different in never-depressed D-sibs compared with never-depressed C-sibs. This leads to the question of whether the DAS is measuring a trait vulnerability to depression or if the questionnaire is merely capturing an aspect of the current mood state. In contrast, although the SSQ scores are familial, and significantly different in never-depressed D-sibs compared with C-sibs, the relationship between mood measures and the life events known to precipitate depression is more tenuous. Although SSQ scores are significantly negatively correlated with BDI scores, there is no correlation with the type of severe and threatening life events known to precipitate depressive onsets. To further explore the factors that influence DAS and SSQ scores, multiple regression analyses were carried out. The results of these analyses are presented next.

Multiple Regression Analyses

Multiple regression analyses of the data from the four subject groups were carried out as follows: In separate analyses, the DAS and SSQ were taken as the dependent variables. Predictor variables were age, sex, the number of severe threatening (N12c) and the number of less severe events (N34c) in a 12-month time frame, and BDI, as well as five dummy variables. These were created as follows, as dichotomous variables: 141 participants (108 D-probands and 33 siblings) had reported receiving treatment for depression. Of these, 43 were experiencing a first episode of depression (DEP1st) and 74 were currently depressed and had had an episode in the past (DEPCR). An additional 24 were well when interviewed but had been depressed in the past (DEPEV). PROSIB identified whether the participant was a proband or sibling and PRODEP whether the participant was from a depressed or control sibling pair. The predictor variables were entered into separate multiple regression analyses with DAS and SSQ respectively as dependent variables. The results are shown in Table 7.4.

The results show that for the DAS, all predictor variables apart from BDI have a small effect and are nonsignificant. In contrast, for SSQ, age, sex, whether the participant is from a depressed or control sibling pair (PRODEP), and the number of less severe life events (N34c) in 12 months are all significant predictors of SSQ scores.

Table 7.4. Multiple Regression Analysis of Dysfunctional Attitudes Scale Total Score (DASTOT) and Sensation Seeking Questionnaire Total Score (SSQ) as Dependent Variables.

DASTOT			
	Standardized coefficients (beta score)	T	Significance (p)
Constant		13.54	0.00
Sex	−0.02	−0.51	0.61
Age	−0.62	−1.69	0.09
N12c	0.05	1.37	0.17
N34c	−0.01	−0.28	0.78
BDI score	0.68	11.88	0.00
PRODEP	−0.02	−0.39	0.70
PROSIB	−0.01	−0.21	0.84
DEPEV	0.02	0.41	0.68
DEPCR	−0.00	−0.04	0.97
DEP1st	−0.07	−1.40	0.16

SSQ			
	Standardized coefficients (beta score)	T	Significance (p)
Constant		17.46	0.00
Sex	−0.29	−7.28	0.00
Age	−0.47	−11.87	0.00
N12c	0.05	1.29	0.20
N34c	0.09	2.34	0.02
BDI score	−0.05	−0.80	0.43
PRODEP	0.21	3.89	0.00
PROSIB	0.06	1.13	0.26
DEPEV	0.04	0.87	0.38
DEPCR	0.01	0.11	0.91
DEP1st	−0.02	−0.39	0.70

Note. Predictor variables are sex, age, the number of severe threatening events (N12c) and less severe life events (N34c) in 12 months, and five dummy variables: PROSIB, PRODEP, DEPEV, DEPCR, DEP1st. DASTOT data are from "Dysfunctional Attitude Scale (DAS). A Comparison of Forms A and B and Proposals for a New Sub-Scale Version," by M. J. Power, R. Katz, P. McGuffin, C. F. Duggan, F. Lam, and A. T. Beck, 1994, *Journal of Research in Personality, 28.* SSQ data are from "Sensation Seeking in England and America: Cross Cultural, Age and Sex Comparisons," by M. Zuckerman, S. Eysenck, and H. J. Eysenck, 1978, *Journal of Consulting and Clinical Psychology, 46.* PRODEP = depressed or control sibling pair; PROSIB = proband or sibling; DEPEV = past history of depression, currently well; DEPCR = currently depressed and past history of depression; DEP1st = currently depressed, no previous episode.

Conclusion

The CARDEP Study has found little evidence to support the hypothesis that dysfunctional attitudes have traitlike qualities. Although DAS scores are significantly correlated with mood and life-event measures, they are not familiar, and never-depressed D-sibs do not differ in their scores from never-depressed C-sibs. Indeed, multiple regression analysis has shown that the main influence on DAS scores is current depressed mood. These findings suggest that dysfunctional attitudes reflect present mood state rather than a familial vulnerability trait underpinning depression. Consequently, in the CARDEP Study, it appears that the DAS is merely measuring another aspect of depressed mood (Farmer, Harris, et al., 2001).

The findings for the SSQ scores are in part expected and in part somewhat unexpected. The lower SSQ scores in depressed participants, presumably a consequence of depressed individuals tending to avoid risk-taking activity, have been shown in other studies (Carton, Jouvert, Bungener, & Widlöcher, 1992), as have the significant associations with age and gender (Zuckerman, 1994). Contrary to the original hypothesis that high scores on the SSQ would generate excess severe and threatening events caused by the "hazard prone" behaviors, however, the CARDEP Study has shown that although sensation seeking is associated with high rates of life events, these pose low threat and are not the type of event noted to be associated with depressive onsets. Consequently, sensation seeking is not associated with a "hazard-prone" lifestyle and does not provide an explanation for the familial clustering of both depression and life events (Farmer, Harris, et al., 2001).

The CARDEP Study has also shown that SSQ scores are familial, and what is more striking is that the never-depressed siblings of D-probands also have significantly lower scores than the never-depressed siblings of controls. This suggests that sensation seeking in the depressed sib pairs is not low merely because of the effects of the mood state but that there is a traitlike component of low sensation seeking that runs in the families. This finding is further underscored by the results of the multiple regression analysis (see Table 7.4), which shows that the dummy variable PRODEP (coming from a depressed or control sib pair) is also a significant predictor of SSQ scores.

This poses the question, Is the SSQ capturing an aspect of an environmental or genetic "asset" in relation to depression, as posited by Dr. Gottesman in 1991 and as discussed previously? As already noted, high scorers on the SSQ have eventful rather than hazardous lives. It is possible to speculate that having personality characteristics that lead individuals to experience and deal with a lot of trivial events makes them more able to cope and manage the more severe events when they occur.

These speculations lead to further thoughts, namely, that the next step in the search for the causes of major depression should include attempts to identify individuals exhibiting "resilience." This can be done by examining participants who, despite exposure to genetic and environmental risk factors, do not develop depression. Dr. Gottesman's life's work has been dedicated to furthering our understanding of the genetic and environmental risk factors for mental disorder, and he would no doubt approve of such an approach. He has readily acknowledged the need to think laterally and try to address problems from different directions. Dr. Gottesman reminded us in *Schizophrenia Genesis* of Thomas Huxley's perspective that the tragedy of science is the "slaying of a beautiful hypothesis by an ugly fact." As Dr. Gottesman pointed out, however, such "tragedy" quickly gives way to another newer, potentially viable and more beautiful hypothesis requiring new "ugly facts" (Gottesman, 1991).

References

Bebbington, P. E., Brugha, T., McCarthy, B., Potter, J., Stuart, E., Wykes, J., et al. (1988). The Camberwell Collaborative Depression Study. 1. Depressed probands: Adversity and the form of depression. *British Journal of Psychiatry, 152,* 754–765.

Beck, A. (1987). Cognitive models of depression. *Journal of Cognitive Psychotherapy, 1,* 5–37.

Beck, A. T., Ward, C. H., Mendelson, M., Mock, J., & Erbaugh, J. (1961). An inventory for measuring depression. *Archives of General Psychiatry, 4,* 561–71.

Brown, G., & Harris, T. (1978). *Social origins of depression.* London: Tavistock Publications.

Carton, S., Jouvent, R., Bungener, C., & Widlöcher, D. (1992). Sensation seeking and depressed mood. *Personality and Individual Differences, 13,* 843–849.

Eysenck, H. J., & Eysenck, S. B. G. (1975). *Manual of the Eysenck Personality Inventory.* London: Hodder & Stourton.

Farmer, A. E., Harris, T., Redman, K., Mahmood, A., Sadler, S., & McGuffin, P. (2001). The Cardiff Depression Study: A sib-pair study of dysfunctional attitudes in depressed probands and healthy control subjects. *Psychological Medicine, 31,* 627–637.

Farmer, A. E., Harris, T., Redman, K., Sadler, S., Mahmood, A., & McGuffin, P. (2000). The Cardiff Depression Study: A sib-pair study of life events and familiality in major depression. *British Journal of Psychiatry, 176,* 150–156.

Farmer, A. E., Redman, K., Harris, T. Sadler, S., Mahmood, A., & McGuffin, P. (2001). Sensation seeking, life events and depression. The Cardiff Depression Study. *British Journal of Psychiatry, 178,* 549–552.

Goldberg, D., & Huxley, P. (1992). *Common Mental Disorders. A Bio-Social Model.* London: Routledge.

Gottesman, I. I. (1991). *Schizophrenia genesis.* San Francisco: Freeman.

Gottesman, I. I., & Shields, J. (1972). *Schizophrenia and genetics: A twin study vantage point.* New York: Academic Press.

Gottesman, I. I., & Shields, J. (1982). *Schizophrenia: The epigenetic puzzle.* New York: Cambridge University Press.

Jablensky, A., & Eaton, W. W. (1995). Schizophrenia. In A. Jablensky (Ed.), *Epidemiological psychiatry* (pp. 283–306). London: Bailliere Tindall.

Kendler, K. S., Neale, M., Kessler, R., Heath, A. C., & Eaves, L. J. (1994) The clinical characteristics of major depression as indices of familial risk to illness. *British Journal of Psychiatry, 165,* 66–72.

Kessler, R. C., McGonagle, K. A., Zhao, S., Nelson, C. B., Hughes, M., Eshleman, S., et al. (1994). Lifetime and 12 month prevalence of DSM-III-R psychiatric disorders in the United States: Results from the National Comorbidity Survey. *Archives of General Psychiatry, 51,* 8–19.

McGuffin, P., & Katz, R. (1986). Nature, nurture and affective disorder. In J. F. W. Deakin (Ed.), *The biology of depression* (pp. 26–51). London: Gaskell

McGuffin, P., Katz, R., & Bebbington, P. (1988). The Camberwell Collaborative Depression Study III. Depression and adversity in the relatives of depressed probands. *British Journal of Psychiatry, 152,* 766–774.

McGuffin, P., Katz, R., Watkins, S., & Rutherford, J. (1996). A hospital-based twin registry study of the heritability of DSM-IV unipolar depression. *Archives of General Psychiatry, 53,* 129–136.

Plomin, R., & Bergeman, C. S. (1991). The nature of nurture: Genetic influence on "environmental" measures. *Behavior and Brain Science, 14,* 373–427.

Power, M. J., Katz, R., McGuffin, P., Duggan, C. F., Lam, F., & Beck, A. T. (1994). Dysfunctional Attitude Scale (DAS). A comparison of forms A and B and proposals for a new sub-scale version. *Journal of Research in Personality, 28,* 263–276.

Regier, D. A., Kaelber, C. T., Rae, D. S., Farmer, M. E., Knauper, B., Kessler, R. C., et al. (1998). Limitations of diagnostic criteria and assessment instruments for mental disorders. Implications for Research and Policy. *Archives of General Psychiatry, 55,* 109–115.

Singer, M. T., & Wynne, L. C. (1965). Thought disorder and family relations of schizophrenics: IV Results and implications. *Archives of General Psychiatry, 12,* 201–212.

Thapar, A., & McGuffin, P. (1996). Genetic influences on life events in childhood. *Psychological Medicine, 26,* 813–820.

Tsuang, M. T., & Faraone, S. V. (1990). *The genetics of mood disorders.* Baltimore: The Johns Hopkins University Press.

Wing, J. K., Babor, T., Brugha, T., Burke, J., Cooper, J. E., Giel, R., et al. (1990). SCAN: Schedules for the clinical assessment in neuropsychiatry. *Archives of General Psychiatry, 47,* 589–593.

Wing, J. K., Cooper, J. E., & Sartorius, N. (1974). *The measurement and psychiatric symptoms.* Cambridge, UK: Cambridge University Press.

Wing, J. K., Mann, S. A., & Leff, J. (1978). The concept of a case in psychiatric population surveys. *Psychological Medicine, 8,* 203–217.

Zuckerman, M. (1994). *Behavioural expressions and biosocial basis of sensation seeking.* Cambridge, UK: Cambridge University Press.

Zuckerman, M., Eysenck, S., & Eysenck, H. J. (1978). Sensation seeking in England and America: Cross cultural, age and sex comparisons. *Journal of Consulting and Clinical Psychology, 46,* 139–149.

8

Contributions of Danish Registers to Understanding Psychopathology: Thirty Years of Collaboration With Irving I. Gottesman

Aksel Bertelsen

The Danish Registers

Denmark has been ideal for epidemiologic and genetic research because of the stability of the population and the existence of a number of effective registers. The nationwide population registers know the whereabouts of every inhabitant. The Danish people do not move about very much; the emigration rate is low, and very few people disappear. Until recently, people have been quite homogeneous, of Caucasian, mainly Nordic, ethnicity, speaking and understanding the same language, and friendly, open-minded, and easily accessible. During the last 20 to 30 years, however, this has changed. The Danish people have become more reluctant and less willing to take part in various investigations because of a change in the attitude toward registration and medical science. Furthermore, increasing red-tape restrictions make it difficult to obtain person-identifiable information from various sources. At the same time, a growing immigration of people and refugees from Southern Europe, the Near East, and other parts of the world has created a number of more or less well-integrated ethnic minorities who do not always speak the Danish language. In the 1960s and even the 1970s, it was still possible to do research with up to 90%–95% coverage of a study population, whereas it now is only possible to include about 60%. The European Union harmonization will make it even more difficult and threatens the usability and even the existence of a number of the famous Danish registers, with their rich possibilities for epidemiological research.

Dr. Bertelsen is affiliated with the WHO Collaborating Centre for Research and Training in Mental Health, the WHO Reference and Training Centre for ICD-10 Classification of Mental and Behavioural Disorders, and the WHO Reference and Training Centre for Schedules for Clinical Assessment in Neuropsychiatry (SCAN).

These registers include the Danish Central Psychiatric Register, The Twin Register, The Danish Adoption Register, The Police Register, The Register of Causes of Death, The National Patient Register, and various other registers.

The Central Psychiatric Register

The history of the Danish Central Psychiatric Register (Munk-Jørgensen & Mortensen, 1997) goes back to 1920, when it began with the Anthropological Committee, registering various disorders, including some psychiatric diseases. From 1938, the Institute of Human Genetics in Copenhagen registered mental illnesses with increasing coverage, and in 1953 began systematic registration of all admissions to the Mental State Hospitals. In 1966, the same year the ICD-8 Psychiatric Classification was brought into use, the register was transferred to the Institute of Psychiatric Demography at the Aarhus Psychiatric Hospital. In 1969, registration became electronic, based on person numbers covering all psychiatric departments and institutions, most recently (from 1994) also covering outpatient activities.

The Danish Twin Register

The Danish Twin Register (Hauge et al., 1968) was established in 1954 by Harvald and Hauge at the Institute of Human Genetics in Copenhagen, and was based there until 1967. It included all twins born from 1870 to 1910 and all same-sex twins born from 1910 to 1920. Twin pairs were collected manually from all over Denmark from the parish protocols. In 1970, the Twin Register moved to the Institute of Medical Genetics in Odense, with Hauge, who continued including twins born from 1921 to 1930. In 1991, the New Danish Twin Register was established by Kyvik (Kyvik, Green, & Nielsen, 1995) in Odense and included twins born from 1953 to 1982, with complete coverage for those born in 1968 and after, based electronically on person numbers.

The Danish Twin Register of 1967 included 30,772 same-sex pairs of twins, of which pairs unbroken before the age of 6 constituted about one third (11,288 pairs). Of these, 6723 were traced in the early 1960s, thus being age 40 or older. A questionnaire was sent to the twins themselves or to their nearest living relatives asking for information about similarities and various disorders. The traced twins were further matched with the Central Psychiatric Register, and from these two sources, the Psychiatric Twin Register was created with 395 pairs.

The Psychiatric Twin Register and Irving Gottesman

The Psychiatric Twin Register became the basis for a number of twin studies, and here it was that Irving Gottesman came into the picture. At about the same time he, together with James Shields in London, had completed the Maudsley Twin Study on Schizophrenia and published the results in *Schizophrenia and Genetics, A Twin Study Vantage Point* (Gottesman & Shields, 1972). The same year, he became a visiting professor at the University of Copenhagen, and from there visited the Institute of Psychiatric Demography in Aarhus, where Margit Fischer was doing a twin study on schizophrenia. Irving Gottesman was one of the unofficial opponents at the defense of her doctoral thesis in February 1973 (Fischer, 1973) from which time he took a kind and continued interest also in the Danish Twin Study on Manic–Depressive Disorders, upon which this author happened to be working at that time (Bertelsen, Harvald, & Hauge, 1977).

The Danish Twin Study of Schizophrenia

From these twin studies, both of which were based on personal interviews with the twins or their nearest living relatives and all available material from hospital records and various registers a few special points will be presented. At the defense for the Fischer twin study, one of the opponents, Essen-Möller, wondered why the dizygotic concordance was so high for the broad concordance of .27, compared with the morbid risk of schizophrenia and schizophrenia-related psychoses in other first-degree relatives of the twins that showed a prevalence of 7.4% with a presumed morbid risk of about 11% (see Table 8.1).

A CRITICAL REVIEW OF THE DIZYGOTIC CONCORDANCE. The monozygotic/dizygotic rate proportion was 2:1 compared with about 4–5:1 in the Maudsley twin study. No explanation was given at the dissertation defense apart from chance variation. One explanation, however, may be misclassification by the zygosity determination. This was done whenever possible by serological (blood grouping) determination from blood samples drawn from both partners of twin pairs. Because the study population was quite old, one or both partners in more than half of the pairs were deceased at the time of investigation, and the zygosity had to be determined by anthropological examination (asking the surviving twin or relatives about physical similarity of the twins) and looking at

Table 8.1.   The Danish Twin Study of Schizophrenia: Proband Concordance Rates

	Monozygotic	Same-sex dizygotic	MZ/DZ
Strict	9/25 (36%)	8/45 (18%)	2.0
Broad	14/25 (56%)	12/45 (27%)	2.1

Note. Strict concordance: cotwin schizophrenic; broad concordance: cotwin schizophrenic or schizophreniform, paranoid, or atypical psychosis. Based on "Genetic and Environmental Factors in Schizophrenia. A Study of Schizophrenic Twins and Their Families," by M. Fischer, in *Acta Psychiatrica Scandinavica Supplementum,* Vol. 238 (pp. 148–152), 1973, Copenhagen: Munksgaard.

old photos, if available. Margit Fischer was very conscientious and conservative at the anthropological evaluation and only voted for monozygosity when she was absolutely sure, creating a possibility of misclassifying some monozygotic pairs as dizygotic. For pairs with serological zygosity determination only, covering less than half of the material, proband concordance appears to be quite different, with a proportion between monozygotic and dizygotic rates of more than 6 for broad concordance and more than 4 for strict concordance. For pairs with anthropological zygosity determination only, the dizygotic rates come up at the same level as the monozygotic rates, confirming the suspicion of zygosity misclassifications (see Table 8.2).

In a survey of proband concordances allowing the calculation of a heritability index (Kendler, 1983), Fischer's study shows a remarkably low heritability. Taking only the serological zygosity determination pairs into consideration, the heritability comes up on level with other twin studies, including the latest Danish Twin Study on Schizophrenia by Ulla Kläning (Kläning, 1997) with a heritability index of .75 (see Table 8.3).

MORBID RISK IN OFFSPRING OF SCHIZOPHRENIC DISCORDANT TWINS. Margit Fischer (Fischer, 1973) was the first to investigate the morbid risk in offspring of monozygotic discordant twins following a suggestion by Luxenburger, the father of twin studies. She found a morbid risk of 9.6 among the offspring of all monozygotic schizophrenic twins and of 12.9% in the offspring of their discordant "normal" (i.e., not strictly or broadly concordant) cotwins, which she concluded looked quite similar, with no significant difference. She, however, happened to skip one secondary case, a daughter of one of the schizophrenic twins, whom she could not trace because of a misreading of the handwritten record. Irving Gottesman and I later identified and traced the person, who was schizophrenic at the time of Margit Fischer's study. Inclusion of this case

Table 8.2. The Danish Twin Study of Schizophrenia: Proband Concordance Rates, Distributed as to Serological and Anthropological Zygosity Determination

	Serological zygosity determination		
	Monozygotic	Same-sex dizygotic	MZ/DZ
Strict	7/12 (58%)	2/15 (13%)	4.5
Broad	10/12 (83%)	2/15 (13%)	6.4
	Anthropological zygosity determination only		
	Monozygotic	Same-sex dizygotic	MZ/DZ
Strict	2/13 (15%)	6/30 (20%)	0.8
Broad	4/13 (31%)	10/30 (33%)	0.9

Note. Calculated from "Genetic and Environmental Factors in Schizophrenia. A Study of Schizophrenic Twins and Their Families," by M. Fischer, in *Acta Psychiatrica Scandinavica Supplementum,* Vol. 238 (pp. 148–152), 1973, Copenhagen: Munksgaard.

Table 8.3. Heritability Index Estimation in Schizophrenic Twin Series With Proband Concordance Rates

Proband rates		Monozygotic	Dizygotic	$H_c = 1 - (C_{DZ}/C_{MZ})$
Essen-Möller				
1941–1970	Sweden	.64	.15	.77
Kallmann 1946	USA	.78	.19	.76
Slater 1953	UK	.78	.23	.71
Inouye 1961–1972	Japan	.60	.18	.70
Tienari 1963–1975	Finland	.33	.14	.57
Kringlen 1967	Norway	.45	.15	.68
Allen et al. 1972	USA	.38	.08	.78
Gottesman &				
Shields 1972	UK	.58	.12	.78
Fischer 1973	Denmark	.56 (.83)[a]	.27 (.13)[a]	.52 (.84)[a]
Kendler & Robinette				
1984	USA	.31	.07	.78
Onstad et al. 1991	Norway	.48	.04	.92
Kläning 1997	Denmark	.44	.11	.75
Cannon et al. 1998	Finland	.46	.09	.80
Franzek &				
Beckmann 1998	Germany	.65	.28	.57
Cardno et al. 1999	UK	.42	.02	.95

Note. Adapted from literature, especially "Overview: A Current Perspective on Twin Studies of Schizophrenia," by K. S. Kendler, 1983, *American Journal of Psychiatry, 140,* pp. 1413–1425, and "Twin Studies of Schizophrenia," by A. G. Cardno and I. I. Gottesman, 2000, *American Journal of Medical Genetics, 97,* pp. 12–17.
[a]Values in parentheses are for twins with serological zygosity determination

would make the schizophrenic monozygotic offspring figure even more similar, with a risk of 12.8%.

THE GOTTESMAN BERTELSEN REGISTER FOLLOW-UP STUDY OF MORBID RISK IN THE OFFSPRING OF DISCORDANT TWINS. In the mid-1980s, Dr. Irving Gottesman initiated our follow-up study on the offspring of the Fischer monozygotic twins, supplemented with a study of the offspring of the dizygotic twins, which Fischer could not do because they were too young at the time of her study. This was done as a register-based study. We were able to trace a few more offspring of schizophrenic twins, but three of the offspring of normal cotwins had to be excluded because of emigration, with inaccessibility of information. This time, a proper statistical evaluation was possible, comparing morbid risks in the offspring of the discordant monozygotic twins and dizygotic twins. In the monozygotic twins, the morbid risks were the same in the offspring of the schizophrenic and the "normal" cotwins, about 17%, the same risk as would be expected in children with one schizophrenic parent. In the dizygotic twins, the morbid risk in the offspring of the schizophrenic twins was of the same size, but in the offspring of the "normal" cotwins, was only about 2%, the same as would be expected

Table 8.4.   Morbid Risk % (MR%) of Schizophrenia and Schizophrenia-Like Psychosis in Offspring of Discordant Schizophrenic Twin Pairs

	N	S + S-like	MR%
MZ			
Schizophrenic twins	47	6	16.8
"Normal" cotwins	24	4	17.4
DZ			
Schizophrenic twins	27	4	17.4
"Normal" cotwins	52	1	2.1

Note. Age correction by the Kaplan-Meier Estimate. Data from "Confirming Unexpressed Genotypes of Schizophrenia. Risks in the Offspring of Fischer's Danish Identical and Fraternal Discordant Twins," by I. I. Gottesman and A. Bertelsen, 1989, *Archives of General Psychiatry, 46,* pp. 867–872 .

in second-degree relatives, which these offspring actually are, being nieces or nephews of the schizophrenic twins (see Table 8.4). The differences between the offspring of the "normal" MZ and DZ cotwins are statistically significant at the .05 level by unidirectional log-rank-test. Considering offspring of discordant pairs only makes no difference because it is the same morbid risks that will have to be compared: It is the morbid risks in the offspring of the discordant monozygotic and discordant dizygotic cotwins that have to be compared, not the risks in the offspring of probands and cotwins in the discordant monozygotic and dizygotic groups. We realized this point by a lucky strike of inspiration at one of our meetings in Washington Central Railroad Station.

The possible misclassification of zygosity will not influence the results substantially. The misclassification most probably will include monozygotic pairs misclassified as dizygotic by the anthropological zygosity determination, because monozygotic pairs during a lifetime often deviate more and more from their original similarity and thus in photos and in the memories of relatives become dissimilar and are not mistaken for each other anymore. The misclassified pairs most probably would appear among the concordant dizygotic pairs. If included among the discordant dizygotic pairs, they would tend to inflate the morbid risk in the offspring, which does not seem to be the case.

The results confirmed that unexpressed genotypes may be transmitted to the next generation. They further demonstrated that schizophrenia phenocopies (nongenetic phenotypes, i.e., phenotypes that imitate or copy schizophrenia but are not produced by genes) did not occur to any substantial degree, encouraging molecular research in schizophrenia. The results were published in an article in *Archives of Psychiatry* (Gottesman & Bertelsen, 1989a), which has become a frequently cited classic and a milestone in our collaboration. For this publication, the Kurt Schneider Award in 1991 was awarded to us as well as to the late Margit Fischer, honoring her posthumously.

Table 8.5. The Danish Twin Study of Manic–Depressive Disorders

	Proband concordance rates		
	Monozygotic	Same-sex dizygotic	MZ/DZ
Strict	46/69 (67%)	11/54 (20%)	3.4
Broad	60/69 (87%)	20/54 (39%)	2.2
	Bipolar proband concordance rates		
	Monozygotic	Same-sex dizygotic	MZ/DZ
Strict	27/34 (79%)	7/37 (19%)	4.2
Broad	33/34 (97%)	14/37 (38%)	2.6
	Unipolar proband concordance rates		
	Monozygotic	Same-sex dizygotic	MZ/DZ
Strict	19/35 (54%)	4/17 (24%)	2.1
Broad	27/35 (77%)	6/17 (35%)	2.2

Note. Strict concordance: cotwin manic–depressive; broad concordance: cotwin manic–depressive, other affective psychosis or affective personality disorder. Calculated from "A Danish Twin-Study of Manic–Depressive Disorders," by A. Bertelsen, B. Harvald, and M. Hauge, 1977, *British Journal of Psychiatry, 130,* pp. 346–351.

The Danish Twin Study on Manic–Depressive Disorders

Irving Gottesman then suggested that I should write a similar paper confirming unexpressed genotypes for manic–depressive disorders. The twin study of manic–depressive disorders (Bertelsen et al., 1977) was based on a diagnostic revision of the Psychiatric Twin Register, allowing a further inclusion of 42 manic–depressive pairs. The strict proband concordances of MZ (.67) and DZ (.20) were on level with other manic–depressive twin studies, but a new addition was a subdivision into unipolar and bipolar pairs, revealing a higher bipolar concordance almost reaching 100% for broad concordance (see Table 8.5).

Four of the monozygotic pairs had unipolar probands but bipolar cotwins. If they were considered genetically bipolar and transferred to the bipolar group, it would change the MZ concordance rates only slightly (to .82 for strict bipolar concordance and .48 for unipolar concordance). Bipolar-II probands (with hypomanic episodes only) had the same high MZ concordance rate as bipolar-I probands, and unipolar probands with more than three episodes had higher MZ concordance than those with fewer than three episodes, although this difference almost disappeared for broad concordance.

The concordance rates for serologically and anthropologically determined zygosity probands are very similar (see Table 8.6). This also applies if the twins are subdivided as to polarity. The anthropological determination thus seems to have had better luck in this study.

Table 8.6. The Danish Twin Study of Manic–Depressive Disorders: Proband Concordance Rates Distributed as to Serological and Anthropological Zygosity Determination

	Serological zygosity determination		
	Monozygotic	Same-sex dizygotic	MZ/DZ
Strict	23/32 (72%)	6/29 (21%)	3.4
Broad	28/32 (88%)	11/29 (38%)	2.3
	Anthropological zygosity determination		
	Monozygotic	Same-sex dizygotic	MZ/DZ
Strict	23/27 (62%)	5/25 (20%)	3.1
Broad	32/37 (86%)	9/25 (36%)	2.4

Note. Strict concordance: cotwin manic–depressive; broad concordance: cotwin manic–depressive, other affective psychosis or affective personality disorder. Based on "A Danish Twin-Study of Manic-Depressive Disorders," by A. Bertelsen, B. Harvald, and M. Hauge, 1977, *British Journal of Psychiatry, 130*, pp. 346–351.

Table 8.7. Morbid Risk % of Manic–Depressive Disorder in Offspring of Discordant MZ and DZ Manic–Depressive Twin Pairs

	N		Manic–depressive disorder	
	Total	At risk	N	MR %
MZ pairs				
Probands	47	34.9	4	11.5
Cotwins	42	30.0	5	16.7
DZ pairs				
Probands	74	46.1	5	10.8
Cotwins	103	64.3	1	1.6

Note. Age correction ad modum Strömgren.

Table 8.8. Morbid Risk % of Manic–Depressive Disorder in Offspring of Discordant MZ and DZ Unipolar Depressed Twin Pairs

	N		Manic–Depressive Disorder	
	Total	At risk	N	MR%
MZ pairs				
Probands	40	30.3	3	9.9
Cotwins	38	28.0	5	17.8
DZ pairs				
Probands	31	19.0	3	15.8
Cotwins	41	24.9	1	4.0

Note. Age correction ad modum Strömgren.

The offspring of discordant monozygotic and dizygotic manic–depressive twin pairs, when taken as a whole, seem to present similar results as for the off-spring of schizophrenic discordant pairs (see Tables 8.7 and 8.8). This, however, mainly applies to the unipolar pairs because the majority of the bipolar pairs were concordant, almost reaching 100% if broad concordance is considered. Off-spring analysis therefore is not possible for the bipolar discordant pairs.

Schizoaffective Twin Concordance

The Danish schizophrenia and manic–depressive twin series included seven pairs with schizoaffective probands, broadly defined by the presence of both prominent schizophrenic and affective symptoms. The proband concordances were .71 for monozygotic pairs and .0 for dizygotic pairs. The seven pairs included four monozygotic pairs with apparently discordant diagnoses. Fischer had two pairs in which one of the partners was schizoaffective and the other partner was schizophrenic and bipolar, respectively. In the manic–depressive group, similarly, two pairs had one partner schizoaffective with the other purely affective (Bertelsen & Gottesman, 1995). Thus, no concordant monozygotic pairs with definite diagnostic discrepancy were observed.

The proportionally high monozygotic concordance versus dizygotic con-cordance among schizoaffective twins may be explained by a combination of schizophrenia and affective genetic components, which, coming together in the monozygotic twin partners, passes a threshold and produces high con-cordance, whereas the dizygotic twin partners have a probability of one half for the presence of each locus in both twin partners, which by multiplication for several loci, produces a very low concordance (Bertelsen & Gottesman, 1995).

The Danish Dual Mating Study

Following the untimely death of Margit Fischer in 1983, Dr. Gottesman invited me to take over her part in their Dual Mating Study of mental disor-ders in the offspring of parents who both had been psychiatric inpatients. After a thorough revision, we ended up with 139 parent couples with 378 off-spring, subdivided into various diagnostic parent combination groups (Gottes-man & Bertelsen, 1989b). In the combination with both parents schizophrenic, the morbid risk of schizophrenia in the offspring was 50%. If both parents were manic–depressive, the morbid risk of manic–depressive disorder among the offspring was 67%, with a low risk of schizophrenia and schizoaffective disorder. A parent combination of schizophrenia and manic–depressive disorder did not produce a high proportion of schizoaffective offspring but mainly offspring with manic–depressive disorder and only slightly elevated risks of schizophrenia and schizoaffective disorder.

Parent combinations with reactive psychosis in one parent and schizo-phrenia, manic–depressive disorder, reactive psychosis, or any other diagno-sis in the other parent resulted in morbid risks among the offspring corresponding to those expected of those who have a parent with schizophrenia or manic–depressive disorder, and no specific heritability for reactive psychosis (Gottesman & Bertelsen, 1989b). The figures are based on a small number of combinations but are suggestive all the same.

Conclusion

What do these studies mean for psychopathology? The validity of diagnostic classification is to a major degree based on external validation from epidemiologic and genetic studies, showing where the division lines between the various categories should be drawn. In this way, the studies have contributed to demonstrate the validity of the Danish ICD-8 schizophrenia and manic–depressive disorder groups, which for most of the cases, correspond to the actual ICD-10 and DSM-IV categories. At the same time, the studies have confirmed the presence of a strong genetic factor, have identified subgroups of high heritability and penetrance, and by the discordant twin offspring results disproved the probability of a substantial degree of phenotypical heterogeneity (Gottesman & Bertelsen, 1991).

For schizoaffective disorder, the dual mating study has demonstrated that genetically, it seems to include a mixture of schizophrenia and affective genetic components, producing a majority of affective secondary cases. The schizoaffective disorder diagnosis eventually may turn out to have a low validity.

References

Bertelsen, A., & Gottesman, I. I. (1995). Schizoaffective psychoses. Genetical clues to classification. *American Journal of Medical Genetics (Neuropsychiatric Genetics), 60,* 7–11.

Bertelsen, A., Harvald, B., & Hauge, M. (1977). A Danish twin-study of manic-depressive disorders. *British Journal of Psychiatry, 130,* 330–351.

Cardno, A. G., & Gottesman, I. I. (2000). Twin studies of schizophrenia. *American Journal of Medical Genetics, 97,* 12–17.

Fischer, M. (1973). Genetic and environmental factors in schizophrenia. A study of schizophrenic twins and their families. *Acta Psychiatrica Scandinavica Supplementum* (Vol. 238, pp. 148–152). Copenhagen: Munksgaard.

Gottesman, I. I., & Bertelsen, A. (1989a). Confirming unexpressed genotypes of schizophrenia. Risks in the offspring of Fischer's Danish identical and fraternal discordant twins. *Archives of General Psychiatry, 46,* 867–872.

Gottesman, I. I., & Bertelsen, A. (1989b). Dual mating studies in psychiatry—Offspring of inpatients with examples from reactive (psychogenic) psychoses. *International Review of Psychiatry, 1,* 287–296.

Gottesman, I. I., & Bertelsen, A. (1991). Schizophrenia: Classical approaches with new twists and provocative results. In P. McGuffin & R. Murray (Eds.), *The new genetics of mental illness* (pp. 85–97). Oxford, UK: Butterworth-Heineman Ltd.

Gottesman, I. I., & Shields, J. (1972). *Schizophrenia and genetics: A twin study vantage point.* New York and London: Academic Press.

Hauge, M., Harvald, B., Fischer, M., Gotlieb Jensen, K., Juel-Nielsen, M., Raebild, I., et al. (1968). The Danish Twin Register. *Acta Geneticae Medicae et Gemellologiae, 18,* 315–332.

Kendler, K. S. (1983). Overview: A current perspective on twin studies of schizophrenia. *American Journal of Psychiatry, 140,* 1413–1425.

Kläning, U. (2000). *Schizophrenia in twins, incidence and risk factors*. Unpublished PhD dissertation, University of Aarhus, Denmark. Cited in Cardno, A. G., & Gottesman, I. I. (2000). Twin studies of schizophrenia. *American Journal of Medical Genetics, 97,* 12–17.

Kyvik, K. O., Green, A., & Nielsen, H. B. (1995). The New Danish Twin Register: Establishment and analysis of twinning rates. *International Journal of Epidemiology, 24,* 589–596.

Munk-Jørgensen, P., & Mortensen, P. B. (1997). The Danish Psychiatric Register. *Danish Medical Bulletin, 44*(1), 82–84.

9

Longitudinal Prediction of Schizophrenia in a Prospective High-Risk Study

L. Erlenmeyer-Kimling, Simone A. Roberts, and Donald Rock

Introduction

Most high-risk studies of schizophrenia started with the goal of identifying abnormalities in infancy, childhood, or adolescence that may be predictors of future illness (cf., Goldstein & Tuma, 1987; Watt, Anthony, Wynne, & Rolf, 1984). Some studies, such as our New York High-Risk Project (NYHRP), were also interested in early deficits as possible phenotypic indicators of a genetic liability to schizophrenia (Erlenmeyer-Kimling, 2000; Gottesman, 1991; Gottesman & Erlenmeyer-Kimling, 2001; Moldin & Erlenmeyer-Kimling, 1994).

The value of identifying individuals at especially increased risk to schizophrenia-related disorders (SRP), regardless of acknowledged genetic risk, has assumed a high priority in recent years, as some, though not all, studies have indicated that patients identified and treated early (before the first psychotic episode) have a better long-term prognosis than those who endure a first episode without treatment.

In this chapter, we summarize recent findings from the NYHRP (Erlenmeyer-Kimling et al., 2000) showing deficits in childhood neurobehavioral tests to be relatively good and specific predictors of adulthood schizophrenia in participants at high genetic risk and suggesting that these deficits reflect specific schizophrenia-susceptibility genes. We also consider here several other types of genetic or environmental variables that may act as nonspecific potentiators or buffers (Meehl, 1972) in influencing how the clinical expression of the illness may be affected in the presence of these specific susceptibility genes.

Research for this chapter was supported in part by MH19560 (Dr. Erlenmeyer-Kimling) from the National Institute of Mental Health, U.S. Public Health Service, and by the Office of Mental Health of the State of New York. We express appreciation to all current and previous members of the Project, as well as to the research participants, for the important roles they have played in enabling this study to continue.

Methods and Participants in the New York High-Risk Project

Detailed descriptions of the NYHRP, a longitudinal, prospective high-risk study, have been presented (Erlenmeyer-Kimling & Cornblatt, 1992; Erlenmeyer-Kimling et al., 1997; Erlenmeyer-Kimling et al., 2000; Erlenmeyer-Kimling et al., 1995). The NYHRP consists of two independent samples drawn in 1971–1972 (Sample A) and 1977–1979 (Sample B). The combined samples initially totaled 358 children ages 7 to 12 years (mean ± *SD*, 9.3 ± 1.8 years) who were offspring of schizophrenic, affectively ill, or psychiatrically normal parents and thus, respectively, at high risk for schizophrenia (HRSz) or major affective disorders (HRAff) or at low risk for these disorders (NC). Both samples have been followed to mid-adulthood, through seven rounds of neurobiological tests, interviews, questionnaires, and clinical assessments.

As previously described (Erlenmeyer-Kimling et al., 1995), mentally ill parents were identified by screening admissions to New York State psychiatric hospitals in and around New York City and were later interviewed with the SADS-L (Schedule for Affective Disorders and Schizophrenia—Lifetime Version; Spitzer & Endicott, 1978) interviews and diagnosed according to rules of the RDC (Research Diagnostic Criteria; Spitzer, Endicott, & Robins, 1978). Drs. Irving I. Gottesman, Leonard Heston, John Rainer, Michael Stone, and Jean Endicott were the expert diagnosticians who reviewed the SADS-L interviews and hospital records and reached consensus agreements on diagnoses. Normal comparison parents, drawn from the general population (Erlenmeyer-Kimling et al., 1995), were verified as not having received a psychiatric diagnosis or treatment prior to entering the study.

Follow-up into adulthood was completed on 324 offspring, who received SADS-L interviews in one or more assessment rounds, starting at age 18 years or older. Lifetime diagnoses are based on follow-up in 1995, when the offspring were on average 30.7 ± 3.3 years old (Erlenmeyer-Kimling et al., 2000), but now include follow-up to date. The present analyses include 269 offspring (79 HRSz, 57 HRAff, and 133 NC), who had both the adulthood follow-ups *and* all relevant neurobiological tests (listed later) from the initial assessment round. (Note: Any disorders first noticed and diagnosed in the seventh assessment round are disregarded here.)

Relevant childhood neurobehavioral tests, previously reported as predictors (Erlenmeyer-Kimling et al., 2000) were (a) an *Attentional Deviance Index,* based on several cognitive tests (chiefly our particular childhood version of the Continuous Performance Test), which yielded a measure of global attention (Erlenmeyer-Kimling & Cornblatt, 1992); (b) *Verbal short-term or working memory* based on the WISC (Wechsler, 1949, 1974) Digit Span subtest, considered to assess working memory (Conklin, Curtis, Katsanis, & Iacono, 2000), and a similar memory task (Erlenmeyer-Kimling & Cornblatt, 1992) with distractors; and (c) a scale of gross motor skills from an adaptation of the Lincoln-Oseretsky Test of Motor Impairment (Bialer, Doll, & Winsberg, 1974).

Meehl's (1972) well-known etiopathological model of schizophrenia suggested that the clinical expression of the illness, besides being the effect of specific susceptibility genes, may be influenced by other, nonspecific genetic or environmental factors acting as potentiators or buffers in individuals with the schizophrenia genotype. We have recently begun examining a number of childhood and early adolescent variables that might be considered potentiators or buffers. Several likely candidates (e.g., pre- and perinatal problems for the mother or child, baby's or child's physical health problems, parents' reports of childhood temperament characteristics, and handedness as a measure of lateralization) do not appear to have shown differences between HRSz participants who later developed schizophrenia-related psychoses and other members of the schizophrenia-risk group or between the HRSz and the other two risk groups in our samples. Table 9.1 lists the seven variables extensively examined to date.

Results and Discussion

Adulthood Disorders

All children in the NYHRP were free of mental retardation or any clinical expression of major psychiatric diagnoses at the time of entering the study. As indicated in Table 9.2, however, by the time of the last diagnostic assessment, only 33%, 26%, and 41% of the offspring in the HRSz, HRAff, and NC groups, respectively, remained free of any major Axis I disorder (including substance

Table 9.1. Childhood/Early Adolescent Variables Examined as Possible Potentiators

- Unplanned baby
- "Soft" neurological signs (from childhood neurological exam)—deviance calculated as **greater than 1.5 SD** from the NC Mean = .365.
- *Low verbal IQ (WISC or WISC-R)—deviance calculated as **less than** 1.5 SD from the NC Mean = 94.4.
- *Low performance IQ (WISC or WISC-R)—deviance calculated as **less than** 1.5 SD from the NC Mean = 92.4.
- Poor childhood or early adolescent social behavior
- Serious head injury before age 15
- Cluster A personality disorder (schizotypal, schizoid, paranoid—from personality disorder examination interview)

Note. NC = Offspring of normal parents; SD = Standard Deviation; WISC = Wechsler Intelligence Scale for Children; WISC-R = Wechsler Intelligence Scale for Children—Revised.
*High verbal or performance IQ = possible buffer.

Table 9.2. Adulthood Disorders in Participants With Complete Childhood Neurobehavioral Tests

Adulthood Axis I Disorders	Parental risk group		
	HRSz (N = 79)	HRAff (N = 57)	NC (N = 133)
Schizophrenia-related psychoses (SRP)	15%	7%	1%
Other Axis I disorders	52%	67%	58%
No disorder	33%	26%	41%

Note. HRSz, HRAff, NC = offspring of schizophrenic, affectively ill, and normal parents, respectively; SRP = schizophrenia-related psychosis (schizophrenia; schizoaffective disorder, mainly schizophrenia; unspecified psychosis).

abuse, anxiety disorders, and depressive disorders). Schizophrenia-related psychoses (SRP, i.e., definite schizophrenia; schizoaffective disorder, with the RDC subclassification of "mainly schizophrenia"; and unspecified psychosis) were diagnosed by the SADS-L interviews in 15%, 7%, and 0.6%, respectively, of the three offspring groups (Erlenmeyer-Kimling et al., 2000). Table 9.2 shows many of the participants without SRP to have other Axis I disorders (major affective disorders, anxiety disorders, or substance abuse disorders). Comorbidity (not indicated in the table) was frequent in the NYHRP samples.

Childhood Neurobehavioral Tests

Using logistic regression analyses and ROC (Receiver–Operator Curve) methods described previously (Erlenmeyer-Kimling et al., 2000) to define cut-points for impaired performance on each of the three childhood neurobehavioral measures, we found none of the NC participants to display deficits on any of these measures, whereas in the HRSz group, 24%, 37%, and 34% of the participants had impaired performances on the Attentional Deviance Index, Verbal Working Memory, and Gross Motor Skills, respectively. In contrast, 0%, 12%, and 9% of the HRAff participants exhibited deficits on these measures. Thus, on each childhood neurobehavioral test, significantly more HRSz children showed poor performance compared with the HRAff children.

More to the point, however, as shown previously (Erlenmeyer-Kimling et al., 2000), deficits in each of the three childhood neurobehavioral measures predict, to varying degrees, future development of SRP. Table 9.3 lists sensitivity and false-positive rates for prediction of SRP in the HRSz and HRAff groups. Sensitivity refers to the proportion of participants with future SRP who had been accurately predicted to develop the illness, based on a deviance score on the given childhood measure. "False positive" refers to the proportion of participants without future SRP who had been inaccurately predicted to develop SRP. (Because no NC participants were impaired on the childhood tests, sensitivity and false positive rates were zero for this group.)

Table 9.3. Prediction of SRP: (%) Sensitivity and False Positives Based on Childhood Neurobehavioral Tests

Childhood Neurobehavioral Tests	HRSz* (Group $N = 79$; SRP $N = 12$)		HRAff* (Group $N = 57$; SRP $N = 4$)	
	Sensitivity (SRP correctly predicted	False Positive (SRP incorrectly predicted	Sensitivity (SRP correctly predicted	False Positive (SRP incorrectly predicted
Attention Deviance	58.3	17.9	0.0	0.0
Memory	83.3	28.4	25.0	11.3
Gross motor	75.0	26.9	50.0	5.7
All 3 together	50.0	10.4	0.0**	0.0**

Note. HRSz, HRAff, NC = offspring of schizophrenic, affectively ill and normal parents, respectively; SRP = schizophrenia-related psychosis (schizophrenia; schizoaffective disorder, mainly schizophrenia; unspecified psychosis).
*For the NC group all sensitivity and false positive rates = 0%.
**No HRAff subjects were deviant on all 3 neurobehavioral tests together.

Sensitivity and false-positive rates on each test were higher for HRSz than for HRAff participants, as could be expected from the fact that HRAff participants had less overall impairment of performance. Other major Axis I disorders (not shown in the table), including affective psychoses, were not predicted by any of the childhood tests in either risk group.

As indicated in Table 9.3, within the HRSz group, there was a trade-off among the tests with respect to sensitivity and specificity (specificity = 1 minus the false-positive rate). Verbal working memory had both the highest sensitivity rate and the highest false-positive rate, meaning that although this measure was the best predictor of future SRP, it had the poorest specificity rate. Global attention had a more modest sensitivity in predicting future SRP within the HRSz group; however, it had the lowest false-positive and best specificity rates. Gross motor skills fell between verbal working memory and global attention with respect to sensitivity and specificity.

Deficits in Multiple Childhood Measures

Prediction is more safely based on a composite of measures, however, than on a single measure (Erlenmeyer-Kimling et al., 2000; Faraone et al., 1995). We have, therefore, treated the three childhood measures as a composite and counted the number on which each individual participant showed deficits. In the HRSz group, half of the SRP participants were deviant on all three childhood measures (i.e., a sensitivity rate of 50%), whereas only 10.4% of the non-SRP participants were deviant for all three. In the HRSz group as a whole, 16% of the participants (regardless of future SRP status) were deviant on one or more of the measures. Poor performance on all three together was not seen in any of the HRAff participants, further supporting the hypothesis that these deficits may be relatively specific to schizophrenia risk. This is consistent also with data on nonpsychotic adult relatives of schizophrenic probands, who display deficiencies in several neurobehavioral domains and significant correlations between deficits in different domains, compared with control participants in whom deficits in many of the studied domains tend to be more rare and correlations between problems in different domains tend to be low or nonexistent (Faraone et al., 1995; Manschreck et al., 2000; Toomey et al., 1998).

Whereas poor performance on all of the three childhood neurobehavioral tests together is limited to the HRSz group and occurs mainly in the members of that group who have later developed SRP, the 10% false-positive rate in the non-SRP participants raises a different question. Why don't *all* of the offspring of schizophrenic parents who had deficits on each of the neurobehavioral tests develop schizophrenia by adulthood, if we think of those deficits as expressions of susceptibility genes for schizophrenia? Possibly additional, relatively specific susceptibility genes, whose expressions in childhood or early adolescence either have not been explored in these analyses or have not been examined at all by the NYHRP, are present in the participants with SRP but are absent in participants who are false positive for the three measures (designated the FP3 group). We might find, in further analyses, that other neurobehavioral or personality deficits are shared by all or most of the SRP participants but are absent in the FP3 group. Another possibility is that some of the FP3 participants will later exhibit schizophrenia-related psychosis. (Note that the FP3 participants are not on average younger than the SRP participants.) A third possibility is suggested by Meehl's (1972) model of schizophrenia: Along with the expression of specific susceptibility genes, nonspecific genetic or environmental influences may act as potentiators, augmenting the risk of illness and may be present in all or the majority of SRP participants but not in most non-SRP participants, or they may act as buffers, thus reducing risk in some individuals with the schizophrenia genotype. Although all of these possibilities need to be considered, this report focuses on preliminary analyses of the third possibility, namely, on variables that may be nonspecific potentiators or buffers.

Potentiators or Buffers

Most of the variables we are exploring as possible potentiators or buffers are early background characteristics or traits that would have been present in the offspring long before any of them developed psychotic disorders. Table 9.1 listed the seven possible potentiator or buffer variables that are the focus of the present analyses.

We have thus far treated the variables as having equal effects and as being additive in the direction of potentiating the risk of SRP (rather than the reverse, with the variable acting as a possible buffer, e.g., lower IQ acting as a potentiator rather than higher IQ acting as a buffer). Thus, within the HRSz group, we formulated hypotheses about the quantitative relationships between the potentiator variables and the childhood neurobehavioral impairments as follows:

- Among the HRSz participants who developed SRP in adulthood, those with deficits on none or just one of the childhood neurobehavioral measures were expected to have quantitatively more potentiators than SRP participants with deficits on two or three neurobehavioral measures.
- Participants who were false positive on all three childhood measures (FP3) were expected to have experienced quantitatively fewer potentiators than SRP participants as a whole or SRP participants with deficits on the three neurobehavioral measures.
- FP3 participants were expected to have fewer potentiators than other non-SRP participants in the HRSz group who were deviant on two or fewer neurobehavioral tests and thus were considered to have a lower genetic liability to SRP.

The percentages of participants experiencing the individual potentiator variables listed in Table 9.1 were highest in the SRP subgroup out of all the HRSz subgroups, ranging in SRP participants from 83% (unplanned baby) to 33% (soft neurological signs). The FP3 participants had the lowest percentages on each individual potentiator, ranging from 43% to 0% for unplanned baby and soft neurological signs, respectively. The remaining non-SRP participants (who were deviant on 0–2 childhood neurobehavioral tests) from this parental group fell between the high for SRP participants and the low for FP3 participants on all variables. In the NC group (excluding the single SRP participant, who was positive only for childhood social problems and Cluster A personality disorders), unplanned baby and soft neurological signs were seen in 48% and 8% of all participants, respectively. Cluster A or "odd" cluster personality disorders (schizotypal, schizoid, paranoid) according to DSM-III-R were high in SRP participants from all parental groups. These personality disorders occurred in 22% of the non-SRP offspring of schizophrenic parents who were deviant on 0–2 childhood neurobehavioral tests but in none of the FP3 participants.

Thus, in general, the hypotheses set forth previously were borne out, at least with respect to the direction, if not the size, of the expected differences (Table 9.4). In the SRP subgroup of HRSz offspring, those with impaired performance on none or only one of the neurobehavioral tests experienced 86% and 67%, respectively, of the seven potentiators, compared with 38% and 45% experienced by SRP participants with deficits on two or three of the childhood tests. In this same parental group, among non-SRP participants, differences in the percentage of potentiators experienced were lower and showed less variation as a function of the number of impaired neurobehavioral tests, ranging from 33% for participants with no impaired neurobehavioral tests to 20% for those with impairments on all three tests (FP3s), as shown in Table 9.4. It appears, therefore, that the total *quantity* of the neurobehavioral indicators plus potentiators may be important in determining whether clinical expression of illness occurs, at least in the offspring of schizophrenic parents and for the different measures examined here. It should be noted, however, that in the small group of FP3 participants, no one experienced soft neurological signs or Cluster A personality disorders, hinting that qualitative differences may be implicated as well.

Finally, we have calculated effect sizes with respect to several types of comparisons in the NYHRP data. Our decision to use this analysis was inspired by a recent book (Heinrichs, 2001) presenting meta-analyses based on Cohen's (1988) *d* statistic to calculate effect sizes as measures of the strength of reported findings in comparisons between schizophrenic patients and normal controls with respect to neurocognitive and many other types of variables. Dr.

Table 9.4. HRSz Group: Percentage of Potentiator Variables (out of 7) Experienced by SRP and Non-SRP Participants According to Number of Impaired Childhood Neurobehavioral Tests

Number of impaired childhood neurobehavioral tests	Percentage of potentiator variables experienced	
	SRP participants ($N = 12$)	Non-SRP participants ($N = 67$)
3	45%	20%
2	38%	23%
1	67%	26%
0	86%	33%

Note. HRSz = offspring of schizophrenic parents; SRP = schizophrenia-related psychosis (schizophrenia; schizoaffective disorder, mainly schizophrenia; unspecified psychosis); potentiator variables = unplanned baby, "soft" neurological signs, verbal IQ, performance IQ, poor childhood/adolescent social behavior, head injury before 15, and Cluster A personality disorders (schizotypal, schizoid, paranoid).

Heinrichs has pointed out, however, that effect sizes are likely to be highly unstable when they are based on a single study and, particularly, one with such small numbers as we have in several subgroup cells. It is important to keep that caveat in mind.

We did, nevertheless, calculate effect sizes contrasting (a) all HRSz participants with all NC participants; (b) only those HRSz participants who developed schizophrenia-related psychoses versus all NC participants; (c) within the HRSz group, those who did versus those who did not develop SRP; (d) within the HRSz group, those who developed SRP versus participants who were false positive on all three neurobehavioral measures (FP3); and (e) within the HRSz group, those who developed SRP versus those who were deviant on none, one, or two of the childhood neurobehavioral measures.

Mostly, the effect sizes shown in Table 9.5 are reasonable, in the sense that they go in the expected direction for both neurobehavioral tests and potentiators. For example, the effect size is considerably smaller when the entire HRSz group is contrasted with the NC group than when the SRP subgroup is contrasted with the NC group. Although an effect size of 3 for the mean number of deviant neurobehavioral tests in the contrast between the SRP subgroup and the NC group as a whole seems quite strong and suggests little overlap between these two groups, the obtained value is probably somewhat inflated because of the lack of performance variability in the NC participants.

Table 9.5. Effect Sizes for Comparison of Deviance on Three Neurobehavioral Tests and Seven Potentiators

Comparison groups	Number of deviant neurobehavioral tests		Number of deviant potentiators	
	Effect size (d)	95% Confidence Interval Lower bound– Upper bound	Effect size (d)	95% Confidence Interval Lower bound– Upper bound
HRSz$_{ALL}$ vs. NC$_{ALL}$	1.13	0.89–1.37	0.86	0.60–1.11
HRSz$_{SRP}$ vs. NC$_{ALL}$	3.28	3.02–3.54	2.02	1.52–2.52
Within HRSz group				
SRP vs. Non-SRP	1.24	0.67–1.80	0.86	0.03–1.46
SRP vs. FP3	0.93	0.00–1.85	1.25	0.44–2.06
SRP vs. FP0–2	1.67	1.17–2.16	0.79	0.02–1.40

Note. HRSz, HRAff, NC = offspring of schizophrenic, affectively ill, and normal patients, respectively; SRP = schizophrenia-related psychosis (schizophrenia; schizoaffective disorder, mainly schizophrenia; unspecified psychosis); FP3 = false positives (participants deviant on all three childhood neurobehavioral tests); FP0–2 = participants deviant on 0–2 childhood neurobehavioral tests.

With greater variance in the latter group, as would undoubtedly be found in a larger sample of the general population, this effect size could well be reduced. In any event, all the other effect sizes seen in Table 9.5, although meeting our directional expectations and showing smaller quantitative effects of deviant *potentiators* than for the number of deviant *neurobehavioral* tests, indicate that there would be too much overlap between groups in any particular comparison. Within the HRSz group, comparisons of SRP participants versus non-SRP participants are also reasonable in terms of their relationships to each other; that is, for neurobehavioral tests, the largest effect size is seen for the difference between the SRP subgroup and the subgroup with deviance on 0–2 neurobehavioral tests. In contrast, the largest effect size for potentiators is between the SRP and FP3 subgroups, as expected. (See *Potentiators or Buffers.*)

Overall, the data appear to us to demonstrate that the approach of identifying impairments in multiple childhood measures and other early variables that may act as potentiators in the expression of schizophrenia susceptibility and of treating these additively can be useful. Expansion to include other carefully selected measures, traits, clinical expressions (e.g., positive or negative dimensions of thought disorder [Ott, Roberts, Allen, & Erlenmeyer-Kimling, 2002]), and possible potentiators might further sharpen the subgroup differences (effect sizes). False-positive rates are reduced by demanding evidence of deviation from more than one source (e.g., see Table 9.2, where both sensitivity and false-positive rates decreased when prediction was based on deviant performance on all three childhood neurobehavioral measures together). Prediction was best within the offspring of the schizophrenia parent group. We were not able to identify the four offspring of affectively ill parents or the one NC participant who later developed schizoaffective disorder on the basis of childhood measures taken either alone or quantitatively. We cannot, therefore, draw any conclusions about prediction from these measures or the potentiators in the general population. That question would have to be examined carefully, along with family history information, in a very large sample and would likely produce a low yield relative to the cost of such a study.

The same is true of the possible potentiators. We need to consider a larger set of them, which might lead to increasing the effect sizes for the comparisons within the HRSz group, thus enhancing the accuracy of predicting SRP. Increasing predictability in the general population, however, would require that the additional potentiators have a low base rate in the population at large.

Since the inception of the NYHRP, Dr. Gottesman has played an integral role as advisor, consultant, sometime constructive critic, and always good friend in the development of the study. It is a privilege to be able to include in this volume honoring him this chapter describing the long-term outcomes and nearly end results in a study to which Dr. Gottesman has contributed so greatly.

References

Bialer, I., Doll, L., & Winsberg, B. G. (1974). A modified Lincoln–Oseretsky motor development scale: Provisional standardization. *Perceptual & Motor Skills, 38,* 599–614.

Cohen, J. (1988). *Statistical power analysis for the behavioral sciences* (2nd ed.). New York: Academic Press.

Conklin, H. M., Curtis, C. E., Katsanis, J., & Iacono, W. G. (2000). Verbal working memory impairment in schizophrenia patients and their first-degree relatives: Evidence from the digit span task. *American Journal of Psychiatry, 157,* 275–277.

Erlenmeyer-Kimling, L. (2000). Neurobehavioral deficits in offspring of schizophrenic parents: Liability indicators and predictors of illness. *American Medical Journal, 97,* 65–71.

Erlenmeyer-Kimling, L., & Cornblatt, B. (1992). A summary of attentional findings in the New York High-Risk Project. *Journal of Psychiatric Research, 26,* 405–426.

Erlenmeyer-Kimling, L., Hilldoff-Adamo, U., Rock, D., Roberts, S. A., Bassett, A. S., Squires-Wheeler, E., et al. (1997). The New York High-Risk Project: Prevalence and comorbidity of Axis I disorders in offspring of schizophrenic parents at 25 years of follow-up. *Archives of General Psychiatry, 54,* 1096–1102.

Erlenmeyer-Kimling, L., Rock, D., Roberts, S. A., Janal, M., Kestenbaum, C., Cornblatt, B., et al. (2000). Attention, memory, and motor skills as childhood predictors of schizophrenia-related psychoses: The New York High-Risk Project. *American Journal of Psychiatry, 157,* 1416–1422.

Erlenmeyer-Kimling, L., Squires-Wheeler, E., Hilldoff-Adamo, U., Bassett, A. S., Cornblatt, B. A., Kestenbaum, C. J., et al. (1995). The New York High-Risk Project. Psychoses and cluster A personality disorders in offspring of schizophrenic parents at 23 years of follow-up. *Archives of General Psychiatry, 52,* 857–865.

Faraone, S. V., Seidman, L. J., Kremen, W. S., Pepple, J. R., Lyons, M. J., & Tsuang, M. T. (1995). Neuropsychological functioning among the nonpsychotic relatives of schizophrenic patients: A diagnostic efficiency analysis. *Journal of Abnormal Psychology, 104*(2), 286–304.

Goldstein, M. J., & Tuma, A. H. (1987). High-risk research: Editors' introduction. *Schizophrenia Bulletin, 13,* 369–371.

Gottesman, I. I. (1991). *Schizophrenia genesis: The origins of madness.* New York: W. H. Freeman.

Gottesman, I. I., & Erlenmeyer-Kimling, L. (2001). Family and twin strategies as a head start in defining prodromes and endophenotypes for hypothetical early-interventions in schizophrenia. *Schizophrenia Research, 51,* 93–102.

Heinrichs, R. W. (2001). *In search of madness, schizophrenia, and neuroscience.* New York: Oxford University Press.

Manschreck, T. C., Maher, B. A., Candela, S. F., Redmond, D., Yurgelun-Todd, D., & Tsuang, M. (2000). Impaired verbal memory is associated with impaired motor performance in schizophrenia: Relationship to brain structure. *Schizophrenia Research, 43,* 21–32.

Meehl, P. E. (1972). Specific genetic etiology, psychodynamics, and therapeutic nihilism. *International Journal of Mental Health, 1,* 10–27.

Moldin, S. O., & Erlenmeyer-Kimling, L. (1994). Measuring liability to schizophrenia: Progress report 1994: Editors' introduction. *Schizophrenia Bulletin, 20,* 25–29.

Ott, S. L., Roberts, S. A., Allen, J., & Erlenmeyer-Kimling, L. (2002). Positive and negative thought disorder and psychopathology in childhood among participants with adulthood schizophrenia. *Schizophrenia Research, 58,* 231–239.

Spitzer, R. L., & Endicott, J. R. (1978). *Schedule for affective disorders and schizophrenia, lifetime version (SADS-L)* (3rd ed.). New York: New York State Psychiatric Institute, Biometrics Unit.

Spitzer, R. L., Endicott, J. R., & Robins, E. (1978). *Research diagnostic criteria (RDC) for a selected group of functional disorders* (3rd ed.). New York: New York State Psychiatric Institute, Biometrics Unit.

Toomey, R., Faraone, S. V., Seidman, L. J., Kremen, W. S., Pepple, J. R., & Tsuang, M. T. (1998). Association of neuropsychological vulnerability markers in relatives of schizophrenic patients. *Schizophrenia Research, 31,* 89–98.

Watt, N., Anthony, E. J., Wynne, L., & Rolf, J. (1984). *Children at risk for schizophrenia: A longitudinal perspective.* New York: Cambridge University Press.

Wechsler, D. (1949). *The Wechsler Intelligence Scale for Children.* New York: The Psychological Corp.

Wechsler, D. (1974). *Wechsler Intelligence Scale for Children-Revised (WISC-R) Manual.* New York: The Psychological Corp.

10

Genes and Neurodevelopment in Schizophrenia

Hans Moises, Tómas Zoega, Linheng Li,
and Leroy Hood

Introduction

The current understanding of the origin of schizophrenia is based mainly on the genetic and the neurodevelopmental hypotheses. What is the relationship between these two etiological models? In search of an answer, we briefly review the status of knowledge in these two fields, emphasizing the importance of Dr. Irving I. Gottesman's polygenic or multifactorial threshold model; report about our association study of Notch4, a neurodevelopmental gene; and, finally, discuss an integrative model of genes and neurodevelopment in the etiology of schizophrenia.

In science, puzzles are normally solved by an evolutionary process. "The growth of our knowledge is the result of a process closely resembling what Darwin called 'natural selection'; that is, the natural selection of hypotheses . . . " explained Karl Popper, the leading philosopher of science (Popper, 1979, p. 261). Hence, the growth of knowledge of the causes of schizophrenia can be described as succeeding generations of hypotheses. In each generation, variations of hypotheses are developed. The hypothesis best fit to explain the known facts survives the selection procedure of testing.

The Darwinian Hypothesis

Early psychiatrists observed a clustering of psychoses and mental retardation in families. On the basis of these observations, Benedict Morel suggested in 1857 to split psychoses into hereditary and nonhereditary groups, thereby founding psychiatric genetics (Morel, 1857). His hereditary group included "demence precoce," the precursor of Kraeplin's dementia praecox, later termed

We thank Dr. Pall Matthiasson for the ascertainment of the Icelandic sample, Gaurang Jhala for genotyping Notch4, Professor Tómas Helgason for the management of the Icelandic part of the study and the quality control of diagnoses, and Dr. Irving I. Gottesman for his valuable help and advice. The work was supported in part by the German Research Foundation (DFG), Bonn, Germany. Correspondence should be directed to Dr. H. W. M. Moises, Department of Psychiatry, University of Kiel, Niemannsweg 147, D-24105 Kiel, Germany; E-mail: moises@psychiatry.uni-kiel.de.

schizophrenia by Eugen Bleuler. Summarizing the state of knowledge, Charles Darwin stated in 1871 in the *Descent of Man,* "Insanity and deteriorated mental powers likewise run in families" (p. 28). Darwin's new and powerful theory of evolution resulted in attempts to explain insanity as a consequence of evolutionary change. Hereditary degeneration was assumed to be the cause of schizophrenia. It was postulated that successive generations undergo progressive hereditary degeneration leading in four generations from personality traits, criminality, and psychoses to mental retardation and finally extinction of the family by infertility. Degeneration was thought to spread like cancer in the body of society, resulting in the doom of mankind. Obviously, reality is at variance with the hypothesis.

The Mendelian Hypothesis

The rediscovery of Mendel's laws of heredity in 1900 gave rise to new hope and high expectations that the Mendelian paradigm would be able to unravel the cause of schizophrenia (see Moises, 2003). Attempts were undertaken to bring family and twin data into agreement with Mendelian ratios. Several monogenic models were postulated. However, the major problem of Mendelian models of schizophrenia is that the data do not easily fit Mendelian segregation ratios for dominant or recessive inheritance (see Figure 10.1). The rapid decrease in recurrence risk from identical twins to first-degree relatives and again to the general population is not consistent with a single-gene mode of inheritance. Even the use of more sophisticated methods of modeling did not bring the data into agreement with Mendelian models of inheritance (Elston, Namboodiri, & Spence, 1978; Kay, Atkinson, & Stephens, 1975; O'Rourke, Gottesman, Suarez, Rice, & Reich, 1982; Risch & Baron, 1984; Tsuang, Bucher, & Fleming, 1982). How schizophrenia was genetically transmitted remained a mystery.

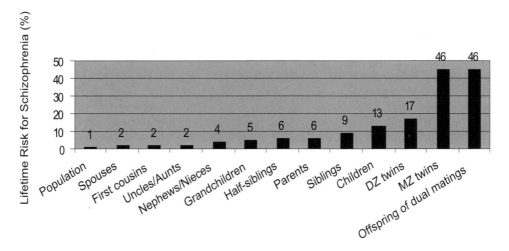

Figure 10.1. Shared susceptibility genes: summary of results of family and twin studies in schizophrenia. Adapted from *Schizophrenia Genesis: The Origins of Madness* (p. 96), by I. I. Gottesman, 1991, New York: W. H. Freeman. Copyright 1991 by I. I. Gottesman. Reprinted with permission.

The Multifactorial Threshold Model

The puzzle was moved in the direction of a solution in 1967 by Dr. Gottesman, at the University of Minnesota, in collaboration with James Shields, at London's Institute of Psychiatry. They applied a multifactorial threshold (MFT) model, following the lead of Douglas Falconer in Edinburgh working on diabetes, to their schizophrenia data and obtained a perfect fit (Gottesman & Shields, 1967). The MFT model is an important contribution of psychiatric genetics to the understanding of schizophrenia and of psychiatric disorders in general. Sometimes called a diathesis-stress model, the MFT model has since become the central paradigm in psychiatry.

The model is based on polygenic inheritance and several environmental factors. Each individual gene has little effect, but gene accumulation can greatly influence the liability to develop schizophrenia. Genetic and environmental factors contribute to the total liability (also termed susceptibility, predisposition, vulnerability, diathesis), the key concept of the MFT model. Liability is a latent (unmeasured) continuous variable (see Figure 10.2). Schizophrenia results if the total liability exceeds a certain point (threshold). Based on the MFT model, heritability between 70% and 89% has been estimated for schizophrenia (McGuffin, Owen, O'Donovan, Thapar, & Gottesman, 1994).

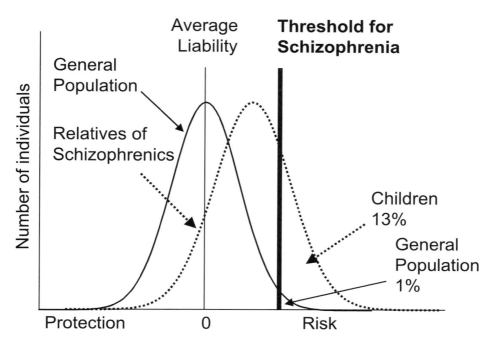

Figure 10.2. Total liability to developing schizophrenia. The multifactorial threshold model consists of several genes and environmental factors and assumes that the total liability is normally distributed in the population, such that those whose liability exceeds a certain threshold develop schizophrenia. Courtesy of Dr. Irving I. Gottesman.

The polygenic model of schizophrenia has now survived more than 30 years of testing by family, twin, adoption, and linkage studies. The first milestone in psychiatric genetics, the elucidation of the mode of genetic transmission of a major psychiatric disorder, has been achieved. However, what is inherited, schizophrenia per se or another phenotype? Family risk, association, and discordant monozygotic (MZ) twin studies attempt to find an answer to the question.

Family Risk Studies and Disease Associations

The biological relatives of schizophrenic patients have not only been found to be at an increased risk for schizophrenia, but they also show an increased frequency of schizophrenia spectrum disorders, which consist of schizophrenia, other non-affective psychoses, schizoaffective disorder, psychotic affective illness, and schizotypal, schizoid, and paranoid personality disorder. In comparison with the normal population, a large number of differences, such as personality traits (passive, anxious, restrained, socially isolated or overactive, irritable, domineering, aggressive); subclinical thought disorder; decreased attention, motor skills, communication abilities, memory, and embryonic growth rate; subcortical ventricular enlargement; multisite neural deficits; and increased incidence of soft neurological signs and of type 2 diabetes have been observed in the biological relatives of schizophrenic patients. In schizophrenic patients, negative associations have been reported with rheumatoid arthritis and cancer, as have positive associations with type 2 diabetes mellitus and tuberculosis.

Studies of family risk and disease associations lead to the conclusion that schizophrenia per se is not inherited but rather is an endophenotype (Gottesman & Gould, 2003) related to a personality phenotype, which has been termed schizoidia (Essen-Möller, 1946), schizothymia (Kretschmer, 1934), psychometric correlates of schizophrenia (Moldin, Gottesman, Rice, & Erlenmeyer-Kimling, 1991), or schizotaxia (Meehl, 1962). If personality correlates or schizotaxia, and not schizophrenia, are inherited, Gottesman and Shield's MFT model predicts that additional environmental liability factors are required for the development of the disease. In search for these environmental factors, Dr. Gottesman advocated and applied the discordant twin approach.

Discordant MZ Twin Studies

Monozygotic twins discordant for schizophrenia are genetically 100% identical. Hence, any observed differences are likely to be the result of environmental factors. In schizophrenia, discordant monozygotic twins (Gottesman, 1991) show a large number of differences before, at, and after birth in brain morphology and function, personality, cognition, and language; in intrauterine development of body and brain (Gilmore et al., 1996), birth weight, and finger ridge counts (Torrey et al., 1994); in whole-brain, frontal lobe, and hippocampus volume (Baare et al., 2001); in memory (Goldberg et al., 1993), especially long-term memory (Cannon et al., 2000); in frontal glucose metabolism (Stabenau & Pollin, 1993); in eye tracking performance (Litman et al., 1997). They also show an increase in minor physical anomalies (Torrey et al., 1994); submissiveness (Gottesman, 1991); perinatal complications, schizoid traits, personality erosion (DiLalla & Gottesman, 1995); ventricular size; and communication failure in the form of "missing information" reference (Docherty & Gottesman, 2000).

In conclusion, the results of these discordant MZ twin studies suggest that schizophrenia is a brain disease influenced by environmental factors. The environmental factors themselves, however, have not been identified yet. A hint is expected to come from the identification of liability genes for schizophrenia as a result of the Human Genome Project. The biochemical function of the liability genes should provide us with important clues about possible gene–environment interactions in schizophrenia.

The Genomic Approach

The first genome scans were completed in 1994 and 1995 by William Byerley and Hans Moises and their groups, respectively (Coon et al., 1994; Moises et al., 1995). The application of highly informative markers and a two-stage strategy by Moises et al. led to the first publication reporting significant linkage findings for a complete genome scan. At present, data from more than 60 linkage studies are available (for review, see Moises, Zoega, & Gottesman, 2002). The pooled results of these linkage studies are displayed in Figure 10.3 and reveal several potential chromosomal locations for schizophrenia liability genes.

Linkage studies are only able to identify a large chromosomal region harboring a liability gene. Such a linkage region contains a large number of genes. To find within such a region the real culprit (liability gene), allelic association (also termed linkage disequilibrium, LD) studies are employed. The LD strategy is not limited to genes within a linkage region but can also be applied to suspected liability genes, so-called candidate genes. Hence, linkage regions and claims of liability genes are not necessarily in perfect agreement. Employing population-based LD studies of candidate genes, 14 claims of liability genes for schizophrenia have been put forward (see Table 10.1.).

What might be the common denominator for the genes listed in Table 10.1 as well as for the other diverse results of schizophrenia research, such as the findings supporting the neurodevelopmental hypothesis?

The Neurodevelopmental Hypothesis

The neurodevelopmental hypothesis, broadly defined, was first proposed in the beginning of the 20th century by Emil Kraepelin and others as an explanation for neuropathological abnormalities found in the brain of some schizophrenia patients. The neurodevelopmental hypothesis of schizophrenia suggests that a disturbance of brain development during early life is causally related to the later emergence of psychosis during adulthood (McGrath, Feron, Burne, Mackay-Sim, & Eyles, 2003). The hypothesis was revived by Murray and Lewis (1987) and Weinberger (1995) to account for newer neuropathological findings. The strength of the neurodevelopmental hypothesis is in its ability to explain clinical, epidemiological, neuropathological, and imaging findings in schizophrenia.

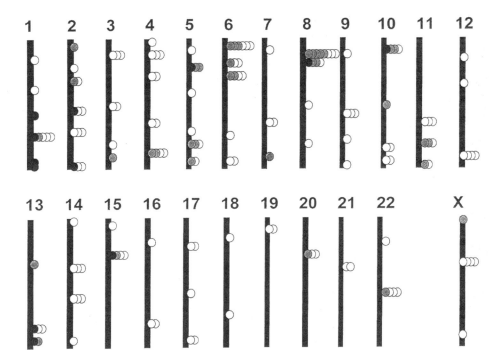

Figure 10.3. Linkage results show that schizophrenia is a complex multigenic disorder as suggested by Gottesman and Shields (1967). The data were compiled from 60 peer-reviewed linkage studies of schizophrenia (as of May 2002). Each dot represents evidence for linkage obtained in an independent sample. The level of significance is shown according to the criteria of Lander and Kruglyak (1995). Black indicates significant (lod score ≥ 3.6) evidence; gray, suggestive (lod score ≥ 2.2) evidence; and white hints ($p \leq 0.05$) for linkage. From *BMC Psychiatry* (http://www.biomedcentral.com/1471-244X/2/8). Copyright 2002 by H. W. Moises, T. Zoega, and I. I. Gottesman. Used with permissions. Published by Biomed Central.

Schizophrenic patients display neurological soft signs such as dysdiado-chokinesia, poor tandem walk, finger–thumb opposition and articulation, increased minor physical anomalies, and dermatoglyphic asymmetry. Children who later develop schizophrenia show multisite neural deficits, increased incidence of soft neurological signs, decreased motor skills, delayed attainment of developmental milestones, and behavioral and intellectual abnormalities (for review, see Boks, Russo, Knegtering, & van den Bosch, 2000).

Several epidemiological findings in schizophrenia, such as an increase in maternal virus infections (e.g. Rantakallio, Jones, Moring, & Von Wendt, 1997), winter births (e.g. McGrath & Welham, 1999), obstetric complications, and low birth weight (e.g., McNeil, Cantor-Graae, & Weinberger, 2000), are compatible with the neurodevelopmental hypothesis.

Neurons in the brains of schizophrenic patients are sometimes misplaced, mis-sized or disorganized without gliosis (Arnold, 2000), which is the scar tissue that develops when the brain reacts to a large variety of insults, including injuries of the developing brain, by the proliferation of astrocytes, the most abundant cells of the CNS. The damaged or lost brain tissue is replaced by a brain-specific scar

Table 10.1.   Postulated Liability Genes for Schizophrenia

Gene symbol	Authors
CHRNA7	Freedman et al., 2001
COMT	de Chaldee et al., 1999; Wonodi et al. 2003
DISC 1 & 2, GRM5	Millar et al., 2000; Devon et al., 2001
DTNBP1	Straub et al., 2002
hKCa3/KCNN3	Dror et al., 1999
HTR2A	Williams et al., 1996
HTR5A	Iwata, Ozaki, & Goldman, 2001
NOTCH4	Wei & Hemmings, 2000
NRG1	Moises, 2001; Moises, Mathiasson, et al., 2002; Moises, Zoega, et al., 2002; Stefansson, Sarginson, et al., 2003; Stefansson, Sigurdsson, et al., 2002; Yang, Si, & Zhang, 2002 Williams et al., 2003
NT-3	Jonsson et al., 1997
PRODH2	Liu et al., 2002
RHD	Palmer et al., 2002
RGS4	Chowdari et al. 2002
WKL1	Meyer et al., 2001

tissue, called gliosis, which consists of astrocytes, a subgroup of glial cells. Volume reductions of gray matter of the whole brain (3%), most pronounced in the temporal lobe (6%) and the amygdala/hippocampal complex (5.5%), as well as enlargements of ventricles (36%), have consistently been described in schizophrenia (for review, see Shenton, Dickey, Frumin, & McCarley, 2001).

NOTCH4 Association Study

NOTCH4 is a neurodevelopmental gene localized within the proximal part of the HLA region (Li et al., 1998) on chromosome 6p21.3, in close proximity to two markers (D6S273 and D6S291), which showed evidence for linkage to schizophrenia in our 1995 genome scan (Moises et al., 1995). As follow-up to our initial linkage finding, we have undertaken an association study of NOTCH4 in a schizophrenia sample from Iceland. As we were completing our work, Wei and Hemmings (2000) reported highly significant evidence for association between NOTCH4 and schizophrenia. The results of our Icelandic association study are briefly presented here.

Polymorphic microsatellite markers were isolated from a genomic library of the NOTCH4 locus. For genotyping, a CTG repeat polymorphism within exon 1 was selected (Li et al., 1998). In 1996, we performed a two-locus lod score analysis between NOTCH4 and markers of the area (D6S291, D6S273, D6S306, D6S274) in four Icelandic multiplex families described elsewhere (Moises et al., 1995) to see whether the NOTCH4 gene could explain our linkage finding of schizophrenia with D6S273 and D6S291. A highly significant lod score of 9.4 was obtained for D6S273 (θ = 0.00), making NOTCH4 an interesting enough candidate gene for schizophrenia to warrant further investigations. In the search for an allelic association, 132 schizophrenic patients from Iceland and one of their parents as controls were investigated. Lifetime diagnoses of schizophrenia were given according to DSM-III-R using information obtained from structured interviews (SADS-LB), from relatives, and from medical records. Genotyping was performed blindly with regard to diagnostic status using an automated DNA sequencer. The Transmission–Disequilibrium Test (TDT) as implemented by Clayton (1999) in the program Transmit (version 2.5.2) was employed for statistical analysis. Dr. Gottesman was part of the project. The results are given in Table 10.2.

Our lack of significant evidence for allelic association between schizophrenia and the CTG repeat polymorphism of NOTCH4 is in agreement with the results of Imai et al. (2001), McGinnis et al. (2001), Sklar et al. (2001), Ujike et al. (2001), and Fan et al. (2002) and in disagreement with the finding of Wei and Hemmings (2000). The latter authors obtained, using TDT, a highly significant allelic association between schizophrenia and the NOTCH4 locus in 80 patients ($p = .0000078$). Given the extensive locus and allelic heterogeneity in polygenic disorders, a high degree of replication cannot necessarily be expected in genome scans and associations studies of schizophrenia. To sum up, genetic, environmental, and neurodevelopmental factors appear to be involved in the pathogenesis of schizophrenia. How these factors interact to cause schizophrenia, however, remains unknown.

An Integrative Model

A unifying hypothesis has recently been proposed by Moises (2001) and Moises, Zoega, et al. (2002). Based on a co-localization of loci approach and a large amount of circumstantial evidence, it was postulated that a functional deficiency of glial growth factors and of growth factors produced by glial cells should cause synaptic destabilization and, later in life, increase the probability of developing schizophrenia. The glial deficiency hypothesis is in agreement with other schizophrenia hypotheses, e.g., the polygenic, epigenetic, viral, nicotinergic, glutamate, synaptic plasticity, and neurodevelopmental hypotheses. Additional evidence supporting the hypothesis can be obtained from a recent review by Davis et al. (2003). Figure 10.4 depicts the hypothesis in the form of the multifactorial-threshold model for schizophrenia developed by Gottesman and Shields (1967).

Table 10.2. Results of Association Study Between Schizophrenia and the CTG Repeat Polymorphism Within Exon 1 of NOTCH4

Allele	Observed	Expected	Var. (O–E)	χ^2 ($df = 1$)	p value
1	7	6.67	0.71	0.16	.69
2	14	18.00	3.00	5.33	.02
3	81	75.06	10.82	3.26	.07
4	116	115.37	15.59	0.025	.86
5	9	8.71	2.84	0.029	.86
6	12	15.53	4.99	2.49	.11
7	1	0.67	0.22	0.51	.48

Note. Global χ^2 test = 9.87 ($df = 6$), $p = 0.13$.

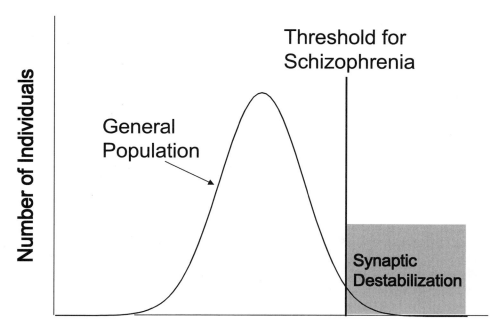

Figure 10.4. Glial and synaptic weakness: The glial and synaptic deficiency hypothesis of schizophrenia. From Biomed Central (http://www.biomedcentral.com/1471-244X/2/8). Copyright 2002 by H. W. Moises, T. Zoega, and I. I. Gottesman. Used with permission. Published by Biomed Central.

The common denominator for the genes listed in Table 10.1 seems to be their involvement in glial or synaptic functioning (Moises, Zoega, et al. 2002). Glial cells play important roles in the developing as well as in the mature adult central nervous system (CNS). In the adult CNS, glial cells, especially astroglia, have supportive, protective, regenerative, and active regulatory roles. In adults, they induce neurogenesis in the hippocampus and the sub-ventricular zone, influence neuronal activity and synaptic strength, and appear to be the third partner in synaptic transmission (tripartite synapse). Synaptic strength and cellular growth depend on the synaptic and the general protein-synthesis rate, which is influenced by growth factors such as neu-rotrophins and neuregulins. Glial cells are part of a positive feedback loop between presynaptic neurons and their postsynaptic targets involving neu-rotrophins and neuregulins.

The glial and synaptic deficiency hypothesis postulates that several genes and environmental factors influence the positive feedback loop between the presynaptic neuron and its target cells and assumes that the baseline strength of synaptic connections is normally distributed in the general population. The strength of the growth signaling correlates with the efficacy and stability of the synaptic connection. A genetically and epigenetically determined low baseline of glial growth factor signaling and synaptic strength, which might be termed glial and synaptic asthenia, is expected to increase the vulnerability for additional reductions (e.g., by viruses infecting glial cells). This should lead to a weakening of the positive feedback loop between the presynaptic neuron and its targets, and, below a certain threshold, to synaptic destabilization and schizophrenia.

The hypothesis suggests glial cells as the locus of the genes–environment interactions in schizophrenia, with glial asthenia as an important factor for the liability to the disorder. This integrative model is able to explain the majority of research findings in schizophrenia. Nevertheless, it is still only a working hypothesis, which might not survive further testing.

The longest survivor of any schizophrenia hypothesis is the genetic hypothesis. It has now survived 146 years of testing since its invention by Bénédict Morel in 1857 for demence precoce. Although Mendelian hypotheses of schizophrenia failed, the first milestone in the understanding of the etiology of schizophrenia was achieved in 1967 by Gottesman and Shield's multifactorial threshold model. The MFT model has now survived 36 years of testing by family, twin, adoption, linkage and association studies and therefore is most likely correct. We all owe tribute to Dr. Gottesman for his groundbreaking contribution, which gave us the intellectual framework for a better understanding not only of the genesis of schizophrenia but of psychiatric disorders in general.

References

Arnold, S. E. (2000). Cellular and molecular neuropathology of the parahippocampal region in schizophrenia. *Annals of the New York Academy of Science, 911,* 275–292.

Baare, W. F., van Oel, C. J., Hulshoff Pol, H. E., Schnack, H. G., Durston, S., Sitskoorn, M. M., et al. (2001). Volumes of brain structures in twins discordant for schizophrenia. *Archives of General Psychiatry, 58,* 33–40.

Boks, M. P., Russo, S., Knegtering, R., & van den Bosch, R. J. (2000). The specificity of neurological signs in schizophrenia: A review. *Schizophrenia Research, 43,* 109–116.

Cannon, T. D., Huttunen, M. O., Lonnqvist, J., Tuulio-Henriksson, A., Pirkola, T., Glahn, D., et al. (2000). The inheritance of neuropsychological dysfunction in twins discordant for schizophrenia. *American Journal of Human Genetics, 67,* 369–382.

Chowdari, K. V., Mirnics, K., Semwal, P., Wood, J., Lawrence, E., Bhatia, T., et al. (2002). Association and linkage analyses of RGS4 polymorphisms in schizophrenia. *Human Molecular Genetics, 11,* 1373–1380.

Clayton, D. (1999). A generalization of the transmission/disequilibrium test for uncertain-haplotype transmission. *American Journal of Human Genetics, 65,* 1170–1177.

Coon, H., Jensen, S., Holik, J., Hoff, M., Myles-Worsley, M., Reimherr, F., et al. (1994). Genomic scan for genes predisposing to schizophrenia. *American Journal of Medical Genetics, 54,* 59–71.

Darwin, C. (1882). *The descent of man and selection in relation to sex.* London: John Murray.

Davis, K. L., Stewart, D. G., Friedman, J. I., Buchsbaum, M., Harvey, P. D., Hof, P. R., et al. (2003). White matter changes in schizophrenia: Evidence for myelin-related dysfunction. *Archives of General Psychiatry, 60,* 443–456.

de Chaldee, M., Laurent, C., Thibaut, F., Martinez, M., Samolyk, D., Petit, M., et al. (1999). Linkage disequilibrium on the COMT gene in French schizophrenics and controls. *American Journal of Medical Genetics, 88,* 452–457.

Devon, R. S., Anderson, S., Teague, P. W., Muir, W. J., Murray, V., Pelosi, A. J., et al. (2001). The genomic organisation of the metabotropic glutamate receptor subtype 5 gene, and its association with schizophrenia. *Molecular Psychiatry, 6,* 311–314.

DiLalla, D. L., & Gottesman, I. I. (1995). Normal personality characteristics in identical twins discordant for schizophrenia. *Journal of Abnormal Psychology, 104,* 490–499.

Docherty, N. M., & Gottesman, I. I. (2000) A twin study of communication disturbances in schizophrenia. *Journal of Nervous and Mental Disease, 188,* 395–401.

Dror, V., Shamir, E., Ghanshani, S., Kimhi, R., Swartz, M., Barak, Y., et al. (1999). hKCa3/KCNN3 potassium channel gene: Association of longer CAG repeats with schizophrenia in Israeli Ashkenazi Jews, expression in human tissues and localization to chromosome 1q21. *Molecular Psychiatry, 4,* 254–260.

Elston, R. C., Namboodiri, K. K., & Spence, M. A. (1978). A genetic study of schizophrenia pedigrees. II. One-locus hypotheses. *Neuropsychology, 4,* 193–206.

Essen-Möller, E. (1946). The concept of schizoidia. *Monatschrift für Psychiatrie und Neurologie, 112,* 258–271.

Fan, J. B., Tang, J. X., Gu, N. F., Feng, G. Y., Zou, F. G., Xing, Y. L., et al. (2002). A family-based and case-control association study of the NOTCH4 gene and schizophrenia. *Molecular Psychiatry, 7,* 100–103.

Freedman, R., Leonard, S., Gault, J. M., Hopkins, J., Cloninger, C. R., Kaufmann, C. A., et al. (2001) Linkage disequilibrium for schizophrenia at the chromosome 15q13-14 locus of the alpha7-nicotinic acetylcholine receptor subunit gene (CHRNA7). *American Journal of Medical Genetics, 105,* 20–22.

Gilmore, J. H., Perkins, D. O., Kliewer, M. A., Hage, M. L., Silva, S. G., Chescheir, N. C., et al. (1996). Fetal brain development of twins assessed in utero by ultrasound: Implications for schizophrenia. *Schizophrenia Research, 19,* 141–149.

Goldberg, T. E., Torrey, E. F., Gold, J. M., Ragland, J. D., Bigelow, L. B., & Weinberger, D. R. (1993). Learning and memory in monozygotic twins discordant for schizophrenia. *Psychological Medicine, 23,* 71–85.

Gottesman, I. I. (1991). *Schizophrenia genesis: The origins of madness.* New York: W. H. Freeman.

Gottesman, I. I., & Gould, T. D. (2003). The endophenotype concept in psychiatry: Etymology and strategic intentions. *American Journal of Psychiatry, 160,* 636–645.

Gottesman, I. I., & Shields, J. (1967). A polygenic theory of schizophrenia. *Proceedings of the National Academy of Sciences USA, 58,* 199–205.

Imai, K., Harada, S., Kawanishi, Y., Tachikawa, H., Okubo, T., & Suzuki, T. (2001). The (CTG)n polymorphism in the NOTCH4 gene is not associated with schizophrenia in Japanese individuals. *BMC Psychiatry, 1*(1), 1. Retrieved September 24, 2003, from http://www.biomedcentral.com/1471-244X/1/1

Iwata, N., Ozaki, N., & Goldman, D. (2001). Association of a 5-HT(5A) receptor polymorphism, Pro15Ser, to schizophrenia. *Molecular Psychiatry, 6,* 217–219.

Jonsson, E., Brene, S., Zhang, X. R., Nimgaonkar, V. L., Tylec, A., Schalling, M., et al. (1997). Schizophrenia and neurotrophin-alleles. *Acta Psychiatrica Scandinavica, 95,* 414–419.

Kay, D. W. K., Atkinson, M. W., & Stephens, D. A. (1975). Genetic hypotheses and environmental factors in the light of psychiatric morbidity in the families of schizophrenics. *British Journal of Psychiatry, 127,* 109–118.

Kretschmer, E. (1934). *Kretschmer's textbook of medical psychology.* London, UK: Oxford University Press.

Lander, E., & Kruglyak, L. (1995). Genetic dissection of complex traits: Guidelines for interpreting and reporting linkage results. *Nature Genetics, 11,* 241–247.

Li, L., Huang, G. M., Banta, A. B., Deng, Y., Smith, T., Dong, P., et al. (1998). Cloning, characterization, and the complete 56.8-kilobase DNA sequence of the human NOTCH4 gene. *Genomics, 51,* 45–58.

Litman, R. E., Torrey, E. F., Hommer, D. W., Radant, A. R., Pickar, D., & Weinberger, D. R. (1997). A quantitative analysis of smooth pursuit eye tracking in monozygotic twins discordant for schizophrenia. *Archives of General Psychiatry, 54,* 417–426.

Liu, H., Heath, S. C., Sobin, C., Roos, J. L., Galke, B. L., Blundell, M. L., et al. (2002). Genetic variation at the 22q11 PRODH2/DGCR6 locus presents an unusual pattern and increases susceptibility to schizophrenia. *Proceedings of the National Academy of Sciences USA, 99,* 3717–3722.

McGinnis, R. E., Fox, H., Yates, P., Cameron, L. A., Barnes, M. R., Gray, I. C., et al. (2001). Failure to confirm NOTCH4 association with schizophrenia in a large population-based sample from Scotland. *Nature Genetics, 28,* 128–129.

McGrath, J. J., Feron, F. P., Burne, T. H., Mackay-Sim, A., & Eyles, D. W. (2003). The neurodevelopment hypothesis of schizophrenia: A review of recent developments. *Annals of Medicine, 35,* 86–93.

McGrath, J. J., & Welham, J. L. (1999). Season of birth and schizophrenia: A systematic review and meta-analysis of data from the Southern Hemisphere. *Schizophrenia Research, 35,* 237–242.

McGuffin, P., Owen, M. J., O'Donovan, M. C., Thapar, A., & Gottesman, I. I. (1994). *Psychiatric genetics.* London: The Royal College of Psychiatrists, Gaskel.

McNeil, T. F., Cantor-Graae, E., & Weinberger, D. R. (2000). Relationship of obstetric complications and differences in size of brain structures in monozygotic twin pairs discordant for schizophrenia. *American Journal of Psychiatry, 157,* 203–212.

Meehl, P. E. (1962). Schizotaxia, schizotypy, schizophrenia. *American Psychologist, 17,* 827–838.

Meyer, J., Huberth, A., Ortega, G., Syagailo, Y. V., Jatzke, S., Mossner, R., et al. (2001). A missense mutation in a novel gene encoding a putative cation channel is associated with catatonic schizophrenia in a large pedigree. *Molecular Psychiatry, 6,* 302–306.

Millar, J. K., Wilson-Annan, J. C., Anderson, S., Christie, S., Taylor, M. S., Semple, C. A., et al. (2000). Disruption of two novel genes by a translocation co-segregating with schizophrenia. *Human Molecular Genetics, 9,* 1415–1423.

Moises, H. W. (2001). Human Genome data analyzed by an evolutionary method suggests a decrease in protein-synthesis rate as cause of schizophrenia and an increase as antipsychotic mechanism. ArXiv e-Print archive at Cornell University. Retrieved September 24, 2003, from http://xxx.arXiv.cornell.edu/abs/cond-mat/0110189

Moises, H. W. (2003). Psychoses. In I. I. Gottesman (Sec. Ed.), *Nature encyclopedia of the human genome* (Vol. 4, pp. 923–929). London: Macmillan.

Moises, H. W., Matthiasson P., Zoega, T., Jhala, G., Yang, L., Gottesman, I. I., et al. (2002) Neuregulin 1 strongly implicated as susceptibility gene for schizophrenia by allelic association study. ArXiv e-Print archive at Cornell University. Retrieved September 24, 2003, from http://xxx.arXiv.cornell.edu/abs/cond-mat/0203527v1 and from http://xxx.arXiv.cornell.edu/abs/cond-mat/0203527

Moises, H. W., Yang, L., Kristbjarnarson, H., Wiese, C., Byerley, W., Macciardi, F., et al. (1995). An international two-stage genome-wide search for schizophrenia susceptibility genes. *Nature Genetics, 11,* 321–324.

Moises, H. W., Zoega, T., & Gottesman, I. I. (2002) The glial growth factors deficiency and synaptic destabilization hypothesis of schizophrenia. *BMC Psychiatry, 2,* 8. Retrieved September 24, 2003, from http://www.biomedcentral.com/1471-244X/2/8

Moldin, S. O., Gottesman, I. I., Rice, J. P., & Erlenmeyer-Kimling, L. (1991). Replicated psychometric correlates of schizophrenia. *American Journal of Psychiatry, 148,* 762–767.

Morel, B. A. (1857). *Traité des dégénérescence physique, intellectuelles et morales de l'espèce humaine.* Paris: Baillière.

Murray, R. M., & Lewis, S. W. (1987). Is schizophrenia a neurodevelopmental disorder? *British Medical Journal (Clinical Research Edition), 295,* 681–682.

O'Rourke, D. H., Gottesman, I. I., Suarez, B. K., Rice, J., & Reich, T. (1982). Refutation of the general single-locus model for the etiology of schizophrenia. *American Journal of Human Genetics, 34,* 630–649.

Palmer, C. G. S., Turunen, J. A., Sinsheimer, J. S., Minassian, S., Paunio, T., Lonnqvist, J., et al. (2002). RHD maternal-fetal genotype incompatibility increases schizophrenia susceptibility. *American Journal of Human Genetics, 71,* 1312–1319.

Popper, K. (1979) *Objective knowledge: An evolutionary approach.* Oxford, UK: Clarendon Press.

Rantakallio, P., Jones, P., Moring, J., & Von Wendt, L. (1997). Association between central nervous system infections during childhood and adult onset schizophrenia and other psychoses: A 28-year follow-up. *International Journal of Epidemiology, 26,* 837–843.

Risch, N., & Baron, M. (1984). Segregation analysis of schizophrenia and related disorders. *American Journal of Human Genetics, 36,* 1039–1059.

Shenton, M. E., Dickey, C. C., Frumin, M., & McCarley, R. W. (2001). A review of MRI findings in schizophrenia. *Schizophrenia Research, 49,* 1–52.

Sklar, P., Schwab, S. G., Williams, N. M., Daly, M., Schaffner, S., Maier, W., et al. (2001). Association analysis of NOTCH4 loci in schizophrenia using family and population-based controls. *Nature Genetics, 28,* 126–128.

Stabenau, J. R., & Pollin, W. (1993). Heredity and environment in schizophrenia, revisited. The contribution of twin and high-risk studies. *Journal of Nervous and Mental Disease, 181,* 290–297.

Stefansson, H., Sarginson, J., Kong, A., Yates, P., Steinthorsdottir, V., Gudfinnsson, E., et al. (2003). Association of neuregulin 1 with schizophrenia confirmed in a Scottish population. *American Journal of Human Genetics, 72,* 83–87.

Stefansson, H., Sigurdsson, E., Steinthorsdottir, V., Bjornsdottir, S., Sigmundsson, T., Ghosh, S., et al. (2002). Neuregulin 1 and susceptibility to schizophrenia. *American Journal of Human Genetics, 71,* 877–892.

Straub, R. E., Jiang, Y., MacLean, C. J., Ma, Y., Webb, B. T., Myakishev, M. V., et al. (2002). Genetic variation in the 6p22.3 gene DTNBP1, the human ortholog of the mouse dysbindin gene, is associated with schizophrenia. *American Journal of Human Genetics, 71,* 337–348.

Torrey, E. F., Taylor, E. H., Bracha, H. S., Bowler, A. E., McNeil, T. F., Rawlings, R. R., et al. (1994). Prenatal origin of schizophrenia in a subgroup of discordant monozygotic twins. *Schizophrenia Bulletin, 20,* 423–432.

Tsuang, M. T., Bucher, K. D., & Fleming, J. A. (1982). Testing the monogenic theory of schizophrenia: An application of segregation analysis to blind family study data. *British Journal of Psychiatry, 140,* 595–599.

Ujike, H., Takehisa, Y., Takaki, M., Tanaka, Y., Nakata, K., Takeda, T., et al. (2001). NOTCH4 gene polymorphism and susceptibility to schizophrenia and schizoaffective disorder. *Neuroscience Letters, 301,* 41–44.

Wei, J., & Hemmings, G. P. (2000). The NOTCH4 locus is associated with susceptibility to schizophrenia. *Nature Genetics, 25,* 376–377.

Weinberger, D. R. (1995). From neuropathology to neurodevelopment. *Lancet, 346,* 552–557.

Williams, J., Spurlock, G., McGuffin, P., Mallet, J., Nöthen, M. M., Gill, M., et al. (1996). Association between schizophrenia and T102C polymorphism of the 5- hydroxytryptamine type 2a-receptor gene. European Multicentre Association Study of Schizophrenia (EMASS) Group. *Lancet, 347,* 1294–1296.

Williams, N. M., Preece, A., Spurlock, G., Norton, N., Williams, H. J., Zammit, S., et al. (2003) Support for genetic variation in neuregulin 1 and susceptibility to schizophrenia. *Molecular Psychiatry, 8,* 485–487.

Wonodi, I., Stine, O. C., Mitchell, B. D., Buchanan, R. W., & Thaker, G. K. (2003) Association between Val[108/158] met polymorphism of the *COMT* gene and schizophrenia. *American Journal of Medical Genetics, 120B,* 47–50.

Yang, J., Si, T., & Zhang, D. (2002, April 14–17). The candidate genes might associate with symptoms of schizophrenia. 7th HUGO's International Human Genome Meeting (HGM), Poster Session, Shanghai, China. Poster No. 378. Abstract retrieved April 17, 2002, from http://hgm2002.hgu.mrc.ac.uk/Abstracts/Publish/WorkshopPosters/WorkshopPoster07/hgm0378.htm

Part V

Molecular Genetics and the Future of the Field

11

Spinach and Ice Cream: Why Social Science Is So Difficult

Eric Turkheimer

Introduction

The nature–nurture debate has entered the postbiometric era. A generation ago, it seemed to behavioral geneticists and their opponents that the outcome of the nature–nurture debate depended on whether or not biometric research designs analyzing covariation among twins, adoptees, and other family members would reveal substantial genetic contributions to important domains of human behavior. That research has now been conducted, with nearly unanimous results: Variation in all behavior, including everything from schizophrenia (Gottesman, 1994) to marital status (McGue & Lykken, 1992; Turkheimer, Lovett, Robinette, & Gottesman, 1992), has a genetic component.

I have summarized the consistent outcome of a generation of behavioral genetic research as "The Three Laws of Behavioral Genetics," stated simply as follows (Turkheimer, 2000):

1. Everything is heritable.
2. The environmental effect of being raised in the same family is substantially smaller than the genetic effect and is often close to zero.
3. Most behavioral variability remains in the error term after genetic effects and the effects of being raised in the same family have been accounted for.

These findings are no longer in serious dispute. What remains is to understand what they mean for the development of human behavior.

The unanimous outcome of biometric family research has led to a realignment of historical positions on both sides of the nature–nurture debate. On one side, traditional population-based behavioral genetics finds itself somewhat exhausted by its own success. For years, the bread and butter of behavioral genetic research consisted of demonstrations of heritability for one behavior after another, each appearing less likely than the last: schizophrenia (Gottesman &

Shields, 1972), intelligence (Cardon & Fulker, 1993), and personality (Loehlin, 1993) were followed by job satisfaction (Arvey, McCall, Bouchard, Taubman, & Cavanaugh, 1994), religiosity (Waller, Kojetin, Lykken, Tellegen, & Bouchard, 1990; Bouchard et al., this volume), and television watching (Plomin, Corley, DeFries, & Fulker, 1990). As it has become apparent that some degree of heritability is practically inevitable, behavioral geneticists have had to turn to other frontiers, most notably multivariate biometric methods (Plomin, 1986) and molecular genetics (Gottesman, 1997; McGuffin, Riley, & Plomin, 2001). Although the prospects for multivariate behavioral genetics and molecular behavioral genetics are both matters of intense and controversial theoretical interest (Turkheimer, 2000; Turkheimer, Goldsmith, & Gottesman, 1995; Turkheimer & Gottesman, 1991), this chapter will place greater emphasis on the challenges faced by environmental social science in the postbiometric era.

On the environmental side, the idea that variability in almost all human behavior has a detectable genetic component no longer evokes the controversy it once did. Most environmentally oriented social scientists are willing to accept the idea that human characteristics such as intelligence, personality, and psychopathology are transmitted in part along genetic pathways (Bronfenbrenner & Ceci, 1994). The controversy that remains concerns the role of the environment. Although modern behavioral geneticists contend that their methods and results are environment-friendly, leaving plenty of variability unexplained after genetic variation has been credited, environmentalists, as a group, have remained dissatisfied (Maccoby, 2000). Why? If the simple fact of genetic "influence" (to use the geneticists' catchall term for the innumerable and largely unknown ways in which gene products can exert causal effects on complex human behavior) no longer troubles environmentalists and if the behavioral-genetic models leave room for environmental influence on behavior, what do contemporary environmentalists have to worry about? Why not do as the behavioral geneticists suggest and render the geneticists what is theirs, leaving environmentalism with its own domain, a domain no longer confounded with genetic variability?

This chapter examines the remaining sources of environmentalist dissatisfaction with behavioral genetic claims, seeks to understand them in terms of some little-examined aspects of population genetic methodology, describes simulations of complex gene–environment systems that reproduce some of the more puzzling results of twin and adoption studies, and offers some recommendations for how the remaining differences between environmentalists and behavioral geneticists might be resolved. I begin by characterizing some of the new alignments of hereditarianism and environmentalism that have been necessitated by the three laws of behavioral genetics.

Nonshared Environmentalism

Behavioral geneticists are correct when they assert that biometric results have not excluded environmental variability from the developmental picture, but the environment has been included in a different form than had been anticipated. In its simplest form, the biometric model partitions phenotypic variability into three components: the additive effect of genes (A), the environment that is shared among family members (C), and the environment that is not shared among family members (E). The shared environment refers to environmental effects that serve to make children reared in the same family more similar; nonshared environment tends to make them different. Most environmentally oriented work in the social sciences—what Rowe (1994) has termed "socialization science"—has focused on the effects of families on children, that is, on the shared environment. If having a depressed mother has a discernible environmental effect on the personality of children, then multiple children reared by the same depressed mother should be similar along this dimension, and the similarity of siblings within such families would be reflected in the biometric variance component attributable to the shared environment.

During the last 15 years, Robert Plomin and his colleagues have argued that environmentalists' historical focus on the shared environment is incorrect (Dunn & Plomin, 1990; Plomin & Daniels, 1987; Rowe & Plomin, 1981). As summarized by the second law of behavioral genetics, biometric components attributable to the shared environment are very difficult to find when appropriate genetic controls are employed. After genetic similarity has been accounted for, biological siblings often appear no more similar than individuals chosen at random from the population. For practically all behavioral traits, monozygotic (MZ) twins are nearly twice as similar as dizygotic (DZ) twins (if not more than twice as similar, which is an indication that something is awry in the twin model, a phenomenon that will be investigated later). Correlations between adoptive parents and children are usually much smaller than correlations between biological parents and children (Braungart, Fulker, & Plomin, 1992). The biometric implication is that little or no variability can be attributed to the shared environment. Nevertheless, genetically identical monozygotic twins usually show substantially less than perfect similarity for these same behavioral traits, so something must account for the residual dissimilarity.

Although the assertion that the residual variability in biometric models can be attributed to systematic effects of the nonshared environment is plausible, it must be noted that the evidence for the claim is still very incomplete. Traditional biometric models of twins and adoptees only demonstrate that a substantial proportion of phenotypic variability cannot be accounted for by the systematic effects of additive genotype or shared environment; they do not demonstrate conclusively that the remaining variability is attributable to the nonshared environment, unless the term "nonshared environment" is applied very loosely.

Direct evidence that nonshared environmental events are the cause of nonshared environmental variability must come from studies that include specific measures of the nonshared environment. Since the publication of Plomin and Daniels (1987), there has been a proliferation of studies of this type, which Mary Waldron and I (Turkheimer & Waldron, 2000) have reviewed. The conclusions to be drawn from this literature are crystal clear: Although the variance component called *nonshared environment* is indeed a substantial component of most behavioral variability, the specific effects of measured environmental variables cannot come close to accounting for it (Turkheimer & Waldron, 2000). Furthermore, when traditional biometric designs are generalized to the multivariate case, nonshared environment is found to contribute to univariate variability but not to multivariate covariability among variables (Waldron & Turkheimer, 2000). Both genes and environment constitute the variability in behavioral measures; for the more compelling question of why variables are related to each other, only genes seem to matter.

Developmentalism

One important contemporary line of opposition to behavioral genetics finds its source not in environmentalist social science but in embryology and developmental biology. Historically, theoretical considerations in developmental biology have not focused on the sources of variation in phenotypic individual differences but rather on the viability of distinctions between inborn and acquired characters, or, in embryology, between preformationist and epigenetic accounts of ontogenesis (Oyama, 1985). The predominant modern view is that there is less than meets the eye to distinctions among biological, native, or instinctual characteristics on the one hand and learned or acquired characters on the other. All biological characteristics, according to this account, emerge out of a matrix of developmental interactions between biological and environmental elements, and because both are required for all development, neither can be more fundamental than the other for any particular phenotype.

Developmental biologists with this kind of outlook have always been suspicious of the variance partitioning methods of behavioral geneticists, which appear to violate their insistence on the unity of biology and environment in development and their preference for concrete ontological processes over statistical variance partitioning. Most recently, Gilbert Gottlieb has undertaken the task of extending these arguments from developmental biology to a full-fledged attack on the methodology of behavioral genetics. Replies to some of Gottlieb's objections to behavioral genetics already appear in print (Turkheimer & Gottesman, 1991; Turkheimer, Goldsmith, & Gottesman, 1995), and I only outline the position in this chapter. (For a firsthand account, see Gottlieb, 1991, 1992, 1995, and, for another consideration of the developmentalist position, see Schaffner, 1998).

The basis of the developmentalists' case against behavioral genetics is not to deny that genes play a significant role in the development of behavior, as past environmentalists have argued, but rather to contend that the intricate ontological interplay of genes and environments in development cannot be captured by the mathematics of population genetic research methods. According to the developmentalists, the goal of developmental science is to specify what Gottlieb calls the "developmental processes" that lead to behavioral phenotypes. Developmentalists can point to many carefully specified theories of behavioral development in animals (e.g., Gottlieb's 1985 studies of ducklings) that they contrast unflatteringly with the variance partitioning of behavioral genetics. What do we learn about the development of personality, they might ask, by noting that 40% of phenotypic variability is "explained" by variation in the genotype (Bouchard & Loehlin, 2001)? They offer a radical answer: nothing at all.

Some skepticism about the causal or etiological content of behavioral genetic models may well be warranted, but it would be a significant overreaction to abandon behavioral genetics entirely, as developmentalists sometimes urge. Behavioral genetics has played an important role in demonstrating that radical environmentalism was incorrect, and it would be foolhardy to allow reasonable criticisms of population genetic research methods to lead us back to a time when correlations between biological parents and their children were naively accepted as unalloyed indicators of sociocultural transmission. Moreover, the successes of experimental animal psychology have been in the explanation of species-typical behavior in lower animals, whereas socialization science and behavioral genetics are more focused on individual differences in humans (i.e., personality, intelligence, and psychopathology; Scarr, 1995; Turkheimer & Gottesman, 1991), and it remains to be demonstrated how experimental methods from one domain can be applied to the other. Many, if not most, conclusive animal experiments cannot be performed with humans for obvious ethical reasons. It is still an open question whether multivariate behavioral genetics and molecular behavioral genetics will overcome Gottlieb's objections by providing a quasi-experimental bridge between population-based variance partitioning and causally specified developmental models. Finally, it must be remembered that—thanks to all of these methodological difficulties— there are no solid developmentalist theories of human individual differences to contrast with behavioral-genetic models. The theories that do exist are socioenvironmental, and they are every bit as correlational as the genetic ones.

Antisocialization Theorists

Some theorists have taken the biometric results of twin and adoption studies at face value and concluded that the reason family environment explains little or no variance in twin or adoption studies is just what it seems: It is because parenting and other aspects of normal families have few if any long-term causal effects on children. The preeminent theorist of this kind is Sandra Scarr, whose 1992 presidential address to the Society for Research in Child Development was the apotheosis of decades of behavioral-genetic successes and galvanized a generation of environmentalists in opposition. Scarr (Scarr & McCartney, 1983) suggested that genes drive experience, by which she means that the most important aspects of the environment are those that are actively sought out by organisms and that organisms seek out environments according to their genotype. So the environments that families provide don't much matter, as long as rearing conditions are "good enough" for the child to be able to seek out environments according to his or her genetic endowment. According to Scarr, environmental variability predominates within families because of the accrual of gene–environment correlation during development. As children, driven by their genotype, seek out suitable environments and evoke genotype-appropriate responses from their caregivers, environment and genotype become increasingly correlated within families, so genetic differences among siblings are magnified by the environmental differences they evoke.

More recently, somewhat similar theories have been advanced by behavior geneticist David Rowe and developmental psychologist Judith Rich Harris. Rowe (1994) documented the refusal of traditional socialization science to take seriously the methodological consequences of behavioral genetics, the ongoing failure to detect substantial shared environmental effects when genetic variance is appropriately controlled, and what he views as the disappointing results of environmental intervention programs. Harris' (1998) theory focused less on genetics than on the transient and context-specific effects of the environment. Families matter as long as children remain in the context of the family, but as children grow, they are increasingly exposed to environments outside the family, environments that are to a large degree of their own choosing, as Scarr emphasized. This consideration led Harris to focus on the role of peer groups in the determination of childhood behavior.

Where Things Stand

The three positions outlined in this chapter each offer a more subtle view of the role of genes and environment in development than was implied by the genes versus environment face-off of the old nature–nurture controversy, but a great deal remains to be resolved. Everyone agrees that genes and environment must combine in some way to produce development, but consensus does not extend very far beyond this developmental cliché. The positions remain at odds because to one degree or another, they continue to cling to the old-fashioned contest between nature and nurture for supremacy in developmental models. Developmentalists make a plausible accounting of the shortcomings of population-based behavioral genetics for the explanation of the developmental mechanisms of behavior, but despite their proclamations of gene–environment integration in development, they give in to the environmentalist temptation to conclude that the consequences of genetic variability for behavior can safely be ignored. Antisocialization theorists, conversely, have used the surprisingly consistent, and consistently genetic, outcome of biometric family studies to argue that the shared effects of childrearing practices can safely be ignored. A domain of discourse in which it is seriously contended that either normal family environment or the methods of population genetics are of little relevance to the explanation of human development is in need of some new possibilities, and the goal of this chapter is to provide some.

Methods

The remainder of this chapter reports the results of a series of simulations of the interactions of genes and environment in development. (An earlier version of the method was described in Turkheimer & Gottesman, 1996; source code for the computer programs is available from the author.) The simulations take place in a two-dimensional space, which is illustrated in Figure 11.1A.

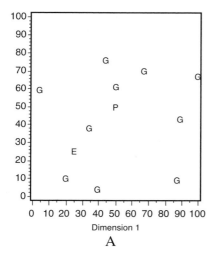

A

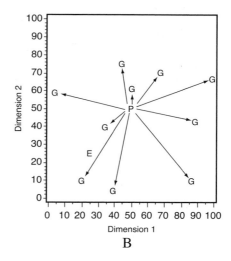

B

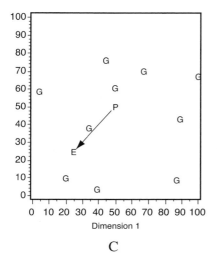

C

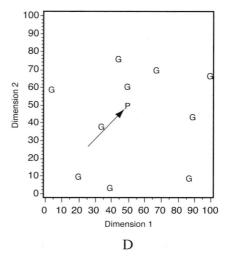

D

Figure 11.1. (A) Initial configuration of system. "G" = genes; "E" = environment; "P" = phenotype. (B) Phenotype is dynamically attracted to genes. (C) Phenotype is dynamically attracted to environment. (D) Environment is dynamically attracted to phenotype.

The dimensions of the space may be thought of as two independent dimensions of phenotype, such as intelligence and extraversion or sociability and conservatism. Three kinds of simulated entities are contained in the space: phenotype (P), genes (G), and environment (E). The locations of each are to be understood in terms of their relevance to the behavioral dimensions of the space, according to rules that will be specified more precisely here. The location of the phenotype at any moment of the simulation indicates the organism's current phenotypic values on the two dimensions. A phenotype in the lower left of the space would indicate that the organism currently has low scores on both phenotypic dimensions, and a phenotype in the upper right would indicate that the organism is currently high on both. The locations of the genes represent the direction of their influence on the phenotype of the organism. A gene in the upper left of the space will tend to pull the phenotype in that direction as it develops. The location of the environment has a similar interpretation: When the environment is in a particular region of the space, the phenotype will be pulled in that direction as it develops. If the environment is located in the lower right of the space, therefore, one can think of it as an environment that is favorable to the development of Dimension 1 but not Dimension 2.

The locations of the genes are fixed throughout the simulation. The locations of the environment and the phenotype change dynamically according to the following set of rules.

1. The phenotype is attracted to the genes. Each gene exerts an attractive force on the phenotype in an amount determined by Rules 2 and 4.

2. The relative attraction of the genes depends on the location of the environment. The attraction that each gene exerts on the phenotype is inversely related to the distance between that gene and the environment. As the location of the environment changes, therefore, it has the effect of "turning on" genes close to it. The attraction of phenotype to genotype is illustrated in Figure 11.1B.

3. The phenotype is attracted to the environment. The current location of the environment exerts an attractive force on the phenotype in an amount determined by Rule 4. The attraction of phenotype to environment is illustrated in Figure 11.1C.

4. At each moment in the simulation, the attraction of the phenotype to the genes and to the environment are stipulated to be equal. This rule is important because it eliminates traditional "How much?" questions from the analysis. At each moment during development, genes and environment exert precisely equal forces on phenotype.

5. The environment is attracted to the current location of the phenotype, as illustrated in Figure 11.1D. Note the contrast between Scarr's model of G → E and the current model, which posits P → E. This distinction is elaborated in the Discussion section of this chapter. For the first quarter of the simulation, the location of the environment cannot change. This condition is referred to as "childhood." (This rule is included for completeness, but it is not investigated in this chapter. See Turkheimer & Gottesman, 1996.)

For each simulated organism, the phenotype begins at the center of the space. The locations of the genes and the first location of the environment are under control of the experimenter or can be specified at random. When the simulation begins, genes and environment exert their attractions on the phenotype and on each other, and the locations of the phenotype and the environment begin to change. Phenotype and environment each trace a complex path that represents changes in the organism's environment and its phenotype in the course of its life, which consists of 300 iterations. Most of the time, the paths eventually settle down close to each other in a region of space close to one of the genes. An example of the paths followed by phenotype and environment for a particular configuration of genotype and environment is illustrated in Figures 11.2A and 11.2B.

Although many aspects of the simulation are under the control of the experimenter (e.g., the number of genes in the space, the relative force of the attraction of genes and environment, the rate at which the environment can change in response to changes in the phenotype), in this chapter, most will remain fixed at intermediate values. The simulated experiments that follow investigate the relationship among two predictors (the initial location of the environment and the average location of the genes) and one outcome, the final location of the phenotype, which is defined as the mean on each dimension of the last 50 iterations.

Results

Experiment 1: Reaction Norm With Cloned Organisms

The disagreement between scientists comfortable with linear and additive models of behavioral variability and developmentalists who insist on concrete models of actual developmental processes has crystallized in the discussion of one of the most fundamental tools of genetic analysis, the reaction norm

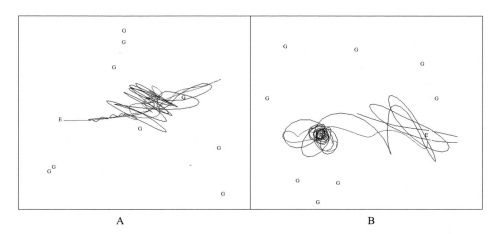

A   B

Figure 11.2.   Two examples of paths followed by phenotype and environment.

(Gottlieb, 1991; Platt & Sanislow, 1988; Turkheimer & Gottesman, 1991). Although reaction norms are nothing more than tabulations or plots of variation in phenotypic outcome as a joint function of genotype and environment, different scientific disciplines have evolved very disparate methods for estimating them. To construct a reaction norm for a trait in lower animals, an animal experimentalist can use a "clones in cages" design: Obtain samples of cloned organisms representing several possible genotypes within a species and raise representatives of each strain in each of a controlled variety of environments. For the experimentalist to whom such research designs are available, no further statistical analysis would be required: One would simply tabulate the phenotypic outcome for each combination of genotype and environment with no expectation that the resulting surface would be linear or even continuous. The experimental developmentalist does not even have to assume that variation in genotypes or environments could be ordered along an axis from "worst " to "best." The goal, after all, is to discover how genotypes and environments combine to produce a phenotype (and to make a point about variability of outcome within genotypes), not to generate statistically based models for predicting phenotype from genotype and environment.

Few of these methodological niceties are available to the social scientist, who must do without cloned organisms (except for MZ twins) or any possibility of "assigning," much less randomly, genotypes to environments. The methodology of behavioral genetics encompasses the alternative quasi-experimental methods that have evolved. With such methods, phenotypic outcome can be plotted as a function of naturally occurring variation in genotype and environment. The regression methods employed are almost always linear and usually additive, so the reaction norms that result generally consist of straight parallel lines. Behavioral geneticists can point out that such linear models, despite their obvious etiological inadequacies, often do a pretty good job of predicting phenotypic outcome from its genetic and environmental antecedents. Developmentalists are appalled by the very smoothness of behavioral-genetic reaction norms, however: Bronfenbrenner and Ceci (1994, p. 571) described one of my own renderings of a reaction norm (Turkheimer & Gottesman, 1991) as resembling "a bent piece of chicken wire that quickly straightens out to become horizontal," a criticism I will readily accept from any behavioral scientist who has never employed linear multiple regression in the analysis of data arising from a complex developmental process. The experimentalist Gottlieb probably qualifies; Bronfenbrenner and Ceci do not.

In the first investigation of the behavior of the simulated gene–environment system, reaction norms were estimated using techniques available to the experimental animal psychologist, that is, a single genotype was reared in a variety of environments. The genotype illustrated in Figure 11.1 was used in a series of 100 simulations, each with a different environmental starting point. The environmental starting points varied along Dimension 1 of the space. The first simulation was run with environmental starting point of (1, 50), the second had a starting point of (2, 50), and so on through (100, 50). A plot of final phenotype versus the starting point of the environment is the reaction norm for this genotype along Dimension 1.

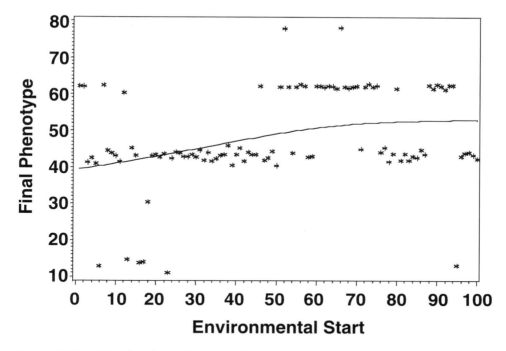

Figure 11.3. Simulated reaction norm illustrating variation in phenotype for a single genotype as environmental starting point varies.

Figure 11.3 shows the reaction norm that results. The line through the scatterplot is a smoothing spline. Because genotype was held constant across simulations, all variability in this reaction norm is "environmental." Although there is obviously a positive relationship between environmental starting location and phenotypic outcome ($r = .68$), several characteristics of the relationship suggest that it would be difficult to model using ordinary social scientific methods. The relation is clearly nonlinear and seems to include a discontinuity at an environmental starting point of about 50: For environmental starting locations below this value, phenotypic outcomes are usually in the low 40s, whereas for starting locations greater than this value, phenotypic outcomes suddenly jump to around 65. Moreover, throughout the relationship, there are many points that vary from the general trend line in apparently unsystematic ways.

Reaction norms are usually drawn for single genotypes as they vary across rearing environments, but it is just as appropriate to investigate phenotypic outcome for a variety of genotypes raised in a single environment (Turkheimer, Goldsmith, & Gottesman, 1995). For the next simulation, therefore, 100 randomly generated genotypes were reared using a single environmental starting location of (25, 25). A plot of the relation between the mean genotypic value on Dimension 1 and final phenotypic value, shown in Figure 11.4, is the "environmental reaction norm" for the starting location (25, 25). Although the correlation between mean genotypic value and final phenotypic

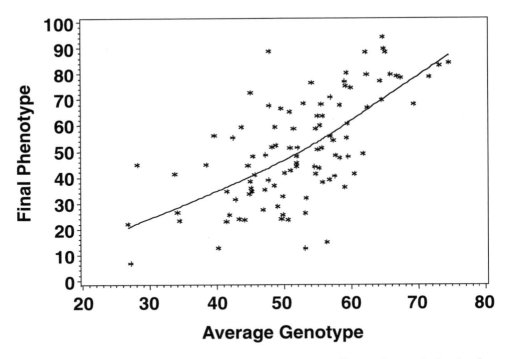

Figure 11.4.   Simulated "environmental " reaction norm illustrating variation in phe-notype for a single environmental starting point as genotype varies.

value ($r = .65$) is roughly the same as the correlation between environmental starting location and phenotypic outcome in the previous reaction norm, exam-ination of the scatterplot reveals that it is much better suited to standard methods of statistical analysis in that it is roughly linear, continuous, and homoscedastic.

Experiment 2: Analysis of Variance

Experiment 1 has demonstrated that the simulated system comprises both environmental and genetic variability, that is, phenotypic outcome varies when genotype is held constant and environmental starting location is allowed to vary and when environmental starting location is held constant and genotype is allowed to vary. It will be useful to summarize this result in the form of an analysis of variance. For this experiment, 10 random genotypes were generated, and each genotype was reared using 10 randomly selected starting environmental locations, for a total of 100 simulations. Note that this design uses information that in the real world can only be obtained from clones: Each genotype is raised 10 different times in a variety of environments. The phenotypic variability resulting from this design can be partitioned into two parts, one attributable to variation between the genotypes and the other attributable to variation in environmental starting location within the geno-

Table 11.1. Genetic and Environmental Variance Produced by Experiment 2

	Genetic Variance	Environmental Variance
Dimension 1	21067 (50%)	21054 (50%)
Dimension 2	18789 (56%)	14586 (44%)

types. Table 11.1 shows that variability was roughly evenly divided between these two sources, so the "heritability" of phenotype on Dimension 1 (the proportion of total phenotypic variability accounted for by genotype) can be taken to be about .5.

Experiment 3: Random Variation in Genotype and Environment

The experiments described so far would not be feasible in humans. We cannot know how variation in environment would effect the phenotypic outcome of a single human genotype or how genetic variation would effect phenotypic outcome in humans reared in identical environments (except, of course, for identical twins, which will be simulated in Experiment 5). Instead, we must infer the general shape of the relation among genotype, environment, and phenotypic outcome by studying variation in environment across different genotypes, each of which only appears once in the design. Because we cannot hold genotype constant experimentally, we do so statistically by using regression methods to isolate the effects of genotype and environment in populations in which both vary randomly.

To simulate this research design, 100 organisms were generated, each with a random genotype and a random environmental starting location. Once again, final phenotypic outcome was recorded for each outcome and regressed on mean genotype and environmental starting location. The partial regression of phenotypic outcome on environmental starting point is a linear estimate of the first, "genetic," reaction norm from Experiment 1, and the partial regression of final phenotype on mean genotype is a linear estimate of the second, "environmental," reaction norm. For genotype, the results of this experiment were similar to the previous two: Figure 11.5 is a scatterplot of the relation between mean genotype and final phenotypic outcome, and as before, it is roughly linear and generally smooth. Except for the environment, the results are very different. As can be seen in Figure 11.6, there is essentially no relationship between the starting location of the environment and phenotypic outcome when genotype is allowed to vary randomly. An analysis of variance showed that 39% of the variability in outcome was accounted for by the mean level of the genotype, whereas none of it was explained by variation in environmental starting location.

How can this be? In Experiments 1 and 2, environment explained as much variation as genotype; in Experiment 3, using precisely the same simulations under different sampling conditions, it explained none at all. The environmental effects in Experiments 1 and 2 were entirely within replicated genotypes, whereas each genotype only appeared once in Experiment 3. It appears that in this simulated system, the effect of the environment is all interaction,

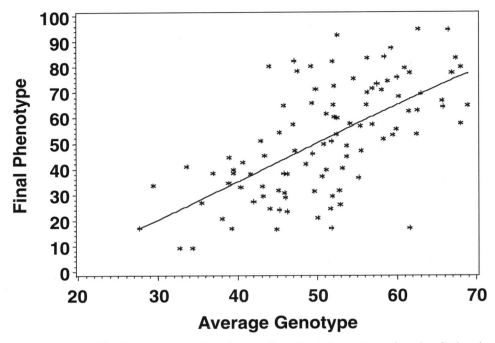

Figure 11.5. Final phenotype plotted as a function of genotype for simulation in which both genotype and starting environment vary randomly.

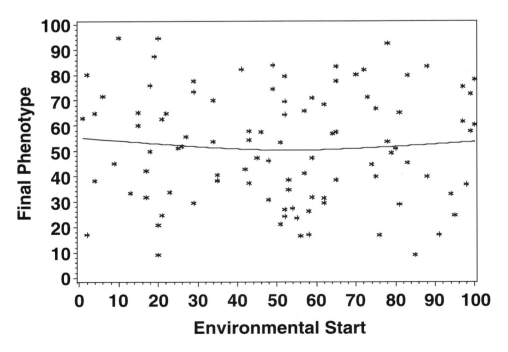

Figure 11.6. Final phenotype plotted as a function of starting environment for simulation in which both genotype and starting environment vary randomly.

with no main effect. The effect of the environment can be detected within a single genotype, but the shape of the environmental effect depends crucially on the genotype with which it is interacting. Across varying genotypes, the effects of starting environmental location cancel each other out and become undetectable.

Experiment 4: A Twin Study

Monozygotic twins occupy a central place in behavioral genetic methodology precisely because they offer the only possibility to replicate the clones in cages design using humans. The replication is very incomplete: Only two "clones" of any particular genotype are usually available, and they cannot be "assigned" to random environments. Nevertheless, the classical twin design is arguably the most successful quasi-experimental research design in the behavioral sciences: Its elegance and the consistency of its results across an astonishing variety of behavioral phenotypes have contributed greatly to the increasing acceptance of behavioral genetics during the last generation.

Nevertheless, the results of twin studies are not without their mysteries. On the one hand, MZ twins are often too similar. Although the biometric model suggests that heritability approaches unity when the similarity between MZ twins is twice as great as that between DZ twins, MZ twins are often more than twice as similar (Lykken, McGue, Tellegen, & Bouchard, 1992). More complex family designs allow such excess similarity to be modeled as multiplicative effects among genes, but like the nonshared environment, genetic nonlinearity is easier to model than it is to specify. On the other hand, it sometimes seems as though identical twins are not similar enough. Schizophrenia, for example, is widely thought to be a genetic disorder of the brain (Liberman & Corrigan, 1992), and no plausible environmental component to its etiology has ever been identified. Yet identical twins are only about 50% concordant for the disorder (Gottesman, 1991). What is the source of the MZ twin discordance?

Stochastic processes in development may be one explanation. The simulations described so far contain no randomness: Phenotypic outcome has been completely determined by the starting configuration and the dynamic rules that describe the behavior of the system. Therefore, two "monozygotic twins reared together," with identical genotypes and the same environmental starting location, would follow exactly the same course. In order to allow for differences between monozygotic twins, some randomness in development must be included. There are several points in the system at which randomness could be introduced, but the most plausible is in the effect of phenotype on the environment. In the system as it has been described so far, changes in the location of the environment are completely determined by the location of the phenotype. In real organisms, of course, phenotype can influence the environment but not determine it.

The following method was employed to determine the amount of randomness to introduce. A random component was added to the module determining changes in environmental location, so that 90% of the change depended on the location of phenotype and 10% depended on a random variate. One hundred pairs of monozygotic twins were generated with identical randomly chosen genotypes and environmental starting locations within pairs, phenotypic outcomes were simulated using the new random component, and the correlation in phenotypic outcome between twins was computed. With the random component at 10%, the correlation was .95, suggesting that 10% randomness did not cause much divergence between the twins. The random component was then increased to 20%, and so on until changes in environmental location were 100% random. When changes in environmental location were 50% random, the correlation was reduced to .7, which seemed to be a reasonable representation of the similarity between MZ twins that is commonly observed, so this value was selected for the remainder of the twin study.

Another 100 pairs of MZ twins were generated using the parameters just described, along with 100 pairs of dizygotic (DZ) twins who shared a randomly selected 5 of their 10 genes. Phenotypic outcomes were generated for each twin pair, and correlations were computed for the MZ and DZ twins. Results are given in Table 11.2. For the MZ twins, as before, the correlations on Dimensions 1 and 2 were about .7, in keeping with the specification of the system. In DZ twins, however, the correlations were substantially smaller. Doubling the difference between the MZ and DZ twin correlations resulted in heritabilities on Dimensions 1 and 2 close to .8, whereas the shared environment once again accounted for no variability in phenotype.

Although Experiments 1 and 2 demonstrated that the simulations contain substantial environmental variability, the twin design, like the random family design in Experiment 3, failed to detect it. Why? It appears that the effect of adding randomness to the determination of changes in the environment had a disproportionate effect on the DZ twins. The exact replication of genotype in the MZ twins was sufficient to maintain the similarity of the twins despite dynamic variation arising from interaction with a partially random environment, whereas the 50% genetic dissimilarity of the DZ twins interacted with environmental randomness and resulted in substantially less similarity in phenotype.

Experiment 5: Indeterminacy in Reaction Norms

In Experiment 1, we saw that one of the difficulties in interpreting the reaction norms produced by the simulations was that they contained "outliers," or points that deviated from the general trend for no apparent reason. Attempts to understand such outliers represent a major portion of the

Table 11.2. Results of Simulated Twin Study

	Correlation	
	Dimension 1	Dimension 2
MZ	.75	.61
DZ	.35	.19
r^2	.80	.84
c^2	.00	.00

activities of working social scientists. Why do some children raised in brutal poverty overcome their background and go on to successful lives? Why are some MZ twins of schizophrenic patients perfectly normal? A very reasonable scientific impulse is to want to investigate the environmental backgrounds of outlier cases in greater detail: Surely, if we study the upbringing of the successful child of poverty with enough care, we will discover the key factors that can "inoculate" children against the risks presented by chaotic environments.

In the simulations, we can model this process by "zooming in" on our view of the reaction norm and focus attention on the region in which the outliers occur. For example, in Figure 11.3, in the region along Dimension 1 from 10 to 20, most of the phenotypic outcomes are between 40 and 50, except for a few that are considerably lower, close to 10. Suppose the view of the x-axis of Figure 11.3 is expanded so that it runs from 10 to 20 in intervals of 0.1. Figure 11.7 shows the result. The expanded region from 10 to 20 looks very much like the original: Some organisms had a final phenotypic value between 40 and 50, others are close to 10 (and a few previously undetected points close to 25 appear!), but no pattern is discernible. We could then choose to zoom in again, perhaps to the region on Dimension 1 between 12 and 13 with an interval of .01. Figure 11.8 shows the result, which is again similar to the original reaction norm. This process of zooming in can continue indefinitely, as illustrated in Figure 11.9, which shows the reaction norm across a region on Dimension 1 extending only from 12.7 to 12.8 and yet contains as much variability in phenotypic outcome as the original figure.

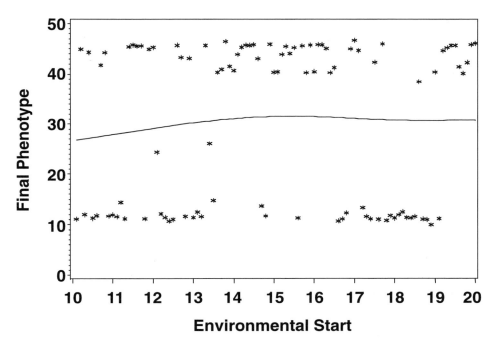

Figure 11.7. Reaction norm from Figure 11.3, with expanded view of region between 10 and 20.

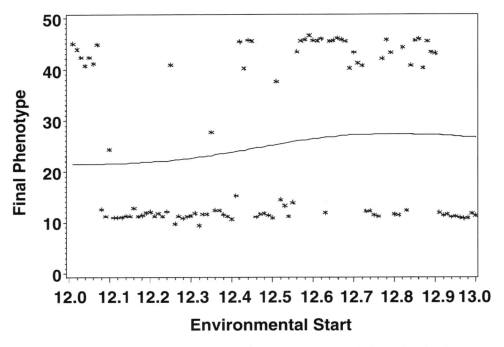

Figure 11.8. Reaction norm from Figure 11.3, with expanded view of region between 12 and 13.00.

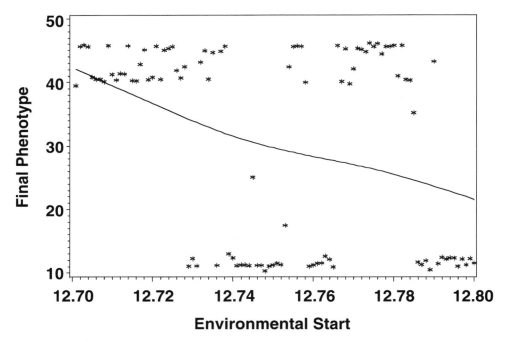

Figure 11.9. Reaction norm from Figure 11.3, with expanded view of region between 12.7 and 12.8.

Suppose you were a social scientist assigned to understand the environmental circumstances that dispose this genotype to arrive at final phenotypic values near 10. How much scientific progress could be made, at least in the region of the environment between 10 and 20? No matter how detailed your environmental data became, you would still be unable to determine the exact environmental values producing the specific phenotypic outcome in question. Correlations between environmental variation and phenotypic outcome, as we have seen throughout this series of experiments, would be completely hopeless. It would be wrong, however, to conclude that the environment is impotent in the determination of phenotype, because all of the variability in phenotypic outcome in the reaction norm is environmental by definition. The reaction norms in Figures 11.7, 11.8, and 11.9, remember, illustrate environmental variability within the single genotype illustrated in Figure 11.3. This paradox is at the heart of the difficulty in developing a rigorous science of environmental effects on development: The environment is a necessary component of all developmental processes, and variation in the environment is demonstrably associated with phenotypic variation, but the nature of the covariation renders it invisible to typical social scientific methods.

Discussion

Spinach and Ice Cream

Gregory Bateson (1972) told a story about a mother who, in her eagerness to instill healthful eating habits in her son, reinforced him for eating a helping of spinach by rewarding him with a bowl of ice cream. Bateson asked, Will the boy grow up to love or hate spinach, love or hate ice cream, or love or hate his mother? If the topic of food preference management were ever taken up as a line of research by an enterprising assistant professor, I submit that we already know more or less what would result. If the research were undertaken in a convenience sample of singleton children and their biological mothers who happened to be spinach reinforcers (i.e., without random assignment of families to food behavior groups), modest but statistically significant linear effects of food preference reinforcement on later patterns of eating behavior would be found, leading to an initial wave of enthusiasm for the environmental potency of maternal food reinforcement behavior. When the skeptical behavioral geneticist at another university got wind of these findings and replicated the study in twins or adoptees, however, it would be discovered that most of the purported environmental effect was in fact attributable to genetic transmission of food preferences from mothers to children and that the familial environmental effects of food reinforcement were practically nil. This new finding would be greeted with stoically repressed glee in the behavioral-genetic community, whereas environmentalists would write angry replies about the limitations of twin and adoption methods for the study of behavioral development.

As the anger subsided over a period of years, positions on the matter might coalesce along the lines I have outlined. Nonshared environment theorists would contend that the environment acts to make siblings more different, not more similar, and would undertake the study of differential feeding practices within families, the effects of peer group standards, or birth order. Antisocialization theorists would declare victory, produce lists of reasons why one wouldn't expect maternal behavior to be a strong determinant of eating behavior in the first place, generate theories of how genetically driven food preferences in children cause food management behavior in their caregivers, and begin linkage and association studies to find the genes responsible for food preference. Developmentalists would declare that the entire research program was meaningless, because the goal of studying the development of eating behavior is to establish the developmental sequence of gene–environment interactions that leads to phenotypic patterns of eating, a goal to which biometric exercises in variance partitioning have little or nothing to contribute.

I submit further that questions like these—they might be called "spinach and ice cream" questions—are paradigmatic of the difficult methodological and interpretive problems faced by behavioral scientists. The hallmark of spinach and ice cream questions is that they induce a conflict between environmentalists, clinicians, and our own intuitions on the one hand and biogenetically oriented scientists on the other. One does not have to be a radical environmentalist to believe that the peculiarities of your parent's cooking had an effect on your adult food preferences. Right or wrong, introspection suggests that our families were important determinants of our adult selves. If taken seriously, however, the upshot of the last 20 years of biometric research is that the effects of early environmental events, at least to the extent they are shared among siblings, are largely illusory. We believe that our parents' peculiarities shaped our adult attitudes and those of our siblings, but the antisocialization theorists tell us that we are mistaken. Instead, our adult phenotypes are the product of our genetic endowment, which is why they are generally similar to those of our parents and to environmental events that we did not share with our siblings, which is why children in the same family are as different as they are.

The simulations that I have described in this chapter suggest another possibility, which may offer a way to take behavioral genetics seriously without dismissing wholesale the causal effects of family environments. The simulations were designed so that at each moment, the genetic and environmental forces exerted on phenotype were precisely equal. When environmental variation was studied within a single genotype, unambiguous environmental variability in phenotypic outcome could be observed, but the shape of the relation between environment and phenotype was nonlinear, discontinuous, and not generalizable from one genotype to another. Because the relation between environment and phenotype was inconsistent across different genotypes, when genotype was allowed to vary randomly, it was no longer possible to detect any effect of the environment at all. When each genotype appears only once in the design, as is the case in most human research, the reaction norms relating environment to phenotype within each genotype average each other out, and nothing observable remains.

Why do the developmental dynamics of the simulations obscure the effects of the environment, whereas genetic effects are relatively unaffected? The genetic configuration is fixed at birth. Although developmental changes in the environment have the effect of turning genes on and off during development, the genotype nonetheless exerts a constant and steady force on phenotypic development. A genotype in which most of the genes are located in the upper left of the space will exert a constant pull on the phenotype in that direction, regardless of the other complex dynamics the system produces. The environment, in contrast, is in a constant state of flux induced by its reciprocal interactions with phenotype, which in turn is the joint product of genotype and environment. The starting location of the environment, therefore, is a source of variability in outcome but not a source of systematic variability.

Suppose a clinician interviewed a pair of siblings raised by a spinach-reinforcing mother. "Oh, yes," one of them might say, crunching a carrot, "Mother always reminded me how important it is to eat well, and that is why I am a vegan today." The other, with equal conviction and ice cream spoon in hand, might report, "Mother was always so annoying with her peculiar ideas about eating, I finally rebelled and gained 150 pounds." If the direction of the effect of the mother's behavior depended crucially on minute phenotypic details of siblings, they both might be correct. Woe to the social scientist who sets out to study the environmental effects of spinach-reinforcement on adult food preferences! The simulations suggest that an attempt to develop a systematic environmental theory would be a frustrating tangle of initial hopes, false leads, small effect sizes, and unreplicated findings, whereas the behavioral geneticist studying the same phenomenon could count on substantial and replicable heritabilities.

The Postbiometric Era Revisited

The possibility that environment is a potent but unsystematic source of variability in behavioral development offers a resolution of the dilemma posed by biometric studies of behavior. It is not that it doesn't matter how humans are raised, but rather that the effects of variation in rearing practices are fiendishly difficult to specify. Behavioral scientists studying clones in cages have the advantage of wielding experimental control over both genotype and environment, and with these tools, it has proved possible to dampen developmental dynamics to an extent that allows inferences to be drawn about the consequences of specific environmental events. In free-ranging humans, for whom genotype and environment are essentially uncontrollable, not to mention correlated with each other, the dynamic complexities of development overwhelm any systematic consequences of environmental variation.

For nonshared environmentalists, this analysis suggests that a careful distinction must be maintained between the nonshared environmental events that have been the focus of empirical research so far and the nonshared effects of shared environmental events. These constructs are frequently discussed as if they were the same thing. Here, for example, are Plomin, DeFries, and McClearn (1990):

> Environmental variance can be decomposed into two components, Ec and Ew. Common or shared environmental influences (Ec) are those that make members of a family similar to each other; the remainder of the environmental variance, the portion not shared by family members is called *within, independent,* or *nonshared* (Ew). . . . Given that environmental variance is important but shared environment is not, critical environmental influences must be of the nonshared variety, making children in the same family as different from one another as are pairs of children selected randomly from the population. The importance of this finding lies in the fact that much previous environmental research has been misguided: Environmental factors relevant to differences in behavioral development lie not *between* families but *within* families. (pp. 249–250, emphasis in original)

According to this definition, if parental divorce served to make children in the same family more different, would divorce count as shared or nonshared environment? In the first part of the paragraph, Plomin seems to want to count anything that makes children different as nonshared. In an important sense, however, divorce is shared among siblings regardless of whether it ends up making them more similar or more different, and researchers have generally taken Plomin's subsequent assertion that "critical environmental influences must be of the nonshared variety" (Plomin, DeFries, et al., 1990, p. 249) to mean that causal factors operating within families should be the focus of future research efforts. As a result, research undertaken under the banner of nonshared environment has focused on the systematic effects of nonshared causes, such as differential parental treatment and the effects of peer groups, to the exclusion of the nonshared effects of shared causes such as divorce, which are dismissed as a "misguided" focus of old-fashioned environmentalism.

Our meta-analyses (Turkheimer & Waldron, 2000) have offered little reason for optimism that nonshared environmental events will go very far toward answering Plomin and Daniels' (1987) seminal question about why children in the same family are so different. The range of possible explanations of within-family sibling differences will be greatly expanded if we can include the differential effects of the large domain of environmental events that are (usually) shared among siblings in a family, including everything from socioeconomic status to marital discord and divorce. The query, "What are the effects of divorce on children?" is a spinach and ice cream question. The effect of divorce on a child may depend nonlinearly on the phenotype of the child at the time of the divorce, leading to differential effects on siblings experiencing essentially the same environmental event. This leads to an empirical prediction: Children experiencing potent environmental events should show greater variability in developmental outcomes, and pairs of siblings should be more different from each other, even if no systematic effects on the mean can be observed.

The spinach and ice cream explanation provides some support for the developmentalists' insistence that partitioning variance is one thing and explaining the development of behavior another. It is hard to see how biometric family studies of the simulations would ever lead to an understanding of the dynamic rules that generated them. Indeed, unless they were interpreted very carefully, biometric studies might mislead us into concluding that the environment played no causal role in the simulations. The simulations also remind us, high-level theorizing about development notwithstanding, that individual differences in genotype are associated with individual differences in behavior. Too often, developmentalists allow their legitimate concerns about the limited etiological consequences of population genetics to justify an unwarranted acceptance of old-fashioned environmentalism. In the simulations, as in the field, when the scientific goal is to predict behavior, as opposed to understanding it, knowledge about the genotype is still the best kind of information to have (Meehl, 1962).

The antisocialization theorists have taken the opposite tack, maintaining that because normal family environment is not a useful predictor of behavior, it is not a important cause of behavior. Plomin (1994) cited Grilo and Pogue-Geile:

> Experiences that are shared among family members do not play an important role in determining individual differences in weight, fatness, and obesity . . . experiences that are not shared among family members comprise most of the environmental influence on weight and obesity . . . . The conclusion that experiences that are shared among family members count for little in determining individual difference in weight, and perhaps obesity, necessitates a drastic rethinking of many current environmental etiological theories of weight. (1991, p. 534)

The spinach and ice cream explanation suggests that this inference may not be correct. It may be that "experiences that are shared among family members" do count for something in determining individual differences in weight but nonetheless serve to make siblings different rather than similar. This is no mere semantic distinction, because the antisocialization theorists' conflation of small variance components with weak causal effects has provided the evidentiary basis for the theorists' dismissal of the causal efficacy of shared family environment and thus to environmentalists' impressions that they are being asked to swallow the contention that normal families have no effect on their children.

In this light, it is instructive to contrast Scarr's model (Scarr & McCartney, 1983) of the role of environment in development with the model that is instantiated in the simulations. Scarr stated simply that $G \rightarrow E$, and to the extent she means that genotype exerts some distal influence on the environment, she is certainly correct. The "genes," as the developmentalists remind us, cannot "influence" an organism's environment in any direct way. What they can do is interact with the environment in a way that sets off a complex chain of interactions that eventuates in environmental change. Although the simulations have demonstrated that the complex dynamics of such a system can preserve linear relations between genotype and outcome, it is hardly the case that $G \rightarrow E$ directly, and indeed there is no direct $G \rightarrow E$ attraction programmed into the simulation. In the simulations, genetically identical organisms born into different environments show variation in phenotypic outcome, but the unpredictability of environmental variation across genotypes obscures environmental effects when clones are not employed. By analogy to humans, our intuition that we would have turned out differently had we been born into a different family may be correct, even though effects of shared environments cannot be detected by biometric designs.

What *does* determine environmental change in a niche-picking organism? In a child with a genetic propensity for high intelligence, for example, it is not the child's genes per se, but rather the child's behavior, that is to say its phenotype, that evokes stimulating verbal productions by caregivers. Phenotype, not genotype, produces changes in the environment, and phenotype at any moment in development is the cumulative result of an organism's developmental history, encompassing genotype, environment, and all the complexities of their epigenetic interactions. Replacing Scarr's theory of G → E with a P → E theory of development would maintain Scarr's concern with the role of organisms in the construction of their own environments while allowing for much greater indeterminancy and environmental variability in behavioral outcome.

Why Environmental Social Science Is So Difficult

By offering a solution to the problem posed by the second law of behavioral genetics, the spinach and ice cream explanation relieves the postbiometric positions on nature and nurture of their original reason for existence: the need to explain, or explain away, the mysterious failure of shared family environment to contribute to biometric analyses of behavior. The rejection of the claim that normal shared family environment plays no role in the development of behavioral variability, however, simply replaces a substantive implausibility with a methodological quandary. If the effects of the shared environment consist of complex developmental interactions with genotype and phenotype, interactions so complex as to be in principle unpredictable, how can they be studied? A domain of environmental causation that was theoretically undeniable but empirically intractable would be a poor consolation prize for environmentalists. If the meat and potatoes of socialization science—correlations between family characteristics and children's development—is doomed to failure when appropriate genetic controls are employed, how is the empirical environmentalist to proceed?

A first step is to realize that spinach and ice cream questions are ill-specified and unanswerable, and moreover they concede a methodological advantage to behavioral genetic rivals. Divorce doesn't have an effect on children: It has a multitude of effects, and the choice among them will be little clarified by correlation matrices of variables describing characteristics of parents and offspring (Wachs, 1993a). Population-based behavioral genetic models of marital status may not elucidate the developmental processes of marital discord and their various effects on children either, but they at least have the advantage of preserving reliable linear relations between the latent variable called "genotype" and behavioral outcome, which allows behavioral geneticists to assert with confidence the developmental banality that genes "influence" behavior.

Theories that attempt to predict behavior from environmental first principles will fail if they neglect the distal but reliable effects of genotype; genetic theories will remain etiologically empty unless they include the complex developmental dynamics of genotype and environment. The goal of an environmentalist theory of behavior, then, is first to catalog the range of outcomes

that are possible within a behavioral domain and then to specify the phenotype by environmental interactions that make some outcomes more likely
than others for individual subjects. Of course, doing justice to phenotype by
environment interactions would mean taking seriously the role of genotype in
generating phenotypes, so the resulting theories would no longer be strictly
"environmental," but that is precisely the point. Partitioning environmental
and genetic variability has served a useful purpose, but that purpose has now
been served.

Nonlinear Models for Nonlinear Processes

One expectation based on the outcome of the simulations is that environment
may be a better predictor of behavior in some regions of the reaction norm
than in others. In Figure 11.3, for example, although the reaction norm may
not be well described by a linear model and may even be formally unpredictable in some regions, there are also regions where reasonable generaliza-
tions can be made. Below the environmental threshold at about 50 on
Dimension 1, the mean phenotypic outcome is about 43; above the threshold,
it is about 63. Note that this mean difference in outcome does not translate
into a correlation between environment and outcome on either side of the
threshold, as would be expected if the overall reaction norm were linear.

Exactly this phenomenon is observed in adoption studies of intelligence
(Turkheimer, 1991). Correlations between the intelligence of adopted children
and characteristics of their adoptive homes are typically close to zero, in accor-
dance with the second law of behavioral genetics. Paradoxically, when the
intelligence of children adopted into middle-class homes is compared with the
intelligence of children adopted into poor homes or to their unadopted siblings,
a substantial mean difference is generally observed. How can these findings be
reconciled? Not with linear models, which require the relation between environment and outcome to be constant across all levels of environment. There
appears to be a nonlinearity, even a threshold, in the reaction norm for intelligence, such that highly deprived—not good enough—environments exert an
effect on intelligence compared with middle-class homes, whereas variation
within middle-class homes does not. Many contemporary regression methods
have completely abandoned the requirement of linearity (Hastie & Tibshirani,
1990) and would thus appear to be especially well suited for work in the softer
social sciences, but they have yet to be widely applied. The lines through the
reaction norms in this chapter were generated by such methods, and they generalize nicely to multivariate models.

Another class of modern regression methods, referred to as classification
and regression trees (CART; Breiman, Friedman, Olshen, & Stone, 1984), cap-
italizes on the characteristic of the simulations that makes them most
intractable for linear models: the fact that it is possible to predict outcome in
some regions of the environmental prediction space but not in others. CART
models work by making predictions sequentially rather than on the basis
of weighted linear combinations of predictors. The estimation program seeks
the cutoff score on a predictor variable that does the best job of classifying

observations according to outcome. It divides the sample into two groups on the basis of this cut score and then seeks the optimum cutoff within each of the two resulting groups, proceeding in this way until no further improvement in prediction can be made.

The Return of Interactionism

Similarities between the nature–nurture debate and the person–situation debate in social psychology have not been sufficiently explored since the publication of Rowe's (1987) proposal for cross-fertilization between fields. As Rowe observed, the two debates are remarkably similar in structure: In both, an internal mechanism to explain behavior (genotype or traits) is pitted against an external mechanism (environment or the situation). Rowe, however, whose primary concern involved the contributions behavioral genetics might make to the person–situation debate, did not emphasize a striking difference: The histories of the debates are reversed. In the nature–nurture debate, an environmental establishment was challenged by a new experimental paradigm (behavioral genetics) that succeeded in demonstrating powerful internal determinants of behavior. In the person–situation debate, a personological establishment was challenged by a new experimental paradigm (situationism) that succeeded in demonstrating potent external determinants of behavior.

It is worth pondering why the course of the debates have been so different. The person–situation debate has taken place largely in the laboratories of social and personality psychologists. In this setting, as in the animal studies of the developmentalists, the environment is under the control of the experimenter rather than the participant. Another characteristic of laboratory studies is that outcome is measured over a much shorter time span: Does the presumably "honest" subject pick up the $5 bill when she believes no one is watching? Human behavioral genetics, in contrast, usually examines uncontrolled behavior as it accrues over a lifetime. It appears that systematic effects of the environment are easier to detect in controlled settings and relatively short periods of time.

In any case, in both debates it became increasingly apparent that from a causal as opposed to a variance partitioning perspective, neither internal nor external determinants of behavior could be expected to prevail over the other and that from the point of view of explaining the genesis of behavior, the very attempt to separate them is a fool's errand. Both fields have thus been led to the conclusion that internal and external mechanisms of behavior necessarily interact etiologically and statistically in the determination of behavior. Interactionism was fashionable in social psychology in the 1970s (Endler & Magnusson, 1976), fell out of favor for a while, and has recently been resuscitated by a series of important theoretical and empirical papers by Mischel and Shoda (1995). These studies, which cannot be described in detail here, demonstrate that consistency in behavior is not explained by personality or by situation but by interaction between the two: Individual consistency in behavior comprises characteristic patterns of responding to variation in environments.

The reader is to be forgiven a groan as yet another nature–nurture discussion concludes with a call for the integration of genes and environment in the science of behavior. One cannot emphasize enough how difficult it is to specify the interaction of phenotypes and environments in the genesis of behavior. Indeed, I am not convinced that the usual well-intentioned endorsements of increased scientific collaboration between geneticists and environmentalists will bear fruit (Rowe & Waldman, 1993; Wachs, 1993b). The goal of the simulations presented in this chapter has been to offer a concrete explanation of why human developmental science is so difficult, that is, it is the result of the scientifically unfortunate but humanistically pleasing convergence of two factors: the complex dynamic genesis of behavior and the impossibility of exerting meaningful experimental control over the genes or environments of humans.

Traditional approaches to human development have circumvented this dilemma by simplifying the empirical domain in ways that made them easy targets for their opponents, who had of course simply chosen a different mode of simplification. Environmentalists, as behavioral geneticists never tire of pointing out, ignored genetic pathways between parents and children; behavioral geneticists, as developmentalists never tire of pointing out, ignored the interactive ontogenetics of behavior; and developmentalists (as traditional environmentalists might point out but have not, apparently content to encourage skepticism about behavioral genetics wherever it takes root) ignored the dynamic complexity of human behavior by limiting themselves to experimentally controlled work in lower animals. Thus is completed the perfect rhetorical circle that has kept the nature–nurture debate spinning for the past century.

References

Arvey, R. D., McCall, B. P., Bouchard, T. J., Taubman, P., & Cavanaugh, M. A. (1994). Genetic influences on job satisfaction and work value. *Personality & Individual Differences, 17*(1), 21–33.

Bateson, G. (1972). *Steps to an ecology of mind.* Chicago: University of Chicago Press.

Bouchard, T. J., & Loehlin, J. C. (2001). Genes, evolution, and personality. *Behavior Genetics, 31*, 243–273.

Bouchard, T. J., Jr., Segal, N. L., Tellegen, A., McGue, M., Keyes, M., & Krueger, R. (in press). Genetic influence in social attitudes: Another challenge to psychologists from behavior genetics. In L. DiLalla (Ed.). *Behavior genetics principles: Perspectives in developments, personality, and psychopathology.* Washington, DC: American Psychological Association.

Braungart, J. M., Fulker, D. W., & Plomin, R. (1992). Genetic mediation of the home environment during infancy: A sibling adoption study of the HOME. *Developmental Psychology, 28*, 1048–1055.

Breiman, L., Friedman, J. H., Olshen, R. A., & Stone, C. J. (1984). *Classification and regression trees.* Monterey, CA: Wadsworth and Brooks/Cole.

Bronfenbrenner, U., & Ceci, S. J. (1994). Nature–nurture reconceptualized from a developmental perspective: A bioecological model. *Psychological Review, 101*, 568–586.

Cardon, L. R., & Fulker, D. W. (1993). Genetics of specific cognitive abilities. In R. Plomin & G. E. McClearn (Eds.), *Nature, nurture and psychology* (pp. 99–120). Washington, DC: American Psychological Association.

Dunn, J., & Plomin, R. (1990). *Separate lives: Why siblings are so different.* New York: Basic Books.

Endler, N. S., & Magnusson, D. (1976). Toward an interactional psychology of personality. *Psychological Bulletin, 83*, 956–974.

Gottesman, I. I. (1991). *Schizophrenia genesis: The origins of madness.* New York: W. H. Freeman.

Gottesman, I. I. (1994). Schizophrenia epigenesis: Past, present, and future. *Acta Psychiatrica Scandinavica, Supplementum, 94,* 26–33.

Gottesman, I. I. (1997). Twins: En route to QTLs for cognition. *Science, 276,* 1522–1523.

Gottesman, I. I., & Shields, J. (1972). *Schizophrenia and genetics: A twin study vantage point.* New York: Academic Press.

Gottlieb, G. (1985). Development of species typical identification in ducklings: XI. Embryonic critical period for species-typical perception in the hatchling. *Animal Behavior, 33,* 225–233.

Gottlieb, G. (1991). Experiential canalization of behavioral development: Theory. *Developmental Psychology, 27,* 4–13.

Gottlieb, G. (1992). *Individual development and evolution: The genesis of novel behavior.* New York: Oxford University Press.

Gottlieb, G. (1995). Some conceptual deficiencies in "developmental" behavior genetics. *Human Development, 38,* 131–141.

Grilo, C. M., & Pogue-Geile, M. F. (1991). The nature of encironmental influences on weight and obesity: A behavior genetic analysis. *Psychological Bulletin, 110,* 520–537.

Harris, J. R. (1998). *The nurture assumption: Why children turn out the way they do.* New York: The Free Press.

Hastie, T. J., & Tibshirani, R. J. (1990). *Generalized additive models.* London: Chapman and Hall.

Liberman, R. P., & Corrigan, P. W. (1992). Is schizophrenia a neurological disorder? *Journal of Neuropsychiatry, 4,* 119–124.

Loehlin, J. C. (1993). What has behavioral genetics told us about the nature of personality? In T. J. Bouchard & P. Propping (Eds.), *Twins as a tool of behavioral genetics. Life sciences research report* (pp. 109–119). Chichester, UK: John Wiley & Sons.

Lykken, D. T., McGue, M., Tellegen, A., & Bouchard, T. J. (1992). Emergenesis: Genetic traits that may not run in families. *American Psychologist, 47,* 1565–1577.

Maccoby, E. E. (2000). Parenting and its effects on children: On reading and misreading behavior genetics. *Annual Review of Psychology, 51,* 1–27.

McGue, M., & Lykken, D. T. (1992). Genetic influence on risk of divorce. *Psychological Science, 3,* 368–373.

McGuffin, P., Riley, P., & Plomin, R. Toward behavioral genomics. *Science, 291,* 1232–1249.

Meehl, P. E. (1962). Schizotaxia, schizotypy, schizophrenia. *American Psychologist, 17,* 827–838.

Mischel, W., & Shoda, Y. (1995). A cognitive–affective system theory of personality: Reconceptualizing situations, dispositions, dynamics, and invariance in personality structure. *Psychological Review, 102,* 246–268.

Oyama, S. (1985). *The ontogeny of information.* Cambridge, UK: Cambridge University Press.

Platt, S. A., & Sanislow, C. A. (1988). Norm-of-reaction: Definition and misinterpretation of animal research. *Journal of Comparative Psychology, 102,* 254–261.

Plomin, R. (1986). Multivariate analysis and developmental behavioral genetics: Developmental change as well as continuity. *Behavior Genetics, 16,* 25–43.

Plomin, R. (1994). Genetic research and identification of environmental influences. *Journal of Child Psychiatry, 35,* 817–834.

Plomin, R., Corley, R., DeFries, J. C., & Fulker, D. W. (1990). Individual differences in television viewing in early childhood: Nature as well as nurture. *Psychological Science, 1,* 371–377.

Plomin, R., & Daniels, D. (1987). Why are children in the same family so different from one another? *Behavioral and Brain Sciences, 10,* 1–16.

Plomin, R., DeFries, J. C., & McClearn, G. E. (1990). *Behavioral genetics: A primer* (2nd ed.). University Park, PA: Pennsylvania State University Press.

Rowe, D. C. (1987). Resolving the person–situation debate: Invitation to an interdisciplinary dialogue. *American Psychologist, 42,* 218–227.

Rowe, D. C. (1994). *The limits of family influence: Genes, experience and behavior.* New York: Guilford Press.

Rowe, D. C., & Plomin, R. (1981). The importance of nonshared (E1) environmental influences in behavioral development. *Developmental Psychology, 17,* 517–530.

Rowe, D. C., & Waldman, I. D. (1993). The question "How?" reconsidered. In R. Plomin & G. E. McClearn (Eds.), *Nature, nurture, and psychology* (pp. 355–373). Washington, DC: American Psychological Association.

Scarr, S. (1992). Developmental theories for the 1990s: Development and individual differences. *Child Development, 63,* 1–19.

Scarr, S. (1995). Commentary. *Human Development, 38,* 154–158.

Scarr, S., & McCartney, K. (1983). How people make their own environments: A theory of genotype → environment effects. *Child Development, 54,* 424–435.

Schaffner, K. F. (1998). Genes, behavior, and developmental emergentism: One process, indivisible? *Philosophy-of-Science, 65*(2), 209–252.

Turkheimer, E. (1991). Individual and group differences in adoption studies of IQ. *Psychological Bulletin, 110,* 392–405.

Turkheimer, E. (2000). Three laws of behavior genetics and what they mean. *Current Directions in Psychological Science, 9,* 160–164.

Turkheimer, E., Goldsmith, H. H., & Gottesman, I. I. (1995). Some conceptual deficiencies in "developmental" behavior genetics: Comment. *Human Development, 38,* 143–153.

Turkheimer, E., & Gottesman, I. I. (1991). Individual differences and the canalization of human behavior. *Developmental Psychology, 27,* 18–22.

Turkheimer, E., & Gottesman, I. I. (1996). Simulating the dynamics of genes and environment in development. *Development and Psychopathology, 8,* 667–677.

Turkheimer, E., Lovett, G., Robinette, C. D., & Gottesman, I. I. (1992). The heritability of divorce: New data and theoretical implications [Abstract]. *Behavior Genetics, 22,* 757.

Turkheimer, E., & Waldron, M. (2000). Nonshared environment: A theoretical, methodological and quantitative review. *Psychological Bulletin, 126,* 78–108.

Wachs, T. D. (1993a). Determinants of intellectual development: Single determinant research in a multidetermined universe. *Intelligence, 17,* 1–9

Wachs, T. D. (1993b). The nature–nurture-gap: What we have here is a failure to collaborate. In R. Plomin & G. E. McClearn (Eds.), *Nature, nurture, and psychology* (pp. 375–391). Washington, DC: American Psychological Association.

Waldron, M., & Turkheimer, E. (2000). Nonshared environment: A theoretical, methodological and quantitative review. *Psychological Bulletin, 126,* 78–108.

Waller, N., Kojetin, B., Lykken, D., Tellegen, A., & Bouchard, T. (1990). Religious interests, personality, and genetics: A study of twins reared together and apart. *Psychological Science, 1,* 138–142.

12

Behavioral Genomics: Where Molecular Genetics Is Taking Psychiatry and Psychology

Peter McGuffin

Introduction

In this chapter, the emphasis is on abnormal behavior. Three main questions are considered:

- Are genes involved in susceptibility?
- If so, can we locate and identify genes and discover what they do?
- If genes are identified, how will this influence clinical practice in psychiatry and psychology?

I address the first question fairly broadly and superficially because it will be evident from other chapters in this book, or indeed to anyone who has followed the life work of Dr. Irving I. Gottesman, that the overall answer for most traits and disorders is "yes." Furthermore, although Dr. Gottesman was among the first to predict that schizophrenia (and probably most other major psychiatric disorders) would turn out to be polygenic (Gottesman & Shields, 1967) and, therefore, that localizing and cloning genes would not be easy, he has more recently contributed to the major endeavor to find the genes involved in schizophrenia and other disorders. Therefore *his* answer to the second question, "Can we locate?" seems to be "yes, eventually," and I concur. However, the story of locating genes involved in abnormal behavior is complicated and deserves more detailed discussion.

Finding the locations of susceptibility genes is the first step in the process of positional cloning in which genes are identified, their structure and sequence studied, the proteins that they encode for identified, and the mechanisms of regulation and expression understood. If all of this can be accomplished with regard to the major psychiatric disorders, it will represent a huge increment in our understanding of the neurobiology of disease. Therefore, the broad answer to my third question on clinical implications is not difficult. The enhanced understanding of the neurobiology of disease will provide new avenues for the development of treatment, provide important anchor points for understanding gene–environment interplay, and have a decided impact on the public as well as on professional perception of abnormal behaviors. Let us examine each of these three areas in more detail.

Are Genes Involved in Susceptibility?

One thing is clear when we consider abnormal behaviors that may have a familial or genetic causation: A wide range of mechanisms are involved. Thus, comparatively uncommon disorders such as Huntington's disease and three forms of early-onset familial Alzheimer's disease each result from mutations in single, dominant, genes (Williams, 2002). However, the single-gene forms of Alzheimer's disease together account for less than 1% of Alzheimer's disease. Most cases occur in later life and have a more complicated genetic basis that involves associations with the E4 allele of apolipoprotein E as well as other loci, including one that is linked to markers on chromosome 10 (Williams, 2002). The patterns in disorders such as schizophrenia (Riley & McGuffin, 2000) and bipolar disorder (Jones & Craddock, 1999) are even more complex, as might be expected if, as predicted by Gottesman and Shields (1967) more than 30 years ago, the genetic component of such conditions involves multiple genes of small effect.

We also have to bear in mind that although the role of a shared environment seems to be small or even nonexistent in contributing to family similarities for many traits, it cannot be disregarded for behavior as a whole. For example, the familial clustering of bulimic symptoms (Rutherford, McGuffin, Katz, & Murray, 1993) or symptoms of disabling fatigue in childhood (Farmer, Scourfield, Martin, Cardno, & McGuffin, 1998) show a pattern of correlation in twins where monozygotic (MZ) similarity is only slightly greater than dizygotic (DZ) similarity, so that it is difficult to distinguish between genetic and family–environmental sources of resemblance. Furthermore, traits that are substantially influenced by a family culture or other shared environmental factors can sometimes show familial clustering and may actually simulate Mendelian inheritance (Edwards, 1960). For example, McGuffin and Huckle (1990) found that attending medical school was 80 times as common in the first-degree relatives of medical students than in the general population. Admittedly, this is a trait for which genes could play an indirect role via their effects on intelligence and personality, but it would seem likely that family culture has a major role. Despite this being the most likely commonsense interpretation, complex segregation analysis showed that attending medical school, at least in Wales, where the study was conducted, passed most of the tests for autosomal recessive inheritance.

We are, fortunately, better informed about the genetics of most of the major psychiatric disorders than we are about attending medical school, because of twin data. This is particularly well exemplified by twin studies of schizophrenia. Dr. Gottesman, with his colleague James Shields, pioneered much of the methodology that is now taken for granted in modern twin studies of psychiatric disorders (Gottesman & Shields, 1972). Theirs was one of the first twin studies of schizophrenia to utilize a hospital-based twin register (in this case the Maudsley Hospital register in London, set up by Eliot Slater in

1948) to obtain a systematically ascertained sample of twins where the index case, or proband, had a hospital diagnosis of that disorder. Although their study preceded the days of operational diagnostic criteria and standardized interviews, Gottesman and Shields devised their own semistructured system of examination so that all interviewed participants underwent similar clinical assessments, which were backed up by Minnesota Multiphasic Personality Inventory (MMPI). Zygosity determination, where possible, was based on genetic polymorphisms in the blood. Detailed abstracts were prepared on all participants. This last procedure (which nowadays does not sound all that startling but at that time was almost unprecedented) allowed two important innovations to be introduced. First, Gottesman and Shields were able to present edited abstracts, from which zygosity and cotwin information had been removed, to raters who performed "blindfolded" assessment. Second, they used not just one but a panel of raters who had different theoretical and clinical perspectives on schizophrenia. Some had "broad" views and some had "narrow" views on what constituted the greatest MZ/DZ difference in concordance and, by implication, the "most genetic" definition of schizophrenia. These results were important in themselves, but they had an added bonus: The way in which Gottesman and Shields collected and stored their data allowed subsequent studies on the same material that were more than a recycling exercise.

The Maudsley Schizophrenia Twin Series Revisited

The introduction of new and more explicit, so-called *operational,* diagnostic criteria in the 1970s and 1980s produced some unexpected results. First, various authors proposed their own versions of what were, on the face of it, similar but subtly different criteria for diagnosing schizophrenia. Although applying any one of these was found to give high reliability as reflected in good interrater agreement, the agreement *between* these different definitions of schizophrenia was surprisingly poor. Some definitions appeared to be very restrictive and others very broad (Brockington, Kendell, & Leff, 1978). Even the extent to which a definition proved to be either "strict" or "broad" was not consistent but appeared to depend also on the characteristics of the patient sample (e.g., whether it consisted of a consecutive series of admissions or of an accumulated series on a case register) and on the way the clinical assessment was carried out (i.e., whether the interview or rating procedure was sensitive to the constituent items that made up the diagnostic criteria; Farmer, Wesseley, Castle, & McGuffin, 1992).

This puzzle presented by an array of newly formulated and reliable, but mutually discrepant, systems of diagnosis, prompted a reassessment of the case material from the Maudsley Hospital twin series that had originally been studied by Gottesman and Shields (1972), applying multiple sets of operational criteria (Farmer, McGuffin, & Gottesman, 1987; McGuffin, Farmer, Gottesman, Murray, & Reveley, 1984). Using this so-called polydiagnostic approach, we were able to compare the effect of different diagnostic criteria with regard to estimates of genetic parameters such as the MZ:DZ ratio and heritability (or proportion of variances accounted for by genes). The results showed that

Schneider's First Rank Symptoms were excessively restrictive and gave no evidence of genetic determination, whereas the St Louis criteria (Feighner et al., 1972) and Research Diagnostic Criteria (Spitzer, Endicott, & Robins, 1978) defined highly "genetic" forms of the disease. Using DSM-III criteria, the percent of the highest estimate of heritability was in the order of 80%.

Twin Studies Using Modern Diagnostic Criteria

The first twin study of schizophrenia to use modern criteria from the outset was carried out in Norway (Onstad, Skre, Torgersen, & Kringlen, 1991). The concordance rates in this study were very close to those found when Farmer et al. (1987) applied DSM-III criteria. Both of these research groups also made an attempt to define the most genetically determined definition of schizophrenia. They considered the effect of varying the definition of affected status on the MZ:DZ ratio by broadening the diagnosis to include other psychotic and affective disorders. Both groups found that including schizoaffective disorder, atypical psychosis, and schizotypy gave the greatest difference between MZ and DZ concordance rates. Further broadening the definition to include affective disorders and personality disorders greatly increased the DZ concordance rate, resulting in a lowering of the MZ:DZ ratio. These results are pertinent to the question of how to define the phenotype for genetic analysis, where the ability to define precisely what is being inherited greatly increases the chances of detecting genes. The MZ:DZ ratio is, in fact, a rather crude way of determining what is inherited, but, in keeping with earlier observations by Gottesman and Shields (1972), the results suggest that the "most genetic" definition is not restricted to tightly defined schizophrenia alone but, on the other hand, is not excessively broad.

More recently, there have been five additional twin studies in which the cases have been defined using operational criteria (Table 12.1). One of these was a further updating and extension of the Maudsley series. Cardno et al. (1999) found proband-wise concordances of 20/47 (43%) in MZ twins compared with 0/50 (0%) in DZ twins using DSM-III-R criteria. For ICD-10 defined schizophrenia, the rates were 21/50 (42%) in MZ twins and 1/58 (2%) in DZ twins. Applying genetic model fitting, they estimated that the broad heritability, or proportion of variation in liability to schizophrenia, was about 84% for the DSM-III-R and 83% for the ICD-10 definition of schizophrenia.

Modern Twin Studies of Other Disorders

Figure 12.1 shows a selection of other disorders, or sets of symptoms, for which the twin similarity has been expressed as correlations. With the exception of chronic fatigue and bulimic symptoms (which, as we have already briefly discussed, show only modest differences in MZ versus DZ correlations), there is a general tendency toward much greater MZ than DZ similarity, suggesting important genetic effects. The data nearly all come from the studies with which I am most familiar because I have been personally involved in them. The exceptions are the data on autism, which were collected by the research group of the former holder of my present post, Michael Rutter (Bailey et al., 1995).

Table 12.1. Twin Studies 1996–1999

Authors	Country	Ascertain-ment	Diagnostic criteria	MZ concordance (%)	DZ concordance (%)	Herita-bility %
Kläning (1996)	Denmark	Population register	ICD-10	7/16 (44)	2/19 (11)	83
Cannon et al. (1998)	Finland	Population register	ICD-8/DSM-III-R	40/87 (46)	18/195 (9)	
Franzek & Beckmann (1998)	Germany	Hospital admissions	DSM-III-R	20/31 (65)	7/25 (28)	
Cardno et al. (1999)	UK	Hospital register	DSM-III-R ICD-10	20/47 (43) 21/50 (42)	0/50 (0) 1/58 (2)	84 83
Tsujita et al. (1992)	Japan	Hospital admissions	DSM-III-R	11/22 (50)	1/7 (14)	
Combined			DSM-III-R ICD -10	57/114 (50) 28/66 (42.4)	4/97 (4.1) 3/77 (3.9)	88 83

Note. Adapted from "Twin Studies of Schizophrenia: From Bow-and-Arrow Concordances to Star Wars Mx and Functional Genomics," by A. G. Cardno and I. I. Gottesman, 2000, *American Journal of Medical Genetics, 97,* p. 13. Copyright 2000 by *American Journal of Medical Genetics.* Adapted with permission of Wiley-Liss, Inc., a subsidiary of John Wiley & Sons, Inc.

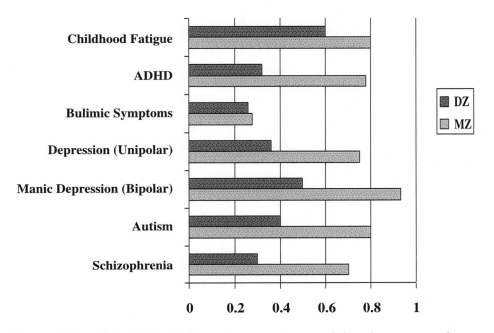

Figure 12.1. Twin similarity for various symptoms and disorders expressed as correlations.

The genetics of childhood autism and the influence of genetic studies on how autism has been conceptualized have an interesting recent history. It was once fashionable to attribute autism to the effects of being raised by cold, aloof "refrigerator" parents. In contrast, Hanson and Gottesman (1976) argued that autism had many organiclike features. However, these authors also suggested that because there is an increased risk of autism in children of below-average IQ and because twins, on average, show lower IQs than singletons, the twin method may be a misleading way of exploring the genetics of autism. A different view was taken by Folstein and Rutter (1977), whose twin study, again at Maudsley Hospital, produced results that were striking despite the small sample size. They found that 36% of MZ pairs were concordant for strictly defined autism compared with no DZ pairs. Nevertheless, the MZ/DZ difference was of marginal statistical significance, and Dr. Gottesman remained a skeptic. I subsequently found myself in an interesting position that required delicate handling when Michael Rutter invited Dr. Gottesman and myself to write the genetics chapter for the second edition of Rutter and Hersov's textbook, *Child and Adolescent Psychiatry, Modern Approaches* (Rutter & Hersov, 1985). When it came to the section on the genetics of autism, I found myself between a highly eminent editor, at this stage better known for his epidemiological work but now arguing that there probably was a strong genetic contribution to autism, and my mentoring coauthor, the doyen of psychiatric genetics, who was skeptical that genes played any role at all in autism. It was only when Dr. Gottesman and I calculated the correlations in liability and found that these were about 0.42 for siblings and 0.88 for MZ twins, fitting neatly with an additive genetic model that I began, with relief, to see some rapprochement between the views of my two senior colleagues. It is a measure of Dr. Gottesman's scientific integrity that he came to accept that the weight of the evidence favored our editor's position. Subsequently, family and twin studies, and, as we shall see, linkage studies now all point in the direction of a sizeable genetic component to childhood autism.

Attempting to Locate and Identify Genes

The bare essentials of the process of positional cloning have already been mentioned. Figure 12.2 helps us consider this in a bit more detail. A chromosomal region containing a gene that confers susceptibility to a disorder is identified by linkage mapping or by linkage disequilibrium mapping. Using a variety of methods, the region is then narrowed down until the gene itself is identified. Subsequently, the mutations, or variations, that confer susceptibility to the disease are identified. Distribution, level of expression, and functions of the gene product can then be studied. The whole process of positional cloning carries with it the possibility of incremental benefits for clinical practice in ways that will be discussed more fully later. As hinted at in the figure, however, these include the possibility of predictive testing, refined diagnosis, and, eventually, the development of specific targeted treatments. The positional cloning approach is, in theory, and increasingly in practice, straightforward in single-gene disorders. The burning issue is whether the approach is feasible in common complex disorders that involve multiple genes.

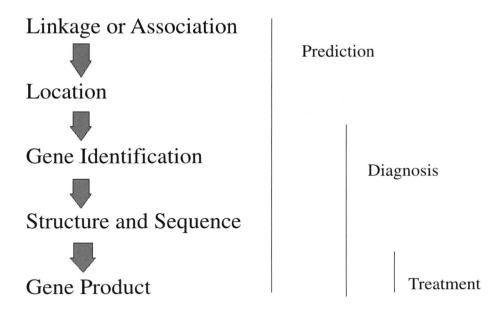

Figure 12.2.   An outline of the process of positional cloning.

Unfortunately, conventional linkage analysis requires several assumptions. These are that major gene effects (rather than just multiple small gene effects) exist, that there is some way of ensuring a genetic homogeneity, and that the mode of transmission of the disorder is known. Concentrating on large multiply affected pedigrees with early onset has enabled these problems to be overcome in some complex disorders such as Alzheimer's disease and breast cancer, in which single-gene forms of disease have been identified, but to date, this has not been the case with such psychiatric disorders as schizophrenia or bipolar disorder, in which, as I discuss later in the chapter, the picture appears to be more complicated. An alternative to studying large families is sib-pair analysis, which has been successful in identifying susceptibility loci involved in such disorders as type 1 diabetes and is being used in a range of other common disorders. This type of study simply detects linkage by testing whether pairs of siblings, in which both are affected by the disorder, share genetic marker alleles more than would be expected by chance. Focusing on affected sib pairs has several advantages, including not needing to make any assumptions about the mode of inheritance of the disease. The main drawback of sib-pair analysis is that susceptibility genes of very small effect may require very large samples to be detected. For example, Williams et al. (1999) completed a whole genome scan involving nearly 200 sib pairs affected by schizophrenia. They found no definite positive linkage findings, but they were able to exclude a gene conferring a relative risk of two or more from more than 80% of the genome. If it is correct that the genes involved in schizophrenia confer relative risks of less than two, then it may be that very large samples in the region of 600 to 800 are required for linkage to be detected. Although this may seem surprising at first sight, it is not, in fact, out of keeping with the basic genetic epidemiology of schizophrenia as summarized by Dr. Gottesman

(1991). For example, the relative risk in a sibling of a schizophrenic is about 10, so it could be that if several additive genes are involved, none will individually have a relative risk of more than two. This is so because relative risks across different loci are multiplicative. Thus, for example, six loci each conferring a relative risk of 1.5 would give a total relative risk of more than 11.

In fact, promising findings are now beginning to emerge in schizophrenia, and recent meta-analyses suggest greater consistency of linkage findings than has been previously recognized (Badner & Gershon, 2002; Lewis et al., 2003). In particular, there appears to be reasonable evidence for loci involved in liability to schizophrenia on chromosomes 1q, 3p, 5q, 6p, 8p, 11q, 13q, 14p, 20q, and 22q. Another psychiatric disorder where sib-pair analysis has been most successful so far is autism, for which several groups have now reported positive linkage findings on the same region of chromosome 7 (Barrett, et al., 1999; International Molecular Genetic Study of Autism Consortium, 1998; Philippe et al., 1999). There are also fairly consistent linkage results regarding dyslexia implicating loci on chromosome 6p (Cardon et al., 1994, 1995; Fisher et al., 1999; Gayan et al., 1999; Grigorenko et al., 1997) and chromosome 15q (Grigorenko et al., 1997; Morris et al., 2000).

Nevertheless, it is desirable to look for approaches that might be complimentary to linkage and have greater power to detect small effects and to narrow down linkage regions. Allelic association is the main such approach. Allelic association is the phenomenon of a particular marker allele occurring more commonly in individuals with a disease or trait than would be expected by chance. Classically, this is detected in a case control study, which compares the frequency of marker alleles and healthy controls. Allelic association can arise because of linkage disequilibrium when the marker and the susceptibility loci are so closely linked that their relationship is preserved over many generations of recombination. Alternatively, the marker itself may confer susceptibility to the disorder if there is a functional variant in a gene encoding a protein that is involved in the pathophysiology of the disorder. Unfortunately, there is also a "nuisance" cause of allelic association known as population stratification. This results from recent admixtures of populations in which the component subpopulations have different frequencies of the disorder and a different frequency of marker alleles. Consequently "false-positive" associations may be found. Although stratification can be overcome by careful ethnic matching of cases and controls, new approaches have been put forward that derive the controls "internally" from family members. One example is the transmission disequilibrium test, in which affected individuals who have two parents available for study are investigated. Only those families where at least one parent is heterozygous for the marker are informative, but there is a simple comparison that cross tabulates whether the marker allele versus the alternative (or "nontest" allele) is transmitted or not transmitted to the affected individuals.

As I have mentioned, the advantage of mapping genes using linkage disequilibrium is that it can detect very small effects, down to odds ratios of a little more than 1, or as little as 1% of the variance in liability to a disorder. The disadvantage of basing gene finding on linkage disequilibrium is that it takes place only over very short chromosome distances. The length of the genome, measured in units called centiMorgans (cM), is about 3500 cM. Linkage can readily be detected, given the right conditions, over distances of 10 to 15 cM. Association in most populations does not usually occur between loci more than a fraction of 1 cM apart, however. Therefore, in contrast to linkage, in which genome searches can be accomplished with a few hundred markers, many thousands of roughly evenly spaced markers are required to effect dense enough coverage for a complete search using association and linkage disequilibrium. Nevertheless, methods that permit high through-put genotyping using many thousands of markers are rapidly becoming available, so genome scans using linkage as equilibrium should be able to be performed routinely within the foreseeable future.

In the meantime, allelic association has been used to test for so-called positional candidates, genes that map to a linkage region and encode for proteins that potentially have relevance to the pathogenesis of a disorder. In particular, there have been exciting new results relating to schizophrenia. As I have mentioned, several regions of the genome have been implicated by more than one linkage study and remain promising following meta-analyses. Chromosome 22q has been implicated both by linkage and by studies of patients with microdeletions. Recent work attempting to refine regions of interest using linkage disequilibrium mapping has identified four promising and novel positional candidates. They are neuregulin-1 on chromosome 8p-p21, G72 located at chromosome 13q34, dysbindin at 6p22.3, and proline dehydrogenase, which is a gene that maps to chromosome 22q11. There is also renewed interest in a fifth gene, catechol-O-methyltransferase (COMT), also on chromosome 22q11. In addition, a sixth gene regulator of G protein signaling 4 (RGS4) implicated by gene expression studies is known to map to a linkage region on chromosome 1q and contains polymorphisms that have been found to be associated with schizophrenia (see reviews by Harrison & Owen, 2003, and McGuffin, Tandon, & Corsico, 2003). COMT is involved in the breakdown of dopamine, and much of the focus in candidate gene studies of schizophrenia has been on genes involved in dopaminergic transmission. However, it is of interest that all of the novel positional candidates listed previously are involved in transmission via excitatory glutamate pathways (Harrison & Owen, 2003). It has also been postulated that they influence glial cells and that these are a locus of the genes–environment interactions in schizophrenia, with glial dysfunction as an important factor for the genetic liability to the disorder (Moises, Zoega, & Gottesman, 2002).

Table 12.2 summarizes the current state of play for some selected psychiatric disorders and allied traits. For single-gene conditions, the positional cloning approach starting with linkage has proved dramatically successful. There are major advances in the understanding of the neurobiology of disorders such as Huntington's disease and early-onset familial Alzheimer's disease. As noted, dyslexia (or reading disability) provides a good example of progress being made in a more complex and common trait. Schizophrenia provides an example of a disorder in which, despite a frustrating array of results from earlier linkage studies (Riley & McGuffin, 2000), some linkage regions now receive support from several studies and interesting positional candidates are beginning to emerge.

Table 12.2. Some Behavioral Disorders and Traits, Their Pattern of Inheritance, and the Status of Gene Mapping Studies

Behavioral trait	Pattern of inheritance	Gene mapping
Huntington's disease	Rare autosomal dominant dynamic mutation	Gene identified (Huntington) with unstable trinucleotide repeat.
Early-onset (familial) Alzheimer's disease	Rare autosomal dominant	Three distinct genes identified (presenilins 1 and 2 and amyloid precursor protein).
Fragile X mental retardation	Nonstandard X-linked dynamic mutation	Two genes identified (FMR1 and 2), both with unstable trinucleotide repeats.
Late-onset Alzheimer's disease	Common complex	Increased risk with apolipoprotein E4 allele firmly established.
Attention deficit hyperactivity disorder	Common complex	Three contributory loci in the dopamine system, DRD4, DAT1, and DRD5; DRD4 best replicated, others less certain.
Dyslexia	Common complex	Two contributory loci suggested on chromosomes 6 and 15; findings replicated.
Schizophrenia	Common complex	Reported linkages including chromosomes 1, 5, 6, 8, 13, 15 and 22; consensus emerging from metanalysis and few promising positional candidate genes include neuregulin, dysbindin, G72, RGS4.
Aggression	Common complex	Mutation reported in X-linked MAO A gene in one family; recent evidence of broader relevance with a common low-activity allele interacting with early environmental adversity.

Note. Adapted from "Toward Behavioral Genomics," by P. McGuffin, B. Riley, and R. Plomin, 2001, *Science, 291*, p. 1232. Copyright 2001 by the American Association for the Advancement of Science. Adapted with permission.

The field has been further complicated by reports of single-gene mutations or subtle chromosomal anomalies such as microdeletions that appear to be infrequent or very rare in the population but that result in behaviors that resemble common disorders. For example, the microdeletion on chromosome 22 that causes velocardiofacial syndrome is associated with a schizophrenic-like psychosis in as many as a third of cases (Murphy, Jones, & Owen, 1999). An even rarer abnormality, a point mutation in the monoamine oxidase A (MAOA) gene on the X-chromosome, has been found to be associated with anti-social or aggressive behavior in one family (Brunner, Nelen, Breakefield, Ropers, & van Oost, 1993). Until recently, MAOA was not thought to be associated with antisocial behavior more generally. However, it now appears that there is an interaction effect with early adversity whereby men with a low activity MAOA allele who are exposed to bad parenting are at increased risk of later developing aggressive or antisocial behavior (Caspi et al., 2002).

Ultimately, the combination of ever more complete information on the genome, the genes, and the control elements contained therein, together with accessibility of our computers on the Internet, means that genes involved in psychiatric disorders and even those involved in normal behaviors will be tracked down and identified. The systematic genome search or positional cloning approach and candidate gene strategies will, in effect, converge very rapidly once all genes have been identified and characterized. Even though the number of genes is likely to be large, high throughput genotyping methods will make tractable the process of finding genes. The only obstacle, therefore, for detecting and identifying genes even of small effect would be of having samples of DNA from well-characterized large-scale collections of cases, controls, and families containing affected individuals. Such studies will depend on collaborations among epidemiological, clinical, and genetic researchers, but, once they have succeeded, what will be the other implications for clinical psychology and psychiatry?

The Impact of Psychiatric Genomics

At its most basic level, progress in genomic research should lead to a profound improvement in understanding of the neurobiology of psychiatric disorders. Knowing the structure and function of all human genes has been compared with discovering a "periodic table of life" (Peltonen & McKusick, 2001, p. 1224) and will pave the way for a shift in emphasis from the structure of the genome to a functional genomics and proteonomics, the study of proteins at a functional level. Combining this type of "bottom-up" approach with top-down studies comparing human behavior with animal models would take us into an era of behavioral genomics (McGuffin et al., 2001).

Genomic advances in psychiatry will also have important implications for pharmacotherapy. At present, the drugs used in the treatment of psychiatric and other central nervous system diseases have actions that are limited to a number of target sites that include cell surface receptors, nuclear receptors, ion channels, and enzymes. It is likely that identifying the genes involved in the pathogenesis of psychiatric disorders will identify new targets, some of which will fall within these categories, but they will also include others that are entirely novel (Roses, 2000). In addition, advances in genomics will allow tailoring of pharmaceuticals that are likely to be relevant to the development of both treatment response and side effects. For example, there is already some evidence that response to atypical antipsychotics such as clozapine is influenced by an individual's genotypes at a combination of loci (Arranz et al., 2000).

In addition, the susceptibility of side effects to tricyclic antidepressants is influenced by genes in the cytochrome P450 system. In contrast, in my view, gene therapy proper, that is, using genetic engineering methods to carry out gene transfer of "healthy" genes into tissues containing mutant genes, is unlikely to have a place in psychiatric disorders. Treatments involving gene transfer have already proven enormously problematic even in single gene disorders affecting more accessible organs such as the lungs (Somia & Verma, 2000) and seem unlikely to be successful in polygenic disorders involving a relatively inaccessible organ, the brain.

Last, there has been a degree of concern that recent advances will tend to "geneticize" psychiatry and encourage deterministic attitudes. One worry is that insurance companies or employers may wish to force DNA testing in individuals at high genetic risk. This is most problematic ethically for single-gene disorders such as Mendelian forms of Alzheimer's disease or Huntington's disease, for which a DNA-based test can tell with virtually 100% certainty whether or not an individual will become affected. With highly heritable polygenic disorders such as schizophrenia, the situation will prove much more complicated. At best, DNA tests may be used to modify the predicted risk in individuals who already have a high risk by virtue of having a schizophrenic close relative. However, the limit of accuracy of this prediction is unlikely to ever be better than 50%, which we know from twin studies is about the accuracy with which the occurrence of schizophrenia can be predicted in the genetic clone, the MZ twin, of a schizophrenic index case.

The other way in which aspects of psychiatry may possibly become geneticized is that the stigma associated with disorder will increase. Nevertheless, it is possible that just the opposite will occur. Part of the postgenomic impact on psychiatry could be that an improved understanding of the neurobiological pathogenesis would help legitimize schizophrenia, depression, and bipolar disorder in the public view. Two examples from the extreme ends of life, where I have the impression that genetic research has had a favorable impact on stigma, are childhood autism and Alzheimer's disease. Both are now regarded and portrayed in the popular media as "real" brain disorders and no longer a result of adverse parenting in the case of autism or a form of decay over which the sufferer should somehow be able to exercise some more control in the case of the more common form of senile dementia. Of course, public opinion is likely to be influenced by, and to some extent led by, the attitude of researchers and clinicians. Therefore, the question of whether genomic advances become associated with a decrease rather than a worsening of stigma is to some extent in the hands of the psychological and psychiatric professions as a whole. Most of the negative attitudes among psychologists and psychiatrists toward genetic research are based on two fearful myths. The first is that geneticists are out to prove that human behavior is *determined* by genes. The second is that they might be right! In contrast, psychologists and psychiatrists who are at least moderately genetically knowledgeable are likely to welcome the potential benefits of genetic and genomics and play their part in implementing them. We will then all receive bonuses as the scientific capital of discoveries in the postgenomic era is translated into improvements in the prestige of psychology and psychiatry as well as improvements in the status and public image of those who suffer from psychological problems.

References

Arranz, M. J., Pons, J., Gutierrez, B., Mulcrone, J., Cairns, N., Makoff, A., et al. (2000). Investigation of 5-HT2A differential expression and imprinting in schizophrenia. *American Journal of Medical Genetics, 96*(4), 391.

Badner, J. A., & Gershon, E. S. (2002). Meta-analysis of whole-genome linkage scans of bipolar disorder and schizophrenia. *Molecular Psychiatry, 7*(4), 405–411.

Bailey, A., Le Couteur, A., Gottesman, I. I., Bolton, P., Simonoff, E., Yuzda, E., et al. (1995). Autism as a strongly genetic disorder: Evidence from a British twin study. *Psychological Medicine, 25*, 63–77.

Barrett, S., Beck, J. C., Bernier, R., Bisson, E., Braun, T. A., Casavant, T. L., et al. (1999). An autosomal genomic screen for autism. Collaborative linkage study of autism. *American Journal of Medical Genetics, 88*(6), 609–615.

Brockington, I. F., Kendell, R. E., & Leff, J. P. (1978). Definitions of schizophrenia: Concordance and prediction of outcome. *Psychological Medicine, 8,* 387–398.

Brunner, H. G., Nelen, M., Breakefield, X. O., Ropers, H. H., & van Oost, B. A. (1993). Abnormal behavior associated with a point mutation in the structural gene for monoamine oxidase A. *Science, 262,* 578–580.

Cannon, T. D., Kaprio, J., Lonnqvist, J., Huttunen, M., & Koskenvuo, M. (1998). The genetic epidemiology of schizophrenia in a Finnish twin cohort: A population-based modeling study. *Archives of General Psychiatry, 55,* 67–74.

Cardno, A., Coid, B., Macdonald, A. M., Ribchester, T. R., Davies, N. J., Venturi, P., et al. (1999). Heritability estimates for psychotic disorders: The Maudsley Twin Psychosis series. *Archives of General Psychiatry, 56,* 162–168.

Cardno, A. G., & Gottesman, I. I. (2000). Twin studies of schizophrenia: From bow-and-arrow concordances to star wars Mx and functional genomics. *American Journal of Medical Genetics, 97,* 12–17.

Cardon, L. R., Smith, S. D., Fulker, D. W., Kimberling, W. J., Pennington, B. F., & DeFries, J. C. (1994). Quantitative trait locus for reading disability on chromosome 6. *Science, 266,* 277.

Cardon, L. R., Smith, S. D., Fulker, D. W., Kimberling, W. J., Pennington, B. F., & DeFries, J. C. (1995). "Reading disability, attention-deficit hyperactivity disorder, and the immune system": Response. *Science, 268,* 787–788.

Caspi, A., McClay, J., Moffitt, T. E., Mill, J., Martin, J., Craig, I. W., et al. (2002). Role of genotype in the cycle of violence in maltreated children. *Science, 297,* 851–854.

Edwards, J. H. (1960). The simulation of mendelism. *Acta Genetica et Statistica Medica, 10,* 63–70.

Farmer, A. E., McGuffin, P., & Gottesman, I. I. (1987). Twin concordance for DSM-III schizophrenia: Scrutinizing the validity of the definition. *Archives of General Psychiatry, 44,* 634–641.

Farmer, A. E., Scourfield, J., Martin, N., Cardno, A., & McGuffin, P. (1998). Is disabling fatigue in childhood influenced by genes? *Psychological Medicine, 29,* 279–282.

Farmer, A. E., Wesseley, S., Castle, D., & McGuffin, P. (1992). Methodological issues in using a polydiagnostic approach to define psychotic illness. *British Journal of Psychiatry, 161,* 824–830.

Feighner, J. P., Robins, E., Guze, S. B., Woodruff, R. A., Winokur, G., & Munoz, R. (1972). Diagnostic criteria for use in psychiatric research. *Archives of General Psychiatry, 26,* 57–63

Fisher, S. E., Marlow, A. J., Lamb, J., Maestrini, E., Williams, D. F., Richardson, A. J., et al. (1999). A quantitative-trait locus on chromosome 6p influences aspects of developmental dyslexia. *American Journal of Human Genetics, 64*(1), 146–156.

Folstein, S. E., & Rutter, M. (1977). Infantile autism: A genetic study of 21 twin pairs. *Journal of Child Psychology and Psychiatry, 18,* 297–321.

Franzek, E., & Beckmann, H. (1998). Different genetic background of schizophrenia spectrum psychoses: A twin study. *American Journal of Psychiatry, 155,* 76–83.

Gayan, J., Smith, S. D., Cherny, S. S., Cardon, L. R., Fulker, D. W., Brower, A. M., et al. (1999). Quantitative-trait for specific language and reading deficits on chromosome 6p. *American Journal of Human Genetics, 64,* 157–164.

Gottesman, I. I. (1991). *Schizophrenia genesis.* New York: W. H. Freeman.

Gottesman, I. I., & Shields, J. (1967). A polygenic theory of schizophrenia. *Proceedings of the National Academy of Sciences USA, 1,* 199–205

Gottesman, I. I., & Shields, J. (1972). *Schizophrenia and genetics. A twin study vantage point.* New York and London: Academic Press.

Grigorenko, E. L., Wood, F. B., Meyer, M. S., Hart, L. A., Speed, W. C., & Shuster, A. (1997). Susceptibility loci for distinct components of developmental dyslexia on chromosomes 6 and 15. *American Journal of Human Genetics, 60,* 27–39.

Hanson, D. R., & Gottesman, I. I. (1976). The genetics, if any, of infantile autism and childhood schizophrenia. *Journal of Autism and Child Schizophrenia, 6,* 209–234.

Harrison, P. J., & Owen, M. J. (2003). Genes for schizophrenia? Recent findings and their pathophysiological implications. *Lancet, 361,* 417–419.

International Molecular Genetic Study of Autism Consortium. (1998). A full genome screen for autism with evidence for linkage to a region on chromosome 7q. *Human Molecular Genetics, 7,* 571–578.

Jones, I., & Craddock, N. (1999). Genetics of bipolar disorder. *Journal of Medical Genetics, 36,* 585–594.

Kläning, U. (1996). Schizophrenia in twins: Incidence and risk factors. Unpublished doctoral dissertation, University of Aarhus, Denmark.

Lewis, C. M., Levinson, D. F., Wise, L. H., DeLisi, L. E., Straub, R. E., Hovatta, I., et al. (2003). Genome scan meta-analysis of schizophrenia and bipolar disorder. Part II: Schizophrenia. *American Journal of Human Genetics, 73,* 34–48.

McGuffin, P., Farmer, A. E., Gottesman, I. I., Murray, R. M., & Reveley, A. M. (1984). Twin concordance for operationally defined schizophrenia: Confirmation of familiality and heritability. *Archives of General Psychiatry, 41,* 541–545.

McGuffin, P., & Huckle, P. (1990). Simulation of Mendelism revisted: The recessive gene for attending medical school. *American Journal of Human Genetics, 46,* 994–999.

McGuffin, P., Riley, B., & Plomin, R. (2001). Toward behavioral genomics. *Science, 291,* 1232–1233.

McGuffin, P., Tandon, K., & Corsico, A. (2003). Linkage and association studies of schizophrenia. *Current Psychiatry Reports, 5,* 121–127.

Moises, H. W., Zoega, T., & Gottesman, I. I. (2002). The glial growth factors deficiency and synaptic destabilization hypothesis of schizophrenia. *BioMed Central Psychiatry, 2,* 8. Retrieved October 17, 2003, from http://www.biomedcentral.com/1471-244x/2/8

Morris, D. W., Robinson, L., Turic, D., Duke, M., Webb, V., Milham, C., et al. (2000). Family-based association mapping provides evidence for a gene for reading disability on chromosome 15q. *Human Molecular Genetics, 9,* 855–860.

Murphy, K. C., Jones, L. A., & Owen, M. J. (1999). High rates of schizophrenia in adults with Velo-Cardio-Facial Syndrome. *Archives of Genetics Psychiatry, 56,* 940–945.

Onstad, S., Skre, I., Torgersen, S., & Kringlen, E. (1991). Twin concordance for DSM-III-R schizophrenia. *Acta Psychiatrica Scandinavica, 83,* 395–601.

Peltonen, L., & McKusick, V. A. (2001). Genomics and medicine—Dissecting human disease in the postgenomic era. *Science, 291,* 1224.

Phillippe, A., Martinez, M., Guilloud-Bataille, M., Gillberg, C., Rastam, M., Sponheim, E., et al. (1999). Genome-wide scan for autism susceptibility genes. *Human Molecular Genetics, 8,* 805–812.

Riley, B., & McGuffin, P. (2000). Linkage and associated studies of schizophrenia. *American Journal of Medical Genetics, 97,* 23–44

Roses, A., D. (2000). Pharmacogenetics and future drug development and delivery. *Lancet, 355,* 1358–1361.

Rutherford, J., McGuffin, P., Katz, R., & Murray, R. M. (1993). Genetic influences in eating attitudes in a normal female twin population. *Psychological Medicine, 23,* 425–436.

Rutter, M., & Hersov, L. (1985). *Child and adolescent psychiatry—Modern approaches* (2nd ed.). Oxford, UK: Blackwell Scientific Publications.

Somia, N., & Verma, I. M. (2000). Gene therepy: Trials and tribulations. *Nature Reviews Genetics, 1,* 91–99.

Spitzer, R. L., Endicott, J. R., & Robins, E. (1978). Research diagnostic criteria: Rationale and reliability. *Archives of General Psychiatry, 35,* 773–782.

Tsujita, T., Okazaki, Y. Fujimaru, K., Minami, Y., Mutoh, Y., Maeda, H., et al. (1992). Twin concordance rate of DSM-III-R schizophrenia in a new Japanese sample. Abstracts Seventh International Congress on Twin Studies (152). Tokyo, Japan.

Williams, J. (2002). Dementia and genetics. In R. Plomin, J. C. DeFries, I. Craig, & P. McGuffin (Eds.), *Behavioral genetics in the postgenomic era* (pp. 503–528). Washington, DC: American Psychological Association.

Williams, N. M., Rees, M. I., Holmans, P., Norton, N., Cardno, A. G., Jones, L. A., et al. (1999). A two-stage genome scan for schizophrenia susceptibility genes in 196 affected sibling pairs. *Human Molecular Genetics, 8,* 1729–1739.

13

Getting the Bugs Into Our Genetic Theories of Schizophrenia

Daniel R. Hanson

Introduction

For a common disorder, schizophrenia is uncommonly stubborn in yielding its mysteries to inquiring science. Is this form of insanity so complex in cause, so twisted in its development, so elusive in phenotype, that it is beyond the rational minds of those of us who try to solve its puzzle? We have not figured it out in the 100 or so years that have elapsed since Kraepelin and Bleuler set the descriptive foundations for identifying the illness. The efforts of countless excellent minds, the spending of vast research funds, and the application of technology that has unlocked the very secrets of life have failed, so far, to explain schizophrenia. Perhaps the problem is just too tough for us. Or, perhaps, we need to step back from our current concepts and find new ways to think about the origins of schizophrenia.

Before stepping too far away from current strategies for studying schizophrenia, we should take stock of what we know (or think we know) with some certainty about this illness. Table 13.1 lists a series of observations about schizophrenia that must be addressed by any theory that attempts to explain the illness. I look briefly at these facts, but the scope of this chapter does not allow full exploration of each of these observations. The informed reader will recognize truth in these observations. Those new to the literature can find further elaboration in the works of our honoree (cf., Gottesman, 1991).

Table 13.1. Realities to Explain About Schizophrenia

- Schizophrenia is a common disorder
- Rapid vs. insidious onset
- Variable course within individuals
- Variability in symptoms/course within families
- Inconsistent findings for every variable ever studied
- Genetic component
- Environmental component
- Widely variable age of onset (8–80)

What We Know About Schizophrenia

Schizophrenia is a common illness. About 1% of the population will experience schizophrenia during their lifetime. Except for a few rare exceptions, this 1% risk is remarkably constant around the globe regardless of culture, geography, or climate. Men and women are affected equally.

In contrast to the consistency of the risk for schizophrenia, the range in age of onset of schizophrenia is unusually broad. Symptoms usually start in the late teenage years or early 20s, but the illness can start in middle childhood (Hanson & Gottesman, 1976) and may rarely start in old age (Slater & Cowie, 1971). The DSM-III statement that the illness could not start after age 45 is clearly false, and this claim has been expunged from subsequent editions.

Genetic factors are important in the development of schizophrenia, as evidenced by family, adoption, and twin studies. The 50% (approximately) concordance rate in identical twins is also the best evidence that genetics are not the whole story. Environmental factors, yet to be identified, must also play a role. It is obviously possible for a person to have the gene(s) for schizophrenia and to pass those genes to offspring yet to remain symptom free (offspring of discordant twins). If we understood how this works, we would be better able to prevent or treat the illness.

The symptoms of the illness are highly variable. Within families (and thus presuming relative homogeneity of genetic and environmental factors), symptoms can vary widely (cf., Rosenthal, 1963). Even within affected individuals, symptoms will wax and wane and may even remit (Bleuler, 1978).

Not only is there enormous variability of symptoms within individuals and within families, but there is also variability within variables. That is, for every variable ever studied, not all people with schizophrenia show the same abnormality. Not all people with schizophrenia have deviant eye tracking, large ventricles, abnormal P300s, and hippocampal pyramidal cell abnormalities. No worries. Not everyone with HIV-I has Kaposi's sarcoma or *Pneumocystis carni,* though these syndromes are much more common in people with AIDS than in the general population. Phenotypic variability and inconsistencies do not require etiologic heterogeneity.

Our successful explanation of schizophrenia must accommodate the observed facts. We are charged with the task of explaining an illness that is relatively common, spans an enormous range in age of onset, has environmental etiologic contributors, is influenced by genetic factors, and encompasses enormous phenotypic variability ranging from no illness to profound disability. Furthermore, the phenotype will change over the life span, with waxing and waning of symptoms and, occasionally, remission.

What kind of pathophysiology produces such circumstances? We have a good model in the outstanding behavioral genetic triumph that has virtually eradicated a severely disabling illness from the planet. That model is polio.

Polio as a Genetic Disorder

What? Polio is a genetic disorder? Couldn't be. We all know a virus causes polio. That is why Salk and Sabin were able to develop vaccines that prevent the illness. The truth that polio is a viral disease is only a partial truth. Polio is also a genetic disease—or so suggests Herndorn and Jennings's (1951) twin data with an MZ (monozygotic) concordance of 36% and a DZ (dizygotic) concordance of 6%. The concept that infectious disease may have a genetic component is, of course, not new. Many agricultural geneticists make their living breeding disease resistance into both plants and animals (cf. Mackenzie & Bishop, 2001; Richter & Ronald, 2000). One of our behavioral genetics founders, Franz Kallmann (Kallmann & Reisner, 1943) showed that genetic factors influenced acquiring tuberculosis (DZ concordance = 26%, MZ concordance = 87%), an observation confirmed in modern times (Werneck-Barroso, 1999). Many other infectious diseases appear to have genetic factors influencing susceptibility/resistance (Bion & Brun-Buisson, 2000; Blackwell, 2001; Burt, 1999; Cook & Hill, 2001; Hawken, Beattie, & Schook, 1998; Hill, 1996, 1999; Kitagawa, Aizawa, Ikeda, & Hirokawa; 1996; Seymour, 1995; Smith & Germolec, 1999). Mechanisms for genetically mediated responses to infection occur through genetic variations in immune mediators such as cytokines (Knight, 2001) and HLA factors (Beskow & Gyllensten, 2002; F. S. Wang, 2003). Let us therefore suppose that schizophrenia develops from an infectious agent (the environmental contributor) but that genetic factors influence who is susceptible. That infectious agents may be operative in schizophrenia is supported by several lines of evidence. Summaries can be found in numerous sources (Morris, 1996; Munk-Jørgensen & Ewald, 2001; O'Reilly & Singh, 1996; Rubenstein, 1997; Torrey, Miller, Rawlings, & Yolken, 1997; Yolken, Karlsson, Yee, Johnston-Wilson, & Torrey, 2000; Yolken & Torrey, 1995).

The polio story provides us with several important insights. Figure 13.1 illustrates the various developmental features of polio. Once the virus infects the host, there may be no symptoms or a minor flulike illness. Host factors such as age, gender, fatigue, and others affect whether or not the infection will progress to paralysis. Some individuals remain paralyzed for life, some recover. Among the recovered, many develop new symptoms late in life. Only 1% to 2% of infected people develop paralysis. Some of these people have a

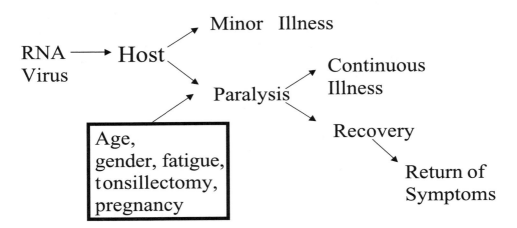

Figure 13.1. Polio: Developmental pathway.

flulike prodrome that resolves prior to development of motor weakness, whereas some who develop paralysis have no notable prodrome. About 4% to 8% of infected people develop the flulike syndrome but never have paralysis. The vast majority of infected people have no significant illness at all. Yet the latter two groups will mount antibodies to the virus and develop immunity to future infections. Some antibody markers of infection persist for life, but others disappear over time (see Horstman, 1963, for a further description of the early epidemiology that solved the polio riddle).

Suppose we tried to tackle the polio problem with standard behavioral-genetic strategies. What would we choose as our phenotype? We might pick as the phenotype a paralytic disorder that typically starts in late childhood or early adolescence but could start at almost any time of life. However, knowing that only 1% to 2% of infected people develop the motor disorder, paralysis is probably not a good phenotype for genetic analysis. The agricultural geneticists who develop disease-resistant organisms almost never study the genetics of disease. They study the genetics of wellness. They look for factors that provide resistance. Perhaps the genetic factors influencing nonparalysis as an outcome after infection by the polio virus are protective factors that could be located in the immune system; the gastrointestinal system, where the virus first invades; or in the invaded nervous system. Nonparalysis after exposure may be a more informative phenotype. There is likely no gene for polio even though genetic factors could be of major importance in conferring resistance. There is no gene for Dutch elm disease, a fungal infection of elm trees, but foresters are successful in breeding trees resistant to infection. Perhaps there is no gene for schizophrenia. We persist in a mode of thinking about disease in a manner shaped by classical Mendelian genetic disorders, in which we postulate some mutant gene, some inborn error of metabolism or structure, causing a specific phenotype. We have modernized the inborn error theme to include sophisticated ideas such as inborn errors of dopamine receptors and transport proteins, but these ideas are only new paint on a rusty theoretical vehicle.

We might go searching for the environmental contributors to paralysis through standard null hypothesis strategies. Thus, we would take people with paralysis and compare their environmental risk factors to people who do not have paralysis. Even if we were clever enough to consider that the paralysis is connected to an environmental factor such as a flulike virus, we still could erroneously reject our hunch. We know that for every proband with viral exposure and paralysis, there may be 90 controls who happen to have the viral exposure but no paralysis. The contrast between affected and controls with respect to viral infection may show no significant difference. We accept the null hypothesis, and we let the necessary and specific causal environmental agent elude us. Turkheimer (see chapter 11) is correct in his assessment of the inadequacies of null hypothesis strategies. The fact that the lifetime risk for schizophrenia is fairly constant around the globe suggests that the environmental contributors are ubiquitous. Many of us have been exposed but only a few get sick. In a population, if the rate of exposure to a causal disease agent is high but the rate of disease is low (e.g. only 1% to 2% of people exposed to the poliovirus get paralysis), then looking for the environmental agent through sick-versus-well null hypothesis testing may be futile.

The polio story is also instructive for its lessons about treatment. Even though the biology of the illness was worked out quite thoroughly in the 1950s, allowing prevention, the knowledge of the pathophysiology provided no help for those already affected. Treatment was ultra-low-tech and consisted of simple but skilled and dedicated physical therapy. With the dedication of therapists following in the Sister Kinney tradition, paralyzed limbs regained function and sometimes normalized. We now understand that any nondamaged neurons in a limb were recruited to enervate muscles that had lost neuronal input. The rescuing neurons hypertrophied and did heroic duty for years. With advancing age, however, these neurons could not sustain the effort, and a late-onset syndrome of weakness set in. Some of the late sequelae of polio are attributable to previously unrecognized damage to monoaminergic neurons in the brain. These brain abnormalities contribute to fatigue and weakness brought on by emotional stress as well as hypersensitivity to pain (Bruno, Frick, & Cohen, 1991). Polio's lessons provide us with a model for trying to explain diseases like schizophrenia that have a widely variable age of onset, genetic and environmental contributors, and great variability in symptoms and severity, with changing features over the life span. Streptococcal infections provide another useful model that brings us even closer to schizophrenia.

Can a Strep Throat Make You Psychotic?

Yes, but not often. Group-A-beta-hemolytic streptococcal pharyngitis is usually a self-limited illness, is easily treated with antibiotics, and is virtually universal. Almost everyone has had a strep throat some time in childhood. Once in a while, however, the illness takes a sinister course and develops into scarlet fever or rheumatic fever. Rheumatic fever is associated with arthritis, possible severe damage of heart valves, and CNS disorders. A psychotic syndrome referred to as "rheumatic schizophrenia" is also described (Davison & Bagley, 1969). Another poststreptococcal syndrome, Sydenham's chorea, causes central nervous damage resulting in a movement disorder and psychiatric symptoms. The choreic symptoms may wax and wane and even disappear, only to return with subsequent exposure to the bacteria. Hormones can also modify symptoms. More recently, a streptococcal associated childhood onset obsessive–compulsive disorder (pediatric autoimmune neurological disorder associated with strep—PANDAS) has been identified (Swedo et al., 1998). It appears that antibodies produced to fight the bacterial infection also cross-react with the basal ganglia of some individuals or produce a more global disseminated encephalomyelitis (Dale et al., 2001; Garvey, Giedd, & Swedo, 1998).

Different strains of the bacteria have different potentials for triggering an autoimmune response (Bisno, Shulman, & Dajani, 1988). Genetic factors in the host have been speculated to increase susceptibility. It is easy to imagine that if you have the bad luck to acquire a highly pathogenic strain of bacteria and had the bad luck to inherit an excessively responsive immune mediator, then you will be at high risk for immunological attack.

The types of adverse sequelae also appear to be a function of developmental stage at which the infection occurs. PANDAS almost always occurs in early childhood. It is suggested that Sydenham's chorea is more often the outcome when the strep infection occurs during adolescence. Life stage "critical periods" will shape longterm outcome.

In this model, an infectious agent interacts with host variables to produce a wide variety of symptoms and syndromes (Figure 13.2). Who would think that childhood obsessive–compulsive disorder would come about through a mechanism similar to cardiac valve disease? The host variables are in part genetic. There is no gene, per se, for rheumatic heart disease.

When infectious agents give rise to inflammatory disease of heart valves, the nature of the infectious agent may be less important that an individual's genetically influenced inflammatory response, as exemplified by Familial Mediterranean Fever (FMF; Scholl, 2002; Toutiou, 2001). The gene for FMF is located on the short arm of chromosome 16 and produces pyrin (marenostrin) that functions in a negative feedback loop to suppress inflammation. Absence of pyrin leads to exaggerated inflammatory responses. In addition, very high rates of rheumatic fever (RF) or rheumatic heart disease (RHD) are found in carrier relatives of patients with FMF (Tutar, Akar, Atalay, Yilmaz, & Yakinkaya, 2002). Having even one mutant gene appears to lead to immune hyperactivity to streptococcal antigens. Antibody production (Veasy & Hill, 1997) and cytokine activity (Yegin, Coskun, & Ertug, 1997) in RF patients is more marked than in nonrheumatics. In this example, the genetic factors that increase the risk for RF lie in the immune response or inflammatory system and not in the heart. Looking for a genetic flaw in the hearts of people with RF would miss the crucial genetic mutation governing inflammatory responses. By analogy, the genetic factors conveying risk for schizophrenia may not be in the brain. Thus, infectious agents could trigger inflammatory mechanisms that damage the brain directly or damage the vascular supply to the brain (Hanson, 2003), leading to CNS dysregulation and psychiatric symptoms. There is growing interest in cytokines and other inflammatory agents in psychoses (Ziad & Remick, 2000), as well as growing awareness that inflammatory reactions are modulated by neuropeptides (H. Wang et al., 2003).

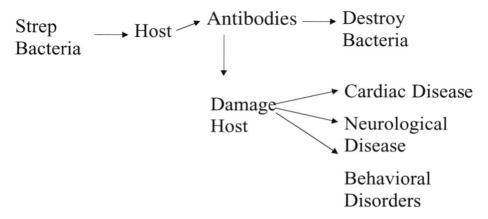

Figure 13.2.   Sequelae of streptococcal pharyngitis.

If, at this juncture, the reader is feeling a bit discouraged at the complexity of it all, just remember that polio is every bit as complicated, the polio puzzle was solved, and polio was virtually eliminated. We are still learning new things about the sequelae of streptococcal infections that involve all of the complexities above. In spite of complexities and incomplete understanding, however, 70-year-old technology (penicillin) and a little vigilance in detecting sore throats are all we need to treat the infection and prevent the sequelae. Rheumatic fever is now a rarity. If we can eradicate polio and nullify strep infections and their consequences, not to mention rapidly and dramatically alter the course of illnesses such as AIDS, we can figure out schizophrenia. However, we may have to think about schizophrenia differently than we do now.

Staying in Touch With Reality

One of the pearls Dr. Gottesman gave to his graduate students was his often-stated philosophy that when trying to solve the schizophrenia puzzle, we should always keep our thoughts anchored in the biological realities of the illness. What are these realities? Some of them were listed in Table 13.1. Table 13.2 lists some possible new realities for consideration.

Just as there is no specific mutant gene for polio or rheumatic fever, there may be no specific mutant gene(s) for schizophrenia, even though genetic factors are important in acquiring the illness. The genetic factors affecting the liability for schizophrenia may not be in the brain but rather, for example, in the immune system if infectious agents are relevant. The gene(s) affecting the acquisition of schizophrenia may not be abnormal mutants but, instead, just part of the range of variation (polymorphisms) of normal individual differences. The wide array of polymorphisms is perpetuated by shuffling the "deck" of genetic cards during meiosis and by the creation of unique combinations of genes through the contribution by each parent of a random assortment of half their genes to each offspring through the process of sexual reproduction. If, at the other extreme of diversity, we were all identical (clones), then, if a bug evolved that could kill one of us, it could kill all. The diversity within our population results in individual differences in susceptibility to infectious or toxic pathogens and helps protect the species as a whole from total devastation. Tooby and Cosmides (1990), among others, suggest that genetic variation is an evolved defense against environmental pathogens. If we accept these lines of reasoning, then we see that luck becomes a major issue. Some of us will be more susceptible to the next strain of rheumatogenic group-A-beta-hemolytic strep. Who will be the lucky one?

Table 13.2.   Realities About Schizophrenia That We May Encounter

- There are no genes for schizophrenia.
- The genetic factors for schizophrenia are not in the brain.
- The genetic factors for schizophrenia are not abnormal.
- Biological markers for schizophrenia are common in both well and ill (nullify the null hypothesis design).

Another reality we may face is that the etiological contributors may be common in both sick and well study groups. It is difficult for many to believe that an important cause of an illness can be about as common in nonaffected as in affected people. The polio example, however, makes it clear that presence of the virus, though necessary to develop paralysis, rarely results in paralysis and thus will be common in both affected and nonaffected people. Who reading this chapter has not had a strep throat? Everyone probably has, whether he or she knows it or not. Yet Sydenham's chorea "caused" by strep throat is rare. If we study the variable "history of strep throat" in a sample of people with Sydenham's chorea compared with a sample of normal controls, we would find no difference, even though streptococcal infection is a major variable associated with Sydenham's chorea.

What does all this mean? Our strategies so far have not unraveled the secrets of schizophrenia. These strategies have largely utilized a mindset that sees schizophrenia as the result of some kind of abnormal gene(s) and assumes that these genetic factors are expressed somewhere in the brain. Furthermore, it is assumed that some kind of environmental factors are at work. For both the genetic factors and environmental factors, it is assumed that the causal agents are more common in sick than in well people, leading to null hypothesis testing as the primary research design. However, necessary environmental contributors may be about equally common in sick versus well populations, and genetic factors may not be in the brain but, instead, in the immune system or elsewhere. Trying to solve schizophrenia by using variations on the inborn error theme should be discarded.

Where to, Next?

Gottesman and Shields (1967, 1972) pointed us in the right direction when they theorized that the heritable factors for schizophrenia were liabilities for the illness. They wrote of specific and general risk and protective factors. This major leap in conceptualization took us beyond simple Mendelian debates. In the "diathesis-stress" model, if the net sum of risk and protective factors exceeded a certain threshold on the risk scale, then schizophrenia would develop. Though not explicitly elaborated, the summation of risk and protective factors is likely a stochastic process. The luck of the draw in receiving genetic "cards" and the "slings and arrows of outrageous fortune" would combine to determine the outcome. Pursuing these lines of reasoning leads us to the conclusion that the risk factors for schizophrenia are common in the general population. Returning to Table 13.1, the first fact about schizophrenia that we must contend with is that schizophrenia is a relatively common disease, affecting about 1% of the population. This means that the risk factors for schizophrenia must also be common. Given that the concordance rate for schizophrenia in identical twins is only about 50%, there must be at least two risk factors for schizophrenia, that is, something genetic and something environmental. Let us assume that these risk factors are independent of each other. If so, the joint probability of acquiring both risk factors is the product of their population frequencies, and, for schizophrenia, this product must equal about 0.01. Taken to the limit, if the environmental contributor was universally present ($f = 1.0$), then the frequency of the genetic factor would have to be at least 0.01. It is unlikely, however, that environmental factors are truly universally present in trait-relevant "doses." Exposure to sunlight is a universally present risk factor for skin cancer, but actual risk is highly dependent on amount of exposure. Strep throat may be exceedingly common, but the rheumatogenic strains of bacteria are not. Thus, the environmental risk factors are likely to affect less than 100% of the population, and the genetic factors will then have to be present at a rate greater than 0.01.

The relation with incomplete penetrance (the risk factor is present but does not become manifest in illness) is such that when penetrance decreases, the frequency of the independent risk factors will have to increase to keep the product of risk factors, multiplied by the fractional penetrance, equal to 0.01.

In our two-factor illustration, then, the population frequencies of the risk factors must be somewhere between 0.01 and 1.0 for their product to equal 0.01. To make a further simplifying assumption, let us say that the two risk factors are present with about equal frequency in the population. This means that the individual frequencies of these factors are about the square root of the population frequency of 1%. That would mean that about 10% of the population would have at least one risk factor. Whereas it is unlikely that all risk factors would have about the same frequency in the population, every time a risk factor's frequency is less that 10% (in our two-factor illustration), then the other factor must be more common than 10% to make the product of the two frequencies equal to 1%. The square root therefore gives us a useful and easy-to-calculate guess for what frequency range to think about as we try to understand how commonthe risk factors for schizophrenia are. The environmental and the genetic risk factors for acquiring schizophrenia cannot be rare.

In general, and with the above assumptions, the number of risk factors (N) contributing to the development of schizophrenia will have a population frequency of the Nth root of 1%. Figure 13.3 illustrates this relationship. The purpose of Figure 13.3 is to illustrate the issues of estimating frequency of risk factors; it is not intended as a rigorous epidemiological model. It serves as a point of departure in thinking about whether we are looking for rare pathogens or normal variation, however. Using this illustration, if schizophrenia results from the independent contribution of, say, four risk factors, then we would expect each of these factors to be present in more than a third of us. Once the number of risk factors exceeds seven, we would expect them to become the norm rather than the exception. Somewhere along the curve in Figure 13.3, we would stop thinking of the risk factors as rare pathological events and start thinking of them as common individual differences within the normal range. Thomson and Esposito (1999), arguing from a molecular perspective, arrived at a similar conclusion.

Should all of this be true, we realize that we need to stop thinking about an abnormal gene that causes schizophrenia and stop applying genetic strategies that are variations on the rare-inborn-error-of-metabolism paradigm. For example, I would not bet on linkage analysis to solve our puzzle. Dr. Gottesman (1978) once wrote a book chapter called "Schizophrenia and Genetics:

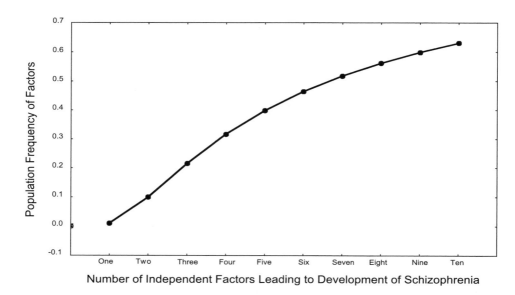

Figure 13.3.   Possible relationship between the number of factors contributing to the development of schizophrenia and their frequency in the general population.

Where Are We? Are You Sure?" where he stated, "Wherever we look with an open mind in psychiatric genetics, we are confronted with uncertainty and challenges to conventional wisdom and traditions" (p. 68). His advice, as always, stands the test of time.

The factors that lead to schizophrenia, as Dr. Gottesman taught us, are multiple. These factors must be quite common in the population and thus are not necessarily abnormal. The risk factors will not be revealed by simple sick-versus-well comparisons, especially if small samples are used. The models of illness that best match the complex realities of schizophrenia are infectious disease models similar to the polio and strep stories. If we can get out of our mindset of searching for abnormal schizophrenia genes and broaden our view to look at normal individual genetic variation in conjunction with exposure to common environmental agents, then we will demonstrate that we can apply what Dr. Gottesman taught us 25 years ago.

References

Beskow, A. H., & Gyllensten, U. B. (2002). Host genetic control of HPV 16 titer in carcinoma in situ of the cervix uteri. *International Journal of Cancer, 101*(6), 526–531

Bion, J. F., & Brun-Buisson, C. (2000). Introduction—Infection and critical illness: Genetic and environmental aspects of susceptibility and resistance. *Intensive Care Medicine, 26*(Suppl. 1), S1–2.

Bisno, A. L., Shulman, S. T., & Dajani, A. S. (1988). The rise and fall (and rise?) of rheumatic fever. *Journal of the American Medical Association, 259*(5), 728–729.

Blackwell, J. M. (2001). Genetics and genomics of infectious disease susceptibility. *Trends in Molecular Medicine, 7*(11), 521–526.

Bleuler, M. (1978). *The schizophrenic disorders: Long-term patient and family studies.* New Haven, CT: Yale University Press.

Bruno, R. L., Frick, N. M., & Cohen, J. (1991). Polioencephalitis, stress, and the etiology of post-polio sequelae. *Orthopedics, 14*(110), 1269–1276.

Burt, R. A. (1999). Genetics of host response to malaria. *International Journal of Parasitology, 29*(6), 973–979.

Cook, G. S., & Hill, A. V. (2001). Genetics of susceptibility to human infectious disease. *Nature Review Genetics, 2*(12), 967–977.

Dale, R. C., Church, A. J., Cardoso, F., Goddard, E., Cox, T. C., Chong, W. K., et al. (2001). Post-streptococcal acute disseminated encephalomyelitis with basal ganglia involvement and auto-reactive antibasal ganglia antibodies. *Annals of Neurology, 50*(5), 588–595.

Davison, K., & Bagley, C. R. (1969). Schizophrenia-like psychoses associate with organic disorders of the central nervous system: A review of the literature. In R. N. Herrington (Ed.), *Current problems in neuropsychiatry* (p. 113–184). Ashford, Kent, UK: Headly.

Garvey, M. A., Giedd, J., & Swedo, S. E. (1998). PANDAS: The search for environmental triggers of pediatric neuropsychiatric disorders. Lessons from rheumatic fever. *Journal of Child Neurology, 13*(9), 413–423.

Gottesman, I. I. (1978). Schizophrenia and genetics: Where are we? Are you sure? In L. Wynne (Ed.), *The nature of schizophrenia* (pp. 59–69). New York: John Wiley.

Gottesman, I. I. (1991). *Schizophrenia genesis: The origins of madness.* New York: W. H. Freeman.

Gottesman, I. I., & Shields, J. (1967). A polygenic theory of schizophrenia. *Proceedings of the National Academy of Sciences, 58,* 199–205.

Gottesman, I. I., & Shields, J. (1972). *Schizophrenia and genetics: A twin study vantage point.* New York: Academic Press.

Hanson, D. R. (2003). A vascular theory of schizophrenia. Manuscript in preparation.

Hanson, D. R., & Gottesman, I. I. (1976). The genetics, if any, of infantile autism and childhood schizophrenia. *Journal of Autism and Childhood Schizophrenia, 6,* 209–234.

Hawken, R. J., Beattie, C. W., & Schook, L. B. (1998). Resolving the genetics of resistance to infectious diseases. *Review of Science and Technology, 17*(1), 17–25.

Herndorn, C. N., & Jennings, R. G. (1951). A twin-family study of susceptibility to poliomyelitis. *American Journal of Human Genetics, 3,* 17–46.

Hill, A. V. (1996). Genetics of infectious disease resistance. *Current Opinion on Genetics of Development, 6*(3), 348–353.

Hill, A. V. (1999). Genetics and genomics of infectious disease susceptibility. *British Medical Bulletin, 55*(2), 401–413.

Horstman, D. M. (1963). Epidemiology of poliomyelitis and allied diseases. *Yale Journal of Biology and Medicine, 36*(5), 5–26.

Kallmann, F. J., & Reisner, D. (1943). Twin studies on genetic variation in resistance to tuberculosis. *Journal of Heredity, 34,* 293–301.

Kitagawa, M., Aizawa, S., Ikeda, H., & Hirokawa, K. (1996). Establishment of a therapeutic model for retroviral infection using the genetic resistance mechanism of the host. *Pathology International, 46*(10), 719–725.

Knight, J. (2001). Polymorphisms in tumor necrosis factor and other cytokines as risks for infectious diseases and the septic shock syndrome. *Current Infectious Disease Reports, 3*(5), 427–439.

Mackenzie, K., & Bishop, S. C. (2001). Utilizing stochastic genetic epidemiological models to quantify the impact of selection for resistance to infectious diseases in domestic livestock. *Journal of Animal Science, 79*(8), 2057–2065.

Morris, J. A. (1996). Schizophrenia, bacterial toxins and the genetics of redundancy. *Medical Hypotheses, 46*(6), 362–366.

Munk-Jørgensen, P., & Ewald, H. (2001). Epidemiology in neurobiological research: Exemplified by the influenza–schizophrenia story. *British Journal of Psychiatry, 178*(Suppl. 40), S30–S32.

O'Reilly, S. L., & Singh, S. M. (1996). Retroviruses and schizophrenia revisited. *American Journal of Medical Genetics, 67*(1), 19–26.

Richter, T. T., & Ronald, P. C. (2000). The evolution of disease resistant genes. *Plant Molecular Biology, 42*(1), 195–204.

Rosenthal, D. (Ed.). (1963). *The Genain Quadruplets.* New York: Basic Books.

Rubenstein, G. (1997). Schizophrenia, rheumatoid arthritis and natural disease resistance. *Schizophrenia Research, 25*(3), 177–181.

Scholl, P. (2002). Periodic fever syndromes. *Current Opinion in Pediatrics, 12,* 563–566.

Seymour, R. M. (1995). Some aspects of the coevolution of virulence and resistance in contact transmission disease processes with ecological constraints. *IMA Journal of Mathematics and Applied Medicine and Biology, 12*(2), 83–136.

Slater, E., & Cowie, V. (1971). *The genetics of mental disorders.* London: Oxford University Press.

Smith, D. A., & Germolec, D. R. (1999). Introduction of immunology and autoimmunity. *Environmental Health Perspectives, 107*(Suppl. 5), 661–665.

Swedo, S. E., Leonard, H. L., Garvey, M., Mittleman, B., Allen, A. J., Parlmutter, S., et al. (1998). Pediatric autoimmune neuropsychiatric disorders associated with streptococcal infections: Clinical descriptions of the first 50 cases. *American Journal of Psychiatry, 155*, 264–271.

Thomson, G., & Esposito, M. S. (1999). The genetics of complex diseases. *Trends in Cell Biology, 9*(12), M17–M20.

Tooby, J., & Cosmides, L. (1990). On the universality of human nature and the uniqueness of the individual: The role of genetics and adaptation. *Journal of Personality, 58*, 17–67.

Torrey, E. F., Miller, J., Rawlings, R., & Yolken, R. H. (1997). Seasonality of births in schizophrenia and bipolar disorder: A review of the research. *Schizophrenia Research, 28*(1), 1–38.

Toutiou, I. (2001, July 9). The spectrum of Familial Mediterranean Fever (FMF) mutations. *European Journal Human Genetics, 9*(7), 473–483.

Tutar, E., Akar, N., Atalay, S., Yilmaz, E., & Yalcinkaya, F. (2002). Familial Mediterranean fever gene (MEFV) mutations in patients with rheumatic heart disease. *Heart, 87*, 568–569.

Veasy, L. H., & Hill, R. (1997). Immunologic and clinical correlations in rheumatic fever and rheumatic heart disease. *Pediatric Infectious Disease Journal, 16*, 400–407.

Wang, F. S. (2003). Current status and prospects of studies on human genetic alleles associated with hepatitis B virus infection. *World Journal of Gastroenterology, 9*(4), 641–644.

Wang, H., Yu, M., Ochani, M., Amella, C. A., Tanovic, M., Susarla, S., et al. (2003). Nicotinic acetylcholine receptor alpha 7 subunit is an essential regulator of inflammation. *Nature, 421*, 328–329.

Werneck-Barroso, E. (1999). Innate resistance to tuberculosis: Revisiting Max Lurie genetic experiments in rabbits. *International Journal of Tuberculosis and Lung Disease, 3*, 166–168.

Yegin, O., Coskun, M., & Ertug, H. (1997). Cytokines in acute rheumatic fever. *European Journal Pediatrics, 156*, 24–29.

Yolken, R. H., Karlsson, H., Yee, F., Johnston-Wilson, N. L., & Torrey, E. F. (2000). Endogenous retroviruses and schizophrenia. *Brain Research Review, 31*(2–3), 193–199.

Yolken, R. H., & Torrey, E. F. (1995). Viruses, schizophrenia, and bipolar disorder. *Clinical Microbiology Review, 8*(1), 131–145.

Ziad, K. R., & Remick, D. G. (2000). Cytokines and the brain: Implications for clinical psychiatry. *American Journal of Psychiatry, 157*, 683–694.

14

Postscript: Eyewitness to the Maturation of Behavioral Genetics

Irving I. Gottesman

Introduction

There must be very few sources of satisfaction greater than receiving the intellectual gifts preceding this last chapter, at least in the life of a professor–scientist transitioning toward a less active stage of enlightenment-seeking. I accept them from my teachers, who were once my students, as a token of our mutual respect and engagement spanning 40 years. The chapters embody and reflect ideas, values, concepts, and facts—all of which I hold dear—about the nature and the sources of individual differences observed within our species with respect to normal-range development of personality, temperament, and health, as well as with respect to differing forms of psychopathology that afflict us, our relatives, and society in general to varying degrees.

True to the canons of the scientific method, the authors rely on the facts and highly informed and defensible conjectures. The last sentence is not an insightless platitude, as I intended to follow the somewhat mischievous maxim of the Foreword author, Brendan A. Maher, from his days as Harvard University's dean of the Graduate School of Arts and Sciences, which distinguishes among facts, "Irish facts," and "mythofacts." The latter are the stock in trade of a majority of critics employed in undermining the domains of behavioral genetics. Common themes running throughout the essays in this book include a focus on matters of real-world importance, a concern for sophisticated methodologies, a lack of dogmatism, a belief that the differences between normal and abnormal behaviors are largely quantitative ones, and a kind of malcontentedness with the status quo—one that will mobilize even greater efforts to "get it right." I must confess to being the likely source of the last theme, but it manifests in a diluted form of the infection. The memorable Beatles' refrain about getting by with a little help from one's friends must be invoked in this postscript, along with the observation that about half of the contributors to this volume, endorsed and published by the American Psychological Association, happened to have been trained as physicians and psychiatrists. Fences between our professions have no place, being both harmful and artificial, when it comes to efforts to understand and to explain variation in human behavior in the service of society.

Roots

Sometime in adolescence, I read Sinclair Lewis's *Arrowsmith* and, in retrospect, I came to appreciate how it had shaped my intellectual valences toward a career that focused on biopsychosocial research into aspects of public health. It did me no harm to start out as a physics major, for sure, but I was not happy until I was exposed to abnormal psychology and Freud. I switched majors to psychology and went off after graduation to three years at sea as a naval officer during the Korean War, returning to life as a graduate student in the clinical program at the University of Minnesota.

That scientist–practitioner (the so-caller "Boulder Model") program suited me to a T. I was enthralled with the two mandatory semesters of individual differences (IDs), and it marked the beginning of a lifelong love affair with the Minnesota Multiphasic Personality Inventory (MMPI) as a means to measure important phenotypes as indicators of personality traits and symptoms of psychopathology. Interacting with Starke Hathaway and Paul Meehl, among others, at the height of their powers was heady stuff for a budding clinical psychologist. Curiosity and a nurturing environment led to an introduction to Sheldon C. Reed, a *Drosophila* geneticist turned human geneticist, by Donald G. Paterson, my professor in IDs and earlier mentor to Leona Tyler, who authored our textbook. Reed, in the Department of Zoology and head of the Dight Institute for Human Genetics, augmented my newly acquired fascination with twin studies (e.g., by Kallmann and by Slater) of mental disorders such as schizophrenia and manic-depression and encouraged me to initiate a sound twin study of intellect and of the personality traits sampled by the MMPI in the normal adolescent population of the Twin Cities. The rest is history (Gottesman, 2001; Healy, 1998).

Progress

This year, 2003, marks the 50th anniversary of the elucidation of the double helix structure of DNA by Watson and Crick. Few would have ventured at the time to predict that their work would open the window to the understanding of life, and, if not tempered by bioethical consciences, Pandora's Box. Behavioral and psychiatric genetics as we know these fields today was not launched until 1960, when John L. Fuller and William R. Thompson published *Behavior Genetics* by pulling together a seemingly disparate literature that spanned many different domains of knowledge: geotaxis in flies, experiments in agronomy, selection of dog breeds for their temperament, activity levels in mice, personality, intelligence, and mental disorders. They provided a framework with their concept of a gene-to-behavior pathway that should have served to prevent simplistic thinking about how genes actually produce variation in behaviors.

A primordium of what would become an informed search for the role of genetic factors in psychopathology, de-Nazified and eschewing genetic determinism, was visible at the First World Congress of Psychiatry in Paris in 1950. At that first post–World War II event, T. Sjögren of Sweden invited Fraser-

Roberts, Penrose, and Slater (United Kingdom); Kallmann (United States); Essen-Möller, Ödegaard, and Strömgren (Scandinavia); and M. Bleuler (Switzerland) to outline a research agenda for their shared interests at the interface of mental disorders and the infancy of human genetics.

The first English language journal for human genetics did not appear until 1949. In retrospect, it is mildly amusing to read Sjögren's introductory remarks to the effect that the possibility of using fly- and mouse-generated ideas about multiple alleles, polygenic systems, and linkage in this field "still appears remote." The preceding chapters sample some of the advances that have been made over the past 43 "DNA years," the interval that coincides with my post-PhD life and makes me an eyewitness to the maturation of this field. It should not go unnoticed that Hans Moises (chapter 10) involved Leroy Hood as one of his coauthors; the latter is a superstar and key player in the Human Genome Project, having won the Lasker, the Kyoto, and the Lemelson–MIT prizes.

Loose Thoughts About Schizophrenia

It is difficult to contain my enthusiasms for my favorite topic, research on schizophrenia, as a prototype for the advances, frustrations, and hopes for the larger domain of behavioral genetics. An integrative model that is comprehensive and fair to the evidence-based facts uncovered and replicated will involve concepts at all levels of genetics (from epidemiology to gene expression) and neurodevelopment, within the context of some kind of biological systems approach. In general, it is very unlikely that dysfunction of any single neurotransmitter system could account for a disorder as complex as schizophrenia. Much more likely is an accumulation over time of numerous failed systems of regulation, some of which are triggered by adverse physical and psychological contributors, as found for other complex diseases. A special issue of *Science* (April 26, 2002) was dedicated to "The Puzzle of Complex Diseases" and is essential reading for gaining a grasp on the difficulties confronting researchers into etiologies; schizophrenia was even singled out as an exemplar.

The most durable clues to the distal causes of schizophrenia, in a set of tortuous genes-to-behaviors pathways scenarios, derive from the cumulative clinical and genetic epidemiological observations that provide strong evidence for genetic predisposition (chapters 8–10, 12–13). Thus, brain dysfunction in schizophrenia can partially be determined by the dynamic genetic "bluescript" of an individual. As long ago as 1895, Jenny Koller, a physician in Zurich, in a prescient epidemiological strategy with a control group, found that schizophrenia "runs" in families, that is, biological relatives of psychotic patients were more susceptible to the disease. Without refining strategies, however, familiality cannot be presumed to mean that genetic forces are the exclusive culprits at work.

On one hand, environmental factors seem to be critically important because there are numerous cases where only one of two genetically identical cotwins is affected with the disease. Up to this point, such clinical differences in outcome have traditionally been explained by differential exposure to physical (brain injury, street drugs, viruses) and psychosocial (deviant parenting, traumatic life events) environments. Adoption studies provided evidence that the absence of many environmental factors alleged to be important did not decrease the chance of developing schizophrenia, leaving other factors to be examined more scrupulously. In this connection, it is necessary to describe elegant studies from Norway and Denmark that investigated the adult offspring of monozygotic (MZ) and dizygotic (DZ) twins, studies in which one or both twins were affected with schizophrenia. The Danish study (chapter 8) involved twins and their offspring who had been followed for so long that both cohorts were beyond the risk period for developing new cases of schizophrenia. It turned out that the rate for schizophrenia in the offspring of unaffected MZ twins was the same as that for the offspring of the affected cotwins (about 17%, whereas the risk to offspring of unaffected DZ cotwins was 2%). Such results strongly suggest that the unaffected MZ cotwins had the necessary genotype but that it was not sufficient for them to develop schizophrenia, yet they transmitted a genotype that permitted their offspring to develop the disease at a very high rate. The biological phenomenon—individuals carry genes that predispose them to a trait or disease, but they do not exhibit that trait or disease—is called "incomplete expression" or "penetrance." The phenomenon has been known for more than 80 years, but the mechanism(s) of why and how some genes remain "silent" in some individuals remains to be understood (Petronis et al. 2003).

Renewed opportunities for understanding various epidemiological, clinical, and molecular puzzles in schizophrenia may spring from a new development in research into human diseases and traits called "epigenetics." I owe a great debt to my colleague Arturas Petronis, of the University of Toronto, for having educated me (Petronis et al., 2003) as to what my use of the term "epigenetic" in 1982 really means. Traditional genetic strategies deal predominantly with gene sequences and investigate what specific proteins are generated, whereas epigenetics investigates factors that regulate (i.e., turn on or off) gene activity, that is, determine how much of each protein is generated. Epigenetic regulation of genes is critically important for the normal functioning of an organism. For example, human cells from different tissues contain the same set of genes, but despite their genetic identity, such cells look different and perform very different functions. It is now believed that this precise level of regulation is achieved by the epigenetic regulation of genes and that this regulation keeps some genes active in one type of cell but switched off in another type of cell.

For example, although dopamine system genes are present in both brain cells and blood cells, such genes are active in the neurons but not in the blood cells. The opposite scenario applies to the gene encoding adult hemoglobin, which is "active" in the erythrocytes but "dormant" in the brain cells. Even slight deviation from the normal epigenetic regulation of a gene can be very harmful to a cell and may result in a disease. For example, individuals who generate more dopamine receptors or who experience a reduction in synaptic stability (Moises, Zoega, & Gottesman, 2002) may be at higher risk to schizophrenia. From the theoretical point of view, epigenetics is able to explain various seemingly unrelated clinical and molecular findings in schizophrenia. The important peculiarity of epigenetic factors is that such factors are not as static as DNA sequences but rather can change over time.

Such partial stability of epigenetic modification may lead to quite different regulation of some critical genes in identical twins, causing the disease in only one of them. Differences in gene activity at the molecular level within pairs of identical twins are beginning to be reported in the literature. The epigenetic theory can also help in understanding the paradox of the elusive role of environmental factors and shed new light on the incomplete expression of genotypes. In general, epigenetic theory is able to unify a wide variety of biological and psychological theories and findings that have emerged about schizophrenia under the epigenetic "umbrella." Our cup, whether it be schizophrenia, temperament, marriage, personality, social attitudes, substance abuse, or depression, is both half full *and* half empty.

Behavioral Genetics and Human Rights

If the judicial system notices facts from academia, it raises the profile of their importance in a way not encountered by esoteric journal presentations. The inferred strength and the inferred positive predictive power of genetic factors in the major mental disorders, using an affected close relative as the point of departure, led to invitations of Peter McGuffin (chapter 12) and myself as expert witnesses in a human rights case in Hong Kong recently (Wong & Lieh-Mak, 2001). Three men who happened to be the offspring of parents with a chart diagnosis of schizophrenia were denied employment in public safety occupations, although each was fully qualified and had passed the required physical, mental, and work-sample tests.

The point of telling the story here is to make it clear that the goal is to highlight evidence-based weighting for the various risk factors involved in the liability, course, and phenomenology of schizophrenia and other disorders without special pleading. The three young men had been found unfit to work because they had a "substantial risk of developing mental illness." Given the conflict of rights, one part of the government charged with ensuring equal opportunities and nondiscrimination in employment sued another part of the government understandably motivated to avoid any avoidable risk of precipitating mental illness in especially vulnerable employees in stress-filled occupations; the case was settled in court after hearing from expert witnesses on both sides. Each man received one million Hong Kong dollars and the right to return to work, and the court awarded our side with a full recovery of the considerable costs of the trial. The victory hinged on our arguing against any current version of genetic determinism and on our demonstration that individualizing risks for a complex disease depended on the best weights to accord to severity of illness in the parent, the proportion of the risk period already survived, the absence of putative nongenetic risk factors, and, finally, the explication of a diathesis-stressor model.

The Near Future

It is clear to me that acceptance of the contemporary results of behavioral genetic strategies by our peers in science as well as by the general public proceeds at a growing and acceptable pace, with a few exceptions to be expected in such a controversial field. The results are embodied in this volume, as well as in recently published, thoughtfully organized books that are must-reads on any enthusiast's reading list (Benjamin, Ebstein, & Belmaker, 2002; Carey, 2003; McGuffin, Owen, & Gottesman, 2002; Pfaff, Berrettini, Joh, & Maxson, 1999; Plomin, DeFries, Craig, & McGuffin, 2003; Plomin, DeFries, McClearn, & McGuffin, 2001; Rao & Province, 2001). Keeping up with the pace of discovery and empirical disconfirmations requires attention to free Internet sources. My favorites include the major gateways, including http://www.ncbi.nih.gov and its companion, http://www.nhgri.nih.gov, maintained by the National Institutes of Health, as well as the rapidly published articles available at http://www.biomedcentral.com and http://www.jbiol.com.

By exposing yourselves and your students to the fonts of knowledge listed here, you too may reach my conclusion that the future lies, not "in plastics" (the advice proffered Dustin Hoffman's character in *The Graduate*) but rather in bioinformatics, proteomics, signal transduction (Manji, Gottesman, & Gould, 2003), and systems biology.

I would also encourage a certain pride in making waves, not to foment chaos and confusion but rather to provoke fact-finding, reconciliation, and consensus. Furthermore, it is important to reject formulaic treatments of data in behavioral genetics and to reach out to other disciplines (cf. Gottesman & Gould, 2003; Rao & Province, 2001); heritability was never intended to be an end, but a means to an end, an end tempered by considerations of developmental processes, gene by environment interactions, and ecological validity. Last, I would counsel the avoidance of isolation from either close or skeptical colleagues, unless some of the latter have fully embraced solipsism and anti-intellectualism (cf. Bressler, 1968). Working with open doors, part of the time, will protect from the idiosyncratic perception of the unmitigated merits of our own ideas.

I remember a line from the old Broadway show *Good Night, Sweet Prince* (1943) to the effect that a man is not old until regrets take the place of dreams. You can see that my dreams are far from over, and they are even getting better with time.

References

Benjamin, J., Ebstein, R. P., & Belmaker, R. H. (Eds.) (2002). *Molecular genetics and the human personality*. Washington, DC: American Psychiatric Publishing.

Bressler, M. (1968). Sociology, biology, and ideology. In D. C. Glass (Ed.), *Genetics* (pp. 178–209). New York: The Rockefeller University Press.

Carey, G. (2003). *Human genetics for the social sciences*. Thousand Oaks, CA: Sage.

Gottesman, I. I. (2001). Psychopathology through a life span–genetic prism. *American Psychologist, 56,* 867–878.

Gottesman, I. I., & Gould, T. D. (2003). The endophenotype concept in psychiatry: Etymology and strategic intentions. *American Journal of Psychiatry, 160,* 636–645.

Healy, D. (1998). Irving Gottesman (USA): Predisposed towards predispositions. In D. Healy (Ed.), *The psychopharmacologists II* (pp. 377–408). London: Chapman & Hall.

Manji, H. K., Gottesman, I. I., & Gould, T. D. (2003). Signal transduction and genes-to-behaviors pathways in psychiatric diseases. *Science STKE, 2003,* pe 49. Retrieved November 3, 2003, from http://stke.sciencemag.org/

McGuffin, P., Owen, M. J., & Gottesman, I. I. (Eds.) (2002). *Psychiatric genetics and genomics.* Oxford, UK: Oxford University Press.

Moises, H. W., Zoega, T., & Gottesman, I. I. (2002). The glial growth factors deficiency and synaptic destabilization hypothesis of schizophrenia. *BMC Psychiatry, 2,* 8. Retrieved September 23, 2003, from http://www.biomedcentral.com/1471-244X/2/8/

Petronis, A., Gottesman, I. I., Kan, P. X., Kennedy, J. L., Basile, V. S., Paterson, A. D., et al. (2003). Monozygotic twins exhibit numerous epigenetic differences: Clues to twin discordance? *Schizophrenia Bulletin, 29,* 169–178.

Pfaff, D. W., Berrettini, W., Joh, T. H., & Maxson, S. C. (Eds.). (1999). *Genetic influences on neural and behavioral functions.* Boca Raton, FL: CRC Press.

Plomin, R., DeFries, J. C., Craig, I. W., & McGuffin, P. (Eds.). (2003). *Behavioral genetics in the postgenomic era.* Washington, DC: American Psychological Association.

Plomin, R., DeFries, J. C., McClearn, G. E., & McGuffin, P. (2001). *Behavioral genetics* (4th ed.). New York: Worth.

Rao, D. C., & Province, M. A. (Eds.). (2001). *Genetic dissection of complex traits: Challenges for the next millennium.* San Diego, CA: Academic Press.

Wong, J. G., & Lieh-Mak, F. (2001). Genetic discrimination and mental illness: A case report. *Journal of Medical Ethics, 27,* 393–397.

Author Index

Numbers in italics refer to listings in the reference sections.

Subject Index

About the Editor

Lisabeth F. DiLalla, PhD, received her graduate degree in developmental psychology from the University of Virginia under Dr. Irving I. Gottesman and then completed a postdoctoral fellowship in behavioral genetics at the Institute for Behavioral Genetics at the University of Colorado. She continued her career at Southern Illinois University and is currently an associate professor in the School of Medicine. Her research on preschoolers has focused on aggressive and cooperative peer behaviors, delinquency, behavioral adjustment to school, and play and imagination. Dr. DiLalla focuses on twins in her research in order to better understand the contributions of genes and environment to the behaviors she studies. She has coedited two other books on life span development.